ACKOFF'S BEST

ACKOFF'S BEST

HIS CLASSIC WRITINGS ON MANAGEMENT

Russell L. Ackoff

John Wiley & Sons, Inc.
New York • Chichester • Weinheim • Brisbane • Singapore • Toronto

Library of Congress Cataloging-in-Publication Data:

Ackoff, Russell Lincoln, 1919–
    Ackoff's best : his classic writings on management
    /   Russell L. Ackoff.
        p.   cm.
    Includes bibliographical references and index.
    ISBN 0-471-31634-2 (cloth : alk. paper)
    1. Management.   2. Business.   I. Title.
    HD31.A2813   1999
    658—DC21   98-24241

Printed in the United States of America.

10   9   8   7   6   5   4   3   2   1

To HELEN
who puts up with my worst.

PREFACE

When Wiley invited me to put to-
gether a volume such as this, the questions that arose immediately were
"Best in who's judgment?" and "Using what criteria?" There was no
choice of the "who"; the task was mine. The choice of criteria, on the
other hand, was wide open. I settled on those publications or parts of
publications that have had the most effect on others—naturally, as I perceived it. Use of this criterion required a good deal of memory and that
was not easy because my first Wiley publication was in 1957, more than
forty years ago.

Using my best recollections of reactions and responses I selected a
number of publications and then tried to make a whole of them rather
than a collection of independent parts. To facilitate the flow, I've removed redundant passages but I have added nothing substantive to the
original publications. The source and date of each selection is provided
on the first page, and each chapter concludes with a list of references. I
have also tried to impose a consistent format on a wide variety of forms
in which the original writing appeared.

I had a great deal of assistance from Tina Fellenbaum in preparing this
manuscript. In writing the originals I had all kinds of help from many
friends, colleagues, and enemies. My greatest debt goes back, as it always
has, to my teachers E.A. Singer, Jr., C. West Churchman, and Thomas
A. Cowan. Unfortunately the two at the end of this list are no longer
alive, but I think of and with them often.

Since "retiring" (sic!) from Wharton I have had relatively little contact with students who were once a major stimulus for me. Meetings

with former students and colleagues are still a major source of pleasure—even though one young man who attended a recent lecture came up afterwards to tell me his grandfather had attended one of my classes.

I am indebted to all my former students and their offspring who have made it possible for me to live inter-generationally, and not be imprisoned in an age group, one to which I belong but do not feel a part of.

And, of course, there is Pat Brandt who has managed my professional life so effectively that I have been able to abdicate responsibility for it.

RLA

Philadelphia
December 1998

CONTENTS

PART I

SYSTEMS

System is more than just a concept. It is an intellectual way of life, a worldview, a concept of the nature of reality and how to investigate it—a *weltanschauung*. In this section, I discuss the emergence and development of that view and its nature (Chapter 1).

In Chapter 2, I differentiate alternatives to the particular approach advocated in Chapter 1. Different types of systems (determinate, animate, social, and ecological) are described, and I discuss the consequences of looking at social systems as either deterministic, animate, or social. The intention is not so much to show that these alternatives are wrong as to show that the approach taken here is more fruitful. The appropriate objective of a social system viewed as an organism is survival, and growth is taken to be essential for survival (because the limit of contraction is death). But since development is the appropriate objective of a social system conceptualized as a social system, I then draw the distinction between growth and development (Chapter 3).

In Chapter 4, I present a system of concepts useful in discussing and studying systems. Chapter 5 is concerned with revealing some of the abuses systems can inflict on mortals and what can be done about them.

CHAPTER 1

OUR CHANGING CONCEPT OF THE WORLD

There is a certain relief in change, even though it is from bad to worse; as I have found in travelling in a stage-coach, that it is often a comfort to shift one's position and be bruised in a new place.

Washington Irving

Change itself is constantly changing. This is reflected in the widespread recognition of its accelerating rate. For example, the speed with which we can travel has increased more in our lifetimes than it has over all the time before our births. The same is true for the speed with which we can calculate, communicate, produce, and consume.

Change has always been accelerating. This is nothing new, and we cannot claim uniqueness because of it. There are, however, some aspects of the changes we are experiencing that are unique. These are responsible for much of our preoccupation with change.

First, although technological and social change have been accelerating almost continuously, until recently this has been slow enough to enable people to adapt, either by making small occasional adjustments or by accumulating the need to do so and passing it on to the next generation. The young have always found it easier than the old to make the necessary adjustments. Newcomers to power have usually been willing to make changes that their predecessors were unwilling to make.

In the past, because change did not press people greatly, it did not receive much of their attention. Today it presses hard and therefore is attended to. Its current rate is so great that delays in responding to it can be very costly, even disastrous. Companies and governments are going out

---

From *Creating the Corporate Future* (Wiley, 1981).

of business every day because they have failed to adapt to it or they have adapted too slowly. Adaptation to current rapid changes requires frequent and large adjustments of what we do and how we do it. As the eminent student of management Peter Drucker put it, managers must now manage discontinuities. The changes in management required to handle change have become a major concern to all those associated with it.

Human beings seek stability and are members of stability-seeking groups, organizations, institutions, and societies. Their objective may be said to be "homostasis," but the world in which this objective is pursued is increasingly dynamic and unstable. Because of the increasing interconnectedness and interdependence of individuals, groups, organizations, institutions, and societies brought about by changes in communication and transportation, our environments have become larger, more complex, and less predictable—in short, more turbulent. The only kind of equilibrium that can be obtained by a light object in a turbulent environment is dynamic—like that obtained by an airplane flying in a storm, not like that of the Rock of Gibraltar.

We can drive a car down a deserted turnpike in good weather with few changes of direction and acceleration; hence we do so without giving it much conscious thought. The worse the weather and the road, and the heavier the traffic (hence the more unpredictable the driving of others), the more we have to concentrate on our driving and the more frequently we have to change our direction and speed.

As Alvin Toffler pointed out, either we do not respond at all or we do not respond quickly enough or effectively enough to the changes occurring around us. He called our paralysis in the face of change-demanding change Future Shock. One of the objectives of this book is to overcome such paralysis.

The second unique characteristic of the changes we face is more subtle than the first and, perhaps, even more threatening. It was first brought to our attention by Donald A. Schön. To paraphrase his argument, as the rate of change increases, the complexity of the problems that face us also increases. The more complex these problems are, the more time it takes to solve them. The more the rate of change increases, the more the problems that face us change and the shorter is the life of the solutions we find to them. Therefore, by the time we find solutions to many of the problems that face us, usually the most important ones, the problems have so changed that our solutions to them are no longer relevant or effective; they are stillborn. In other words, many of our solutions are to problems that no longer exist in the form in which they were solved. As a result we are falling further and further behind our times.

Little wonder, then, that to many experts on change it appears critical that we learn how to forecast it more accurately and as early as possible, to prepare for it more effectively, and to respond to it more rapidly when we have not anticipated it. They see the solution to the problems created by accelerating change in improved forecasting, learning, and adaptation.

There is no doubt that such improvements would reduce some of the social pressure brought about by accelerating change, but it is neither the only path we can follow nor the best one. It is better to develop greater immunity to changes that we cannot control, and greater control over the others. Many changes that occur need not occur; and many that do not occur could have. Most of the changes that people worry about are consequences of what they have done or failed to do, however unintentionally.

Although change in general may be inevitable, particular changes are not. To those changes that do occur we must, of course, learn how to adapt more rapidly and effectively. Therefore, in this book considerable attention is given to learning and adaptation. However, because control of change is preferable to responsiveness to it, control receives even more attention.

Acceleration of change takes place in our minds as well as in our environment. There is no doubt that we have become increasingly sensitive to changes in our environment, and that we now perceive changes that once would have been ignored. We are, perhaps, more finely tuned to pick up change than any previous generation.

The most important change taking place, I believe, is in the way we try to understand the world, and in our conception of its nature. However, the large and growing literature on change and its management focuses on its objective rather than subjective aspects. It assumes that most of the managerial problems created by change derive from its rate. This may be true, but it is apparent that we cannot deal with change effectively unless we understand its nature. This means understanding it in general, not just in particular instances. One of my students, who was better at asking questions than at answering them, grasped this point and put it into a very succinct question: *What in the world is happening in the world?*

It is hard to conceive of a question that is easier to ask and harder to answer. Nevertheless, each of us frames an answer to it, consciously or unconsciously. Our answer constitutes our *Weltanschauung,* our view of the world. This view has either an implicit or explicit impact on just about everything we think and do.

Because the way I proceed in this book is itself greatly affected by my view of the world, I present it here. I do so with the hope that it will enable others to understand better where I am coming from, and that it will support my contention that we cannot cope effectively with change unless we develop a better view of the world. Any view of the world is necessarily hypothetical, and mine is no exception. My view, like any other, will have to stand tests of its effectiveness in developing ways of coping with both the rate and content of change.

About the time of World War II the age we were in began to end, and a new age began to take its place. We are still in the period of transition from one age to another, standing with one foot in each. As the two ages draw further apart we feel increasing strain, and will continue to do so until we place both feet firmly in the age we are entering. We can, of course, step the other way and try to live our lives in a dying age. By so doing, however, we accelerate the demise of the institutions and the culture that are affected by such maladaptive behavior.

By an *age* I mean a period of history in which people are held together by, among other things, use of a common method of inquiry and a view of the nature of the world that derives from its use. Therefore, to say we are experiencing a change of age is to assert that both our methods of trying to understand the world and our actual understanding of it are undergoing fundamental and profound transformations.

THE MACHINE AGE

I believe we are leaving an age that can be called the *Machine Age.* In the Machine Age the universe was believed to be *a machine that was created by God to do His work.* Man, as part of that machine, was expected to serve God's purposes, to do His will. This belief was combined with another even more ancient in origin, man had been created in the image of God. This meant that man believed himself to be more like God than anything else on Earth. This belief is reflected in the way God was depicted in the art of the age: in the image of man. In a sense, men were taken to be "demigods."

From these two beliefs—that the universe was a machine created by God to do His work, and that He had created man in His image—it obviously followed that *man ought to be creating machines to do his work.* The Industrial Revolution was a product of this inference. Not only did the idea of mechanization derive from the world view of the Machine Age, but all the important characteristics of the Industrial Revolution and the culture associated with it were derived from the methodology and basic doctrines on which this view rested. Let us see how.

In the Middle Ages the expected lifespan was short, between twenty and thirty-five years at different times. Infant and child mortality was very high. The population was frequently and devastatingly plagued. During their lives most people never traveled more than a few miles from their places of birth. There was little personal freedom. Poverty and deprivation were widespread. For these and many other reasons the intellectual life of the time focused on the inner spiritual life and afterlife. Let us listen to one witness, the historian Edward Maslin Hulme who illustrates the typicality of these views.

> The intellectual strength of the Middle Ages did not lie in scientific knowledge and achievement, but in a vivid quickening of the spiritual imagination. . . The medieval man had little ability to look things squarely in the face; he had no clear-eyed perception of the visible world. It was not his practice to deal in an objective way with the facts of the actual world about him. All things were veiled with a mist of subjectivity. . . The speculative life was held to be vastly more important than the practical life. The world was but a house of probation. (p. 124)

> The ideal life of the Middle Ages was one closed about with the circumscribing walls of a cloister. . . Its vision . . . ignored as much as possible the world of nature and the world of men, but it opened upon the infinite. (p. 60)

The art of the age reflected this orientation by focusing on man's spiritual and afterlife, not on the content and context of everyday life.

> In the Middle Ages painting was merely the hand maid of the Church. Its function was not to reveal to men the beauty of the present world, but to help him win salvation in the next. (p. 116)

Little wonder, then, that curiosity was not taken to be a virtue.

> In the age of faith curiosity was a cardinal sin. The idea that it is a duty or that it is a part of wisdom to find out the reality of things was quite foreign to the times. (p. 64)

The Renaissance that took place in the fourteenth and fifteenth centuries was a reawakening or, literally, a *rebirth*. In a sense man reentered the world of nature in which he lived by noticing it, becoming curious about it, and inquiring into it. In the Middle Ages

> Revelation was the sole source of truth. But when Peter the Hermit preached the first Crusade he unconsciously helped to set in motion forces that resulted in the Renaissance. Travel incited the curiosity of men. . . Men became filled with curiosity not only to know the civilization of other countries, but to learn something of men who had lived in distant ages and who had been activated by different ideals of life. This curiosity came to be a powerful and important force. . . It produced a revival of learning and research, it resulted in invention and discovery. . . It initiated the experimental method. It implanted in the hearts of men the desire to study and to know the world for themselves, unencumbered by the bonds of authority. (p. 64)

Renaissance men confronted nature with awe, wonder, and childlike curiosity. They tried to unravel its mysteries much as children do today, *analytically*. I do not mean that these intellectual ancestors were unsophisticated. I mean that their science was naive in a literal sense, "having natural or unaffected simplicity."

Analysis

Children given something they do not understand—a radio, a clock, or a toy—are almost certain to try to take it apart to see how it works. From an understanding of how the parts work they try to extract an understanding of the whole. This three-stage process—(1) taking apart the thing to be understood, (2) trying to understand the behavior of the parts taken separately, and (3) trying to assemble this understanding into an understanding of the whole—became the basic method of inquiry of the age initiated by the Renaissance. It is called *analysis*. No wonder that today we use *analysis* and *inquiry* synonymously. For example, we speak of "analyzing a problem" and "trying to solve a problem" interchangeably. Most of us would be hard pressed if asked to identify an alternative to the analytical method.

Commitment to the analytical method induces observation and experimentation, which, in fact, brought about what we think of today as modern science. Over time, the use of this method led to a series of questions about the nature of reality, the answers to which formed the world view of the Machine Age.

Reductionism

According to the viewpoint of the Machine Age, in order to understand something it has to be taken apart conceptually or physically. Then how does one come to understand its parts? The answer to this question is obvious: by taking the parts apart. But this answer obviously leads to another question: Is there any end to such a process? The answer to this question is not obvious. It depends on whether one believes that the world as a whole is understandable in principle, if not in practice. In the age initiated by the Renaissance it was generally believed that complete understanding of the world was possible. In fact, by the mid-nineteenth century many leading scientists believed that such understanding was within their grasp. If one believes this, then the answer to the second question must be yes. Given the commitment to the analytical method, unless there are ultimate parts, *elements,* complete understanding of the universe would not be possible. If there are such indivisible parts and we come to understand them and their behavior, then complete understanding of the world is possible, at least in principle. Therefore, the belief in elements is a fundamental underpinning of the Machine-Age view of the world. The doctrine that asserts this belief is called *reductionism:* all reality of our experience of it can be reduced to ultimate indivisible elements.

Formulated so abstractly, this doctrine may not appear to be familiar; but it is very familiar to most of us in its specific manifestations. In physics, for example, with the work of the nineteenth-century English chemist John Dalton, people generally came to accept a speculation of Democritus and other ancient Greek philosophers as well as the seventeenth century French philosopher Descartes: all physical objects are reducible to indivisible particles of matter, or *atoms.* These elements were believed to have only two intrinsic properties: mass and energy. Physicists tried to build their understanding of nature on a foundation of an understanding of these elements.

Chemistry, like physics, had its elements. They appeared in the familiar Periodic Table. Biologists believed that all life was reducible to a single element, the *cell.* Psychology was not so parsimonious; it postulated a number of elements at different times. It began with psychic atoms, *monads,* but gave them up in favor of *simple ideas* or *impressions,* later called *directly observables* and *atomic observations.* Fundamental *drives, needs,* and *instincts* were added. Later, however, Freud returned to psychic atoms to explain personality. He used three elements—the *id, ego,* and *superego*—and energy, the *libido,* to "explain" human behavior. Linguists tried to reduce language to indivisible elements of sound called *phonemes;* and so on and on.

In every domain of inquiry men sought to gain understanding by looking for elements. In a sense, Machine-Age science was a crusade whose Holy Grail was the element.

Determinism

Once the elements of a thing had been identified and were themselves understood it was necessary to assemble such understanding into an understanding of the whole. This required an explanation of the *relationships* between the parts, or how they interacted. It is not surprising that in an age in which it was widely believed that all things were reducible to elements it was also believed that one simple relationship, *cause-effect,* was sufficient to explain all interactions.

Cause-effect is such a familiar concept that many of us have forgotten what it means. It may be helpful, therefore, to review its meaning. One thing is said to be the cause of another, its effect, if the cause is both *necessary* and *sufficient* for its effect. One thing is necessary for another if the other cannot occur unless the first does. One thing is sufficient for another if the occurrence of the first assures the occurrence of the second. The program directed at explaining all natural phenomena by using only the cause-effect relationship led to a series of questions whose answers provided the remaining foundations for the Machine-Age view of the world.

First, the following question arose: Is everything in the universe the effect of some cause? The answer to this question was dictated by the prevailing belief in the possibility of understanding the universe completely. For this to be possible, everything had to be taken as the effect of some cause, otherwise they could not be related or understood. This doctrine was called *determinism*. It precluded anything occurring by either chance or choice.

Now, if everything in the universe is caused, then each cause is itself the effect of a previous cause. If we start tracing back through the chain of causes do we come to a beginning of the process? The answer to this question was also dictated by the belief in the complete understandability of the universe. It was yes. Therefore, a *first cause* was postulated and taken to be God. This line of reasoning was called the "cosmological proof of the existence of God." It is significant that this proof derived from the commitment to the cause-effect relationship and the belief in the complete understandability of the universe.

Because God was conceptualized as the first cause, He was taken to be the *creator*. As we will see, not all concepts of God attribute this function to Him, or even attribute individuality or "Himness" to Him.

The doctrine of determinism gave rise to yet another critical question to which philosophers of the Machine Age devoted much of their time. How can we explain free will, choice, and purpose in a deterministic universe? There was no generally accepted answer to this question, but this did not create a problem because there was widespread agreement on this much: the concept of free will or choice was not needed to explain any natural phenomenon, including the behavior of man.

Some held that free will was an illusion granted to us by a merciful God who realized how dull life would be without it. Man was thought to be like a fly who, riding on the trunk of an elephant, believes he is steering it. This belief makes the ride more interesting and the elephant does not mind.

Another important consequence of the commitment to causal thinking derives from the acceptance of a cause as sufficient for its effect. Because of this a cause was taken to explain its effect *completely*. Nothing else was required to explain it, *not even the environment*. Therefore, Machine-Age thinking was, to a large extent, *environment-free;* it tried to develop understanding of natural phenomena without using the concept of environment. For example, what does the word "freely" in the familiar "Law of Freely Falling Bodies" mean? It means a body falling in the absence of any environmental influences. The apparent universality of such laws (and there were many) does not derive from their applicability to every environment for, strictly speaking, they apply to none; it derives from the fact that they apply *approximately* to most environments that we experience.

Perhaps even more revealing of the environment-free orientation of Machine-Age science is the nature of the place in which its inquiry was usually conducted, the *laboratory*. A laboratory is a place so constructed as to facilitate exclusion of the environment. It is a place in which the effect of one variable on another can be studied without the intervention of the environment.

Mechanism

The concept of the universe that derives from the exclusive use of analysis and the doctrines of reductionism and determinism is *mechanistic*. The world was viewed *as* a machine, not merely like one. The universe was frequently compared to a hermetically sealed clock. This is a very revealing comparison, implying that it had no environment. Like a clock, its be-havior was thought to be determined by its internal structure and the causal laws of nature.

The Industrial Revolution

This revolution had to do with the replacement of man by man-made machines as a source of work. Its two central concepts were *work* and *machine*. Whatever else was thought of work, it was believed to be *real,* particularly after the Reformation. Because all real things were believed to be reducible to atoms and atoms had only two intrinsic properties, mass (matter) and energy, work was conceptualized as the application of energy to matter so as to change its properties. For example, the move-ment of coal and its transformation into heat (energy) were considered to be work. Thought, however, was not taken to be work because it did not involve the application of energy to matter.

A machine was considered any object that could be used to apply en-ergy to matter. Not surprisingly, it was believed that all machines were reducible to elementary machines: the lever, pulley, wheel and axle, and inclined plane (of which the wedge and screw are modifications).

The mechanization of work was greatly facilitated by reducing it to a set of simple tasks. Therefore, work was *analyzed* to reduce it to its *ele-ments*. These elements were tasks so simple that they could only be done by one person—for example, tightening a screw or driving a nail. Then many of the work elements were mechanized. Not all were because either the technology required was not available or, although available, it was more costly than the use of human labor. Therefore, people and machines, each doing elementary tasks, were aggregated to do the whole job. The result was the industrialized production and assembly line that forms the spine of the modern factory.

The benefits of the Industrial Revolution are too obvious to dwell on here. They were many and significant. The same can be said of its costs. However, there is one cost which we have only recently become aware of, derived from what might be called the irony of the Industrial Revolution. In our effort to replace ourselves with machines as a source of energy, we reduced our work to elementary tasks designed to be simple enough to be done by machines, eventually if not immediately. In this way *we were reduced to behaving like machines,* doing very simple repetitive tasks. Our work became dehumanized. This is the source of one of the most critical problems facing us today, our alienation from work.

The nature of the workplace developed during the Industrial Revolution was dictated by the application of the analytical method to work. If there were another way of thinking about work, it would be possible to conceive of another kind of workplace, one very different from the kind that we know today. This possibility is one that recently has been given much thought. I will return to it after we have seen what the alternative way of thinking is.

On Looking Backward and Forward

The Machine Age is largely history, but part of it still lives. The very brief account of its history that I have given is not a conventional one, hence it is subject to controversy. In contrast, the Systems Age lies largely in the future; nevertheless, my account of it is equally controversial. Such controversy, however, revolves around what we want it to be because, as I will argue, to a large extent the future can be what we want it to be. The Systems Age emerges from a new vision, a new mission, and a new method. Therefore, in describing it my rhetoric changes from narrative to persuasive as I try to convince the reader to share the vision, mission, and method with which I believe we can create this new age.

I present the Systems Age as emerging dialectically from the Machine Age. The Machine Age is a thesis, and its meaning and implications only become clear when its antithesis is fully developed. This development is taking place now, in the period of transition from one age to another, just as it took place for the Machine Age during the Renaissance. The Systems Age, as I see it, is a synthesis of the Machine Age and its antithesis, which is still being formulated. Their synthesis, however, has already begun to emerge and is being disclosed more clearly as time goes on.

The Systems Age is a movement of many wills in which each has only a small part to play, even those who are trying to shape it deliberately. It is taking shape before our eyes. It is still too early, however, to foresee all the difficulties that it will generate. Nevertheless, I believe the new age can be trusted to deal with them. Meanwhile there is much work to be done, much scope for greater vision, and much room for enthusiasm and optimism.

My account of the Machine Age was a hurried resume of the past because I am eager to face the future. The brevity of my account depreciates the magnificent efforts of the past four centuries to cope effectively with reality. The origins of the Systems Age lie in this past, hence the problems it confronts are inherited, but those of us who intend to have a hand in shaping the new age are trying to face them in a new way. Now let us see what that way is.

The Systems Age

No age has a starting point; it emerges imperceptibly in bits and pieces that eventually combine, first to produce an awareness that something fundamental is happening, then to provide a new world view.

Doubts about a prevailing world view usually begin with the appearances of *dilemmas*. A dilemma is a problem or question that cannot be solved or answered within the prevailing world view and therefore calls it into question (see Kuhn). We have already considered one such question: how can we account for free will in a mechanistic universe? In physics, Heisenberg's *Uncertaintly Principle* presented another such dilemma. He showed that within the prevailing paradigm in physics two critical properties of point particles could not be determined simultaneously; as the accuracy of the determination of one increases, the accuracy of the other decreases. This called into question the belief that the world is completely understandable, even in principle.

Then there was the dilemma that arose as all the king's men tried and failed to put Humpty Dumpty together again. Some things, once disassembled, could not be reassembled. The essential properties of other things could not be inferred from either the properties of their parts or their interactions, as for example, the personality or intelligence of a human being. More recently, in their studies of servomechanisms, machines that control other machines, Arturo Rosenblueth and Norbert Wiener argued that such machines could only be understood if they were assumed to display choice and goal-seeking behavior. Choice and mechanism, however, are incompatible concepts. This dilemma had a special significance which is discussed later in this chapter.

In the latter part of the last century and the early part of this one, dilemmas arose with increasing frequency in every field of inquiry. Investigators confronted with dilemmas in one field gradually became aware of those arising in other fields and the similarities among them. They also became aware of the fact that the prevailing mechanistic view of the world and the beliefs on which it was based were increasingly being brought into question. This awareness was intensified by events that took place just before, during, and immediately after World War II.

This war took science and scientists out of their laboratories and into the "real world" in an effort to solve important problems arising in large, complex organizations—military, governmental, and corporate. Scientists discovered that the problems they faced could not be disassembled into ones that fit neatly into any one discipline and that the interactions of the solutions of disassembled parts were of greater importance than the solutions considered separately. This in turn led to the formation of interdisciplinary efforts. In the late 1930s, Operational Research, an interdisciplinary activity, emerged out of the British military establishment to deal with the management and control of its complex operations.

By the 1950s interdisciplinary scientific activities proliferated. These included the management sciences, decision sciences, computer sciences, information sciences, cybernetics, policy sciences, peace science, and many others. The overlap of interest among them and the similarities in their practices led to a search for a theme common to all of them.

By the mid–1950s it was generally recognized that the source of similarities of the interdisciplines was their shared preoccupation with the behavior of *systems*. This concept gradually came to be recognized as one that could be used to organize an increasingly varied set of intellectual pursuits. Of greater importance, however, was the fact that it revealed the fundamental dilemma of the Machine Age and suggested how its world view might be modified to escape the horns of that dilemma. It is for this reason that I refer to the emerging era as the *Systems Age*.

The Nature of a System

Before we can begin to understand the change in world view that the focus on systems is bringing about, we must first understand the concept of systems itself.

A system is a set of two or more elements that satisfies the following three conditions.

1. *The behavior of each element has an effect on the behavior of the whole.* Consider, for example, that system which is, perhaps, the most familiar to us: the human body. Each of its parts—the heart, lungs, stomach, and so on—has an effect on the performance of the whole. However, one part of the body, the appendix, is not known to have any such effect. It is not surprising, therefore, that it is called the appendix which means "attached to," not "a part of." If a function is found for the appendix, its name would probably be changed.

2. *The behavior of the elements and their effects on the whole are interdependent.* This condition implies that the way each element behaves and the way it affects the whole depends on how at least one other element behaves. No element has an independent effect on the system as a whole. In the human body, for example, the way the heart behaves and the way it affects the body as a whole depends on the behavior of the brain, lungs, and other parts of the body. The same is true for the brain and lungs.

3. *However subgroups of the elements are formed, each has an effect on the behavior of the whole and none has an independent effect on it.* To put it another way, the elements of a system are so connected that independent subgroups of them cannot be formed.

A system, therefore, is a whole that cannot be divided into independent parts. From this, two of its most important properties derive: every part of a system has properties that it loses when separated from the system, and every system has some properties—its essential ones—that none of its parts do. An organ or part of the body, for example, if removed from the body does not continue to operate as it did before removal. The eye detached from the body cannot see. On the other hand, people can run, play piano, read, write, and do many other things that none of their parts can do by themselves. No part of a human being is human; only the whole is.

The essential properties of a system taken as a whole derive from the *interactions* of its parts, not their actions taken separately. Therefore, *when a system is taken apart it loses its essential properties.* Because of this—and this is the critical point—*a system is a whole that cannot be understood by analysis.*

Realization of this fact is the primary source of the intellectual revolution that is bringing about a change of age. It has become clear that a method other than analysis is required for understanding the behavior and properties of systems.

Systems Thinking

Synthesis, or putting things together, is the key to systems thinking just as analysis, or taking them apart, was the key to Machine-Age thinking.

Synthesis, of course, is as old as analysis—Aristotle dealt with both—but it is taking on a new meaning and significance in a new context just as analysis did with the emergence of the Machine Age. Synthesis and analysis are complementary processes. Like the head and tail of a coin, they can be considered separately, but they cannot be separated. Therefore, the differences between Systems-Age and Machine-Age thinking derives not from the fact that one synthesizes and the other analyses, but from the fact that systems thinking combines the two in a new way.

Systems thinking reverses the three-stage order of Machine-Age thinking: (1) decomposition of that which is to be explained, (2) explanation of the behavior or properties of the parts taken separately, and (3) aggregating these explanations into an explanation of the whole. This third step, of course, is synthesis. In the systems approach there are also three steps:

1. Identify a containing whole (system) of which the thing to be explained is a part.
2. Explain the behavior or properties of the containing whole.
3. Then explain the behavior or properties of the thing to be explained in terms of its *role(s)* or *function(s)* within its containing whole.

Note that in this sequence, synthesis precedes analysis.

In analytical thinking the thing to be explained is treated as a whole to be taken apart. In synthetic thinking the thing to be explained is treated as a part of a containing whole. The former *reduces* the focus of the investigator; the latter *expands* it.

An example might help clarify the difference. A Machine-Age thinker, confronted with the need to explain a university, would begin by disassembling it until he reached its elements; for example, from university to college, from college to department, and from department to faculty, students, and subject matter. Then he would define faculty, student, and subject matter. Finally, he would aggregate these into a definition of a department, thence to college, and conclude with a definition of a university.

A systems thinker confronted with the same task would begin by identifying a system containing the university; for example, the educational system. Then such a thinker would define the objectives and functions of the educational system and do so with respect to the still larger social system that contains it. Finally, he or she would explain or define the university in terms of its roles and functions in the educational system.

These two approaches should not (but often do) yield contradictory or conflicting results: they are complementary. Development of this complementarity is a major task of systems thinking. Analysis focuses on *structure;* it reveals *how things work.* Synthesis focuses on *function;* it reveals *why things operate as they do.* Therefore, analysis yields *knowledge;* synthesis yields *understanding.* The former enables us to *describe;* the latter, to *explain.*

Analysis looks *into* things; synthesis looks *out of* things. Machine-Age thinking was concerned only with the interactions of the parts of the thing to be explained; systems thinking is similarly concerned, but it is additionally occupied with the interactions of that thing with other things in its environment and with its environment itself. It is also concerned with the *functional* interaction of the parts of a system. This orientation derives from the preoccupation of systems thinking with the *design* and *redesign* of systems. In systems design, parts identified by analysis of the function(s) to be performed by the whole are not put together like unchangeable pieces of a jigsaw puzzle; they are designed to fit each other so as to work together *harmoniously* as well as efficiently and effectively.

Harmony has to do not only with the effect of the interactions of the parts on the whole, but also with the effects of the functioning of the whole and the interactions of the parts on the parts themselves. It is also concerned with the effects of the functioning of the parts and the whole on the containing system and other systems in its environment. This concern with harmony has important implications in the management of systems—implications that are explored below.

There are considerable differences between what might be called analytical and synthetic management. To a large extent this book is devoted to illuminating these differences. One such difference is worth noting here. It is based on the following systems principle:

> If each part of a system, considered separately, is made to operate as efficiently as possible, the system as a whole will *not* operate as effectively as possible.

Although the general validity of this principle is not apparent, its validity in specific instances is. For example, consider the large number of types of automobile that are available. Suppose we bring one of each of these into a large garage and then employ a number of outstanding automotive engineers to determine which one has the best carburetor.

When they have done so, we record the result and ask them to do the same for engines. We continue this process until we have covered all the parts required for an automobile. Then we ask the engineers to remove and assemble these parts. Would we obtain the best possible automobile? Of course not. We would not even obtain an automobile because *the parts would not fit together,* even if they did, *they would not work well together. The performance of a system depends more on how its parts interact than on how they act independently of each other.*

Similarly, an all-star baseball or football team is seldom if ever the best team available, although one might argue that it would be if its members were allowed to play together for a year or so. True, but if they became the best team it is very unlikely that all of its members would be on the new all-star team.

The current methodology of management is predominantly based on Machine-Age thinking. When managers are confronted with large complex problems or tasks, they almost always break them down into solvable or manageable parts; they "cut them down to size." Then they arrange to have each part solved or performed as well as possible. The outputs of these separate efforts are then assembled into a "solution" of the whole. Yet we can be sure that the sum of the best solutions obtained from the parts taken separately is *not* the best solution to the whole. Fortunately, it is seldom the worst.

Awareness of this conflict between parts and the whole is reflected in the widespread recognition of the need for *coordinating* the behavior of the parts of a system. At the same time, however, measures of performance are set for the parts that bring them into conflict. Formulation of these measures is commonly based on the assumption that the best performance of the whole can be reduced to the sum of the best performances of its parts taken separately. The systems principle, however, asserts that this is not possible. Therefore, another and more effective way of organizing and managing the parts is required. One is considered below.

The application of systems thinking, whether to management or the world, like the application of Machine-Age thinking, raises a number of fundamental questions. The answers to these questions provide the doctrines from which a systems view of the world derives. Let us see how.

Expansionism

In systems thinking, increases in understanding are believed to be obtainable by expanding the systems to be understood, not by reducing them to their elements. Understanding proceeds from the whole to its parts, not from the parts to the whole as knowledge does.

If the behavior of a system is to be explained by referring to its containing system (the suprasystem), how is the behavior of the suprasystem to be explained? The answer is obvious: by reference to a more inclusive system, one that contains the suprasystem. Then the fundamental question—Is there any end to this process of expansion? Recall that when the corresponding question arose in the Machine Age—Is there any end to the process of reduction?—the answer was dictated by the belief that, at least in principle, complete understanding of the universe was possible. In the early part of this century, however, this belief was shattered by such dilemmas as that formulated by Heisenberg. As a result, we have come to believe that complete understanding of anything, let alone everything, is an *ideal* that can be approached continuously but *can never be attained*. Therefore, there is no need to assume the existence of an ultimate whole which if understood would yield the ultimate answer.

This means that we are free to believe or not in an all-containing whole. Since our understanding will never embrace such a whole, even if it exists, it makes no practical difference if we assume it to exist. Nevertheless, many individuals find comfort in assuming existence of such a unifying whole. Not surprisingly, they call it God. This God however, is very different from the Machine-Age God who was conceptualized as an individual who had created the universe. God-as-the-whole cannot be individualized or personified, and cannot be thought of as the creator. To do so would make no more sense than to speak of man as creator of his organs. In this holistic view of things man is taken as a part of God just as his heart is taken as a part of man.

Many will recognize that this holistic concept of God is precisely the one embraced by many Eastern religions which conceptualize God as a system, not as an element. It is not surprising, therefore, that in the past two decades many of the young people in the West—products of the emerging Systems Age—turned to religions of the East.

The East has used the concept of a system to organize its thinking about the universe for centuries, but it has not thought about systems scientifically. There is some hope, therefore, that in the creation of systems sciences the cultures of the East and West can be synthesized. The twain may yet meet in the Systems Age.

The doctrine of expansionism has a major effect on the way we go about trying to solve problems. In the Machine Age, when something did not work satisfactorily, we looked for improvement by manipulating the behavior of its parts; we looked for solutions from within and worked our way out from the interior only when we failed there. In the Systems Age we look for solutions from without and work our way in when we fail there. The reasons for and effects of this reversal of direction will become apparent when we consider the differences between Machine-Age and Systems-Age planning.

Producer-Product

The Machine Age's commitment to cause and effect was the source of many dilemmas, including the one involving free will. At the turn of the century the American philosopher E. A. Singer, Jr., showed that science had, in effect, been cheating.* It was using two different relationships but calling both cause and effect. He pointed out, for example, that acorns do not cause oaks because they are *not* sufficient, even though they are necessary, for oaks. An acorn thrown into the ocean, or planted in the desert or an Arctic ice cap does not yield an oak. To call the relationship between an acorn and an oak "probabilistic" or "nondeterministic causality," as many scientists did, was cheating because it is not possible to have a probability other than 1.0 associated with a cause; a cause completely determines its effect. Therefore, Singer chose to call this relationship "producer-product" and to differentiate it from cause-effect.[†]

Singer went on to ask what the universe would look like if producer-product is applied to it rather than cause-effect. One might think of Singer's question in this way: an orange, when sliced vertically, yields a cross-sectional view that is very different from the view revealed when it is sliced horizontally. Yet both are views of the same thing. The more views we have of a thing, the better we can understand it. Singer argued similarly about the universe.

As Singer and Ackoff and Emery have shown, the view of the universe revealed by viewing it in terms of producer-product is quite different from that yielded by viewing it in terms of cause-effect. Because a producer is only necessary and not sufficient for its product, it cannot provide a complete explanation of it. There are always other necessary

---

* Singer showed this in a series of papers published between 1896 and 1904. His work is best presented in a posthumors publication, *Experience and Reflection*.
[†] Much after Singer, Sommerhoff independently came up with very similar results. What Singer called "producer-product," Sommerhoff called "directive correlation."

conditions, coproducers of its product. For example, moisture is a co-producer of an oak along with an acorn. These other necessary conditions taken collectively constitute the acorn's *environment*. Therefore, the use of the producer-product relationship requires the environment to explain everything whereas use of cause-effect requires the environment to explain nothing. Science based on the producer-product relationship is environment-*full*, not environment-*free*.

A law based on the producer-product relationship must specify the environment(s) under which it applies. No such law can apply in every environment, because if it did no environmental conditions would be necessary. Thus there are no universal laws in this view of the universe. For example, we have learned more recently that the law that everything that goes up must come down is not universally true. (Unfortunately, some things that we have put up with the intention that they not come down, nevertheless have done so.) Environmentally relative laws can use probabilistic concepts in a consistent and meaningful way. In an environment in which all the necessary coproducing conditions are not specified—hence may or may not be present—it is not only meaningful but it is useful to speak of the probability of production. For example, we can determine the probability of an acorn producing an oak in a specified environment in which some of the relevant properties are not known. Therefore, the probability determined is the probability that the unspecified but necessary environmental conditions are present.

Teleology

Singer showed by reasoning that is too complicated to reproduce here that in the producer-product-based view of the world, such concepts as choice, purpose, and free will could be made operationally and objectively meaningful. (See also Ackoff and Emery.) A system's *ends—goals, objectives, and ideals*—could be established as objectively as the number of elements it contained. This made it possible to look at systems *teleologically*, in an output-oriented way, rather than deterministically, in an input-oriented way.

Objective teleology does not replace determinism, which is an objective *a*teleology; it complements it. These are different views of the same thing, but the teleological approach is more fruitful when applied to systems.

Centuries ago Aristotle invoked teleological concepts to explain why things, inanimate as well as animate, behaved as they did; but he employed a *subjective* teleology. Among those who carry on in his spirit are some psychologists who try to explain human behavior by invoking such (unobservable, they claim) intervening variables as beliefs, feelings, attitudes, and drives which at best are only observable by those who have them. In an objective teleology, beliefs, feelings, attitudes, and the like are attributable to human beings because of *what they do;* hence are observable. These properties are derived from observed regularities of behavior under varied conditions. Such concepts do not lie behind behavior, but *in* it; hence are observable. In an objective teleology functional characteristics of systems are not treated as metaphysical forces, but as observable properties of the system's behavior.

The ideas and concepts developed by Singer were largely ignored for the first half of this century. Sommerhoff's were ignored as well, but for a shorter time. It was not until the concept of teleological mechanisms* and the dilemma contained in it came into the focus of science's attention that the work of Singer and Sommerhoff came to be recognized as significant. Their work solved this dilemma. A teleological system and a deterministic machine are two different aspects of the same thing. These antithetical points of view are synthesized in the concept of reality emerging in the Systems Age.

Systems-oriented investigators focus on teleological (goal seeking and purposeful) systems. In the Machine Age, even human beings were thought of as machines. In the Systems Age, even machines are thought of as parts of purposeful systems. We now believe that a machine cannot be understood except by reference to the purpose for which it is used by the purposeful system of which it is a part. For example, we cannot understand why an automobile is like it is without understanding the purposes for which it is used. Moreover, some machines, teleogical mechanisms, are seen to have goals, if not purposes, of their own.

Ordinary machines serve the purposes of others but have no purposes of their own. *Organisms* and *organizations* are systems that usually have purposes of their own. However, the parts of an organism (i.e., heart, lungs, brain) do not have purposes of their own, but the parts of an organization do. Therefore, when we focus on organizations we are

---

* Such mechanisms were brought to the attention of science by Frank et al.

concerned with three levels of purpose: the purposes of the system, of its parts, and of the system of which it is part, the suprasystem.

There is a functional division of labor among the parts of all types of systems. A set of elements or parts, all of which do the same thing, does not constitute a system; it is an aggregation. For example, a collection of people waiting for a bus does not constitute a system, nor does a collection of clocks all ticking away on the same shelf. Each part of a system has a function in the system, and some of these must differ. To organize a system, as we will see, is to divide its labor functionally among its parts and to arrange for their coordination.

The Postindustrial Revolution

To complete this account of the change of age that we are in, we should consider the effect of systems thinking on the Industrial Revolution.

The conversion of the Industrial Revolution into what has come to be called the *Postindustrial Revolution* has its origins in the last century. Scientists who explored the use of electricity as a source of energy found that it could not be observed easily. Therefore, they developed such *instruments* as the ammeter, ommeter, and voltmeter to observe it for them. The development of instruments exploded in this century, particularly after the advent of electronics and sonar and radar. Look at the dashboard of a large commercial airplane, or even one in an automobile. These instruments *generate symbols* that represent the properties of objects or events. Such symbols are called *data.* Instruments, therefore, are observing devices, but they are not machines in the Machine-Age sense because they do not apply energy to matter in order to transform it. The technology of instrumentation is fundamentally different from that of mechanization.

Another technology with this same characteristic emerged when the telegraph was invented in the last century. It was followed by the telephone, wireless, radio, television, and so on. This technology, like that of instrumentation, has nothing to do with mechanization; it has to do with the *transmission of symbols,* or *communication.*

The technologies of observation and communication formed the two sides of a technological arch that could not carry any weight until a keystone was dropped into place. This did not occur until the 1940s when the *computer* was developed. It too did no work in the Machine-Age sense; *it manipulated symbols logically,* which, as John Dewey pointed out, is the nature of *thought*. It is for this reason that the computer is often referred to as a thinking machine.

Because the computer appeared at a time when we had begun to put things back together again, and because the technologies of observation, communication, and computation all involve the manipulation of symbols, people began to consider systems that combine these three functions. They found that such systems could be used to *control* other systems, to *automate*. Automation is fundamentally different from mechanization. Mechanization has to do with the replacement of *muscle;* automation with the replacement of *mind*. Automation is to the Postindustrial Revolution what mechanization was to the Industrial Revolution.

Automations are certainly not machines in the Machine-Age sense, and they need not be purposeless. It was for this reason that they came to be called teleological mechanisms. However, automation is no more an essential ingredient of the systems approach than is high technology in general. Both come with the Systems Age and are among its producers as well as its products. The technology of the Postindustrial Revolution is neither a panacea nor a plague; it is what we make of it. It generates a host of problems and possibilities that systems thinking must address. The problems it generates are highly infectious, particularly to less-technologically developed cultures. The systems approach provides a more effective way than previously has been available for dealing with both the problems and the possibilities generated by the Postindustrial Revolution, but it is by no means limited to this special set of either or both.

CONCLUSION

Well, there it is: a tentative answer to the question—what in the world is happening in the world? My response to it is an attempt to make some sense out of what is going on and to equip us to cope with it more effectively. In particular, I hope to show that this response has important and useful implications to managers. Curiously, I have found managers more willing to embrace the systems approach and its implication than academics. Managers are more inclined than academics to try something new and judge it on the basis of its performance. Their egos are not as involved as the academics' in the acceptance or rejection of a view formulated by another. Academic evaluations tend to be based on the subjective opinions of peers, not on any objective measure of performance.

Fortunately, in this connection the corporate manager has a more effective and exacting taskmaster: the "bottom line," the performance of the managed system.

BIBLIOGRAPHY

Ackoff, Russell I. and F. E. Emery. *On Purposeful Systems*. Chicago: Aldine-Atherton, 1972.

Dewey, John. *Logic: The Theory of Inquiry*. New York: Henry Holt, 1938.

Drucker, Peter F. *The Age of Discontinuity*. New York: Harper & Row, 1968.

Frank, L. K., G. E. Hutchinson, W. K. Livingston, W. S. McCulloch, and N. Wiener. "Teleological Mechanisms," *Annals of the New York Academy of Sciences,* 50. Art. 4, 187–278, 1948.

Hulme, Edward Maslin. *The Renaissance, the Protestant Revolution, and the Catholic Reformation in Continental Europe*. New York: The Century Co., 1920.

Kuhn, Thomas S. *The Structure of Scientific Revolutions*. 2nd ed. Chicago: The University of Chicago Press, 1970.

Rosenblueth, A., and N. Wiener. "Purposeful and Non-Purposeful Systems," *Philosophy of Science,* 17, 318–326, 1950.

Schön, Donald A. *Beyond the Stable State*. New York: Random House, 1971.

Singer, E. A., Jr. *Experience and Reflection*. Philadelphia: University of Pennsylvania Press, 1959.

Sommerhoff, Gerd. *Analytical Biology*. London: Oxford University Press, 1950.

Toffler, Alvin. *Future Shock*. New York: Bantam Books, 1971.

CHAPTER 2

REFLECTIONS ON SYSTEMS AND THEIR MODELS

There are different types of systems and different ways of representing (modeling) them. Our concern here is with the consequences of applying a model of one type to a system of a different type. This is a common practice with what we believe to be serious consequences.

TYPES OF SYSTEMS AND MODELS

There are three basic types of systems and models of them, and a metasystem: one that contains all three types as parts of it (see Table 2.1).

1. *Deterministic:* Systems and models in which neither the parts nor the whole are purposeful.
2. *Animated:* Systems and models in which the whole is purposeful but the parts are not.
3. *Social:* Systems and models in which both the parts and the whole are purposeful.

These three types of systems form a hierarchy in the following sense: animated systems have deterministic systems as their parts. In addition, some of them can create and use deterministic systems, but not vice versa. Social systems have animated systems as their parts. All three types of systems are contained in *ecological systems,* some of whose parts are purposeful but not the whole. For example, Earth is an ecological system that has no purpose of its own but contains social and animate systems that do, and deterministic systems that don't.

Consider each of these types of systems in more detail.

From "Reflections On Systems and Their Models," with Jamshid Gharajedaghi, *Systems Research,* March 13, 1996, pp. 13–23.

Table 2.1
Types of Systems and Models

Systems and Models	Parts	Whole
Deterministic	Not purposeful	Not purposeful
Animated	Not purposeful	Purposeful
Social	Purposeful	Purposeful
Ecological	Purposeful	Not purposeful

Deterministic Systems

Systems that have no purpose, and whose parts do not either, are systems whose behavior is determined. They are exemplified by mechanisms. Although deterministic systems, including mechanisms, have no purposes of their own, they normally serve the purpose(s) of one or more entities external to them, their creators, controllers, or users. Provision of that service is their *function*. Although the parts of a mechanistic system do not have purposes of their own, they do have functions serving the function of the whole. Therefore, all the subsystems of a deterministic system are also deterministic systems.

The behavior and properties of a deterministic system are determined by its structure, the causal laws, and its environment if it is an *open system,* but not by its environment if it is *closed*. Even closed deterministic systems have a function: to serve the purposes of the external entity. For example, Descartes and Newton conceptualized the universe as a mechanistic system, as a hermetically sealed clock, and they believed that this system had been created by God and served His purposes, doing His work. Even such commonplace open deterministic systems as automobiles, generators, and computers have no purposes of their own but serve the purposes of their producers and users.

Mechanisms are not the only deterministic systems; plants are also even though they are alive. Neither they nor their parts can display choice; neither they nor their parts have purposes of their own.

Since deterministic systems and their parts cannot display choice, there is only one thing they can do in any particular environment. Their behavior and properties are determined by their internal structure, their environment (if there is any), and the causal laws of nature. *Open* deterministic systems have an environment (external variables that affect their behavior and properties); closed systems don't.

Despite the fact that computers are mechanisms, they appear to make choices. But not so. Their behavior is completely determined by the information and program put into the computer by external sources. If we know these, then, in principle if not in practice, we would be able to predict with certainty what the computer would do in any situation. Programmed instructions in a computer are its causal laws. These together with its internal structure and externally provided inputs completely determine its behavior.

Deterministic systems can be differentiated by the number of functions they have. An ordinary clock has one function: to tell time. On the other hand, an alarm clock is multifunctional, since it also has a wake-up function. Some clocks have many additional functions; for example, they can measure lapsed time, and reveal the temperature.

Animated Systems

Animated systems have purposes of their own, but their parts don't. The most familiar examples are, of course, animals, including human beings. All animated systems are organisms but not all organisms (e.g., plants) are animated systems. (Unless otherwise indicated, we use "organism" to mean an animated organism.) Animated systems are *alive*. Life is currently defined in terms of *autopoiesis:* "the maintenance of units and wholeness, while components themselves are being continuously or periodically disassembled and rebuilt, created and decimated, produced and consumed" (Zeleny, p. 5). As will be apparent, it follows from this definition of life that social and ecological systems are also living systems.

Plants do not have purposes but like all living things have a goal: *survival.* Plants *react* to changing external conditions in such ways as to make their survival possible, but their reactions are determined, not matters of choice, and choice is necessary for purposefulness.

For animals, survival is also a—if not the—most important purpose. They are purposeful organisms whose parts (some of which are called "organs") have functions but no purposes of their own. The behavior of an organism's parts is determined by its state and activity. For example, a person's heart, lungs, brain, etc., have no purposes of their own, but their functions are necessary for the survival and pursuit of the purposes of the whole.

Historically, animated systems have often been treated as though they were nothing but complicated mechanisms. Mechanistic biology dominated biology, the study of living things, for centuries. For example, the biomechanist Roux is said to have taken the following position:

> According to Roux, biology admits of exact formulation because matter alone exists; there is no ground for a fundamental distinction between the living and non-living. The animate, appearing as cells with nuclei, developed from the inanimate by the operation of mechanical laws, and is governed by them. (p. 72)

Included in the long list of eminent biologists who also had a mechanistic point of view were Reil, Lamarck (the evolutionist), Rudolphi, Berzelius, Verworn, and Loeb.

Opposition to a mechanistic conception of organisms surfaced in the mechanist-vitalist controversy which arose out of this conception's inability to account for the nature of life adequately. Today, when life tends to be defined in terms of self-organization and self-renewal (autopoiesis), it is apparent that essential aspects of organisms are not included in mechanistic models of them.

On the other hand, mechanistic entities have seldom been conceptualized as organisms. The only exceptions we can think of occur among primitive people whose beliefs are said to have been "animatistic," which (according to the *Encyclopeadia Britannica,* 11th edition, Vol. 2, p. 53) is "the doctrine that a great part, if not the whole, of the inanimate kingdom, as well as all animated beings, are endowed with reason, intelligence, and volition, identical with that of man."

Social Systems

Social systems—for example, corporations, universities, and societies—have purposes of their own, contain parts (other social systems or animated organisms) that have purposes of their own, and are usually parts of larger social systems that contain other social systems (for example, corporations and nations). (Some primitive societies lived in complete isolation, hence were not part of a larger social system.) We are not aware of anyone trying to model organisms or mechanical systems as social systems, but clearly, social systems have often been modeled organismically (e.g., Stafford Beer, 1972) and even mechanically (e.g., social psysicists and Jay Forrester, 1961, 1971). For example, the sociologist, P. Sorokin, in his book, *Contemporary Sociological Theories* (1928), summarized the mechanistic interpretations of two prominent social physicists, Haret and Barcelo, as follows:

> In their works the translation of the nonmechanistic language of social science into that of mechanics goes on in the following way: The individual is transformed into a material point, and his social environment into a "field of forces," . . . As soon as this is done, there is no difficulty in applying the formulas of mechanics to social phenomena; all that is necessary is to copy these formulas, inserting the word individual instead of material point, and the term social group instead of physical system or a field of forces. "An increase in the kinetic energy of an individual is equivalent to a decrease in his potential energy." "The total energy of an individual in his field of forces remains constant throughout all its modifications . . . and so on." (pp. 17–18)

In addition, Sorokin wrote that "H. C. Carey's *Principles of Social Science* is one of the most conspicuous attempts in the second half of the nineteenth century at a physical interpretation of social phenomena" (p. 13). Carey applied such laws as those of gravitation to social phenomena. If an individual is taken as a molecule and the social group as a body, then the attraction between any two bodies is in direct proportion to their masses (the number of individuals per unit volume) and inversely proportionate to the square of the distance between them. In addition, Carey took centralization and decentralization of populations to be the same as centripetal and centrifugal forces.

Herbert Spencer, the nineteenth-century evolutionary philosopher, provides an excellent example of biological modeling of social systems. His position was summarized by A. M. Hussong (1931) as follows:

> Spencer himself groups together under four heads these comparisons of life and society which result in showing three phenomena well known to characterize *life,* to be no less characteristic of anything to be called a *society.* They are: (1) growth; with which is associated (2) increasing differentiation of structure; and (3) increasing differentiation of function. (p. 23)

Consider the first of Spencer's points to help clarify his position:

> In both biological and social organisms, growth is evidenced by the same phenomena. In both, there are increases in mass—in the biological individual, and expansion from germ to adult form; in the social, and expansion from small wandering hordes to great nations. In both, aggregates of different classes reach various sizes—among biological organisms, the Protozoa rarely increase

beyond a microscopic size; among social organisms the primitive Tasmanians seldom form large groups, while the empires of civilization include millions of people. In both, increases by simple multiplication of units is followed by union of groups and unions of groups of groups. In both, finally, a multiplication of individuals goes on within each group of units. (p. 23)

Organismic models do not take the purposes of the parts of an organism into account. However, these models are useful in social systems in those rare cases in which the purposes of the parts are very limited or not relevant; for example, in organizations that are managed or ruled autocratically. The more autocratic an organization, the more appropriate is the use of an organismic model.

A problem arises with increasing education of the members of a social system, the increasing technology that they must master to do the tasks assigned to them, and the greater the variety of demands made on them. When those managed, governed, or ruled know how to function better than those who manage, govern, or rule them, the less effective autocratic management or rule is. A democratic organization—that is, one in which the members have considerable freedom and opportunity to make choices—can't be adequately modeled organismically precisely because such modeling misses this most important characteristic of such a social system: the ability of its parts to make choices. This inadequacy is particularly apparent where problem solving is involved.

Consider the use of case *studies* in management education. We recently asked a group of managers in an executive development program that had just completed working on a case what would happen if they presented their solution to the relevant corporation's senior management. The class members said that these managers would probably find a number of reasons for not accepting it, and if they accepted it, it would probably not be implemented as intended because of opposition to it by those who would be responsible for its implementation. We then pointed out that *the managers and the implementers were part of the problem, not external to it.* In the organismic model of the corporation which the class had unconsciously used, the purposes of those who had to approve of any proposed action, let alone those who had to carry it out, were not taken into account. Had the class used a social systemic model they would have treated acceptance and implementation of its solution to the problem in the case as part of the problem, not as separate from it.

In the political arena finding what is normally thought of as a solution to a problem, and getting it accepted and implemented, are usually treated separately rather than as necessary aspects of the problem. For example, many laws are simply not obeyed or enforced and therefore solve nothing. President Clinton's recent proposed solution of the national health care problem was rejected by Congress whose approval was required before it could be enacted. Furthermore, many problem solutions that are implemented are sabotaged by those who implement them. This is the case when alleged solutions, when implemented, encourage and facilitate corruption.

Ecological Systems

Ecological systems contain interacting mechanistic, organismic, and social systems, but unlike social systems have no purpose of their own. However, they serve the purposes of the organisms and social systems that are their parts, and provide necessary inputs to the survival of the non-animate biological systems (plants) that it contains. Such service and support is their function.

An ecological system is affected by some of the behavior of its component organismic and social systems, but their effects are determined, as are the behavior and properties of a mechanistic system. For example, the purposeful use of fluorocarbons as a propellant affects the ozone layer in a way that is determined, not as a matter of choice.

Like animated and social systems, ecological systems also live because they are capable of "maintaining their unity and wholeness, while components themselves are being continuously or periodically disassembled and rebuilt, created and decimated, produced and consumed" (Zeleny, p. 5).

Although the function of an ecological system is to serve its parts, many people assume the existence of a deity whose purposes the universal ecological system is believed to serve. The deity is also assumed to have created this system.

Variations within Types of Models

When we talk of deterministic, animate, and social systemic models, we refer to classes of models within which there are many variations. However, these variations derive from different treatments of non-essential variables.

THE EVOLUTION AND CONSEQUENCES OF MISMATCHING MODELS AND SOCIAL SYSTEMS

One can model a part or an aspect of a social system as a mechanism and by so doing improve its performance, but this can reduce the performance of the whole. Optimization of parts can suboptimize the system as a whole. Recall that every essential part of a system can affect the performance of the whole but cannot do so independently of all the other essential parts. Therefore, in changing performance of any of these parts its effect on the system as a whole should be taken into account. Nevertheless, some (non-essential) properties of even a system's essential parts may have no effect on the system as a whole: for example, the color of an automobile's motor may have no effect on its performance and therefore can be modified without affecting performance of the automobile. Similarly, workers may be essential in a corporation, but the color or type of clothing they wear may not be.

The effectiveness of any model used to describe and understand behavior of a particular system as a whole ultimately depends on the degree to which that model accurately represents that system. Nevertheless, there have been and are situations in which application of deterministic or animate models to social systems have produced useful results *for a short period of time*. However, in a longer run, such mismatches usually result in less than desirable results because critical aspects of the social system were omitted in the less complex model that was used. This is the point that we argue and illustrate here.

Deterministic Models Applied to Organizations

In the early stages of industrialization, machines replaced thousands of agricultural workers. This resulted in a very large number of unemployed unskilled agricultural workers and had a destabilizing effect on Western societies. It was then that a new concept of manufacturing "came to the rescue." Production processes were designed much as a complicated tractor is, as consisting of an assembly of parts each of which involves a very simple and repetitive task. Then unskilled workers could be assigned to these elementary tasks and be treated as replaceable machine parts. In time this mechanical model of production converted the army of un-skilled agricultural workers to semi-skilled industrial workers. The im-pact of this mechanistic model of organization on productivity was so great that in one generation it provided an amount of goods and services that surpassed all previous expectations.

Henry Ford's phenomenal success in the creation of a mechanistic mass production system marked the beginning of the production era but con-tained the seeds of its demise. He failed to appreciate the potentiality of the process he initiated when he said, in effect, "they can have any color [of automobile] they want as long as it is black." This gave Alfred Sloan of General Motors the opportunity to gain domination of the market. He took mass production for granted and focused on the question: how to sell. The marketing era emerged. It gave rise to a new set of challenging questions, the most important of which were: (1) how to respond to in-creasing demand for variety and diversity; and (2) how to organize and manage the increases in size and complexity that resulted from increas-ing variety and diversity.

As the size and complexity of organizations increased, the effective-ness of managing them as though they were machines decreased. De-centralization of control became necessary and this was incompatible with a mechanistic conception of organization. A machine requires cen-tralized control and invariance of output. No driver in his right mind would drive a car with decentralized front wheels.

However, in an organization that requires invariant functioning of its parts (as bureaucracies do), decentralization leads to disorganization, if not chaos, and less than the best possible performance of the whole. This is so because improving the performance of one part of an organization taken separately, as occurs in decentralization, often reduces the effec-tiveness of other parts. For example, the best solution to a production problem taken in isolation (such as minimizing inventory) may well be in conflict with the best solution from a marketing point of view (which consists of holding an adequate stock of all items offered for sale). It is for this reason that organizations continually oscillate between centralization and decentralization.

An example of a social-systemic treatment of an inventory problem is provided by an abrasive-manufacturing company that offers a discount on purchases of its products that are proportional to the amount of lead time given by the customer for delivery of the goods ordered. This solution converted "demand" into a partially controllable variable by taking into account the purposefulness of the customers. It reduces inventory several times as much as could be obtained by use of (mechanistic) economic lot sizes, and it had a very positive effect on customer attitudes toward the company.

Summarizing, deterministic and animate models may work very well when applied to parts or aspects of a social system when these parts or aspects are considered in isolation. However, it is possible to improve the performance of each part or aspect of a system taken separately and simultaneously reduce the performance of the whole. This follows from the fact that no part or aspect of a system has an independent effect on the performance of the system. A system's performance is the *product of the interactions* of its parts or aspects.

The extent of the harm done by using a model that is not of the same type as the system modeled depends on the level of development of the system involved. For example, when it was initiated, Henry Ford's production system approximated a mechanical system for the following reasons. First, the workers were poorly educated and relatively unskilled, but adequate for the simple repetitive tasks assigned to them. These tasks required behavior that was more machine-like than human. Second, since there was virtually no social security available, unemployment implied financial destitution for many. This resulted in workers who were willing to tolerate working conditions suitable for machines, but not people. Third, there was a large pool of people looking for work, hence workers could easily be replaced, like machine parts; and the workers knew this. Fourth, business organizations were normally managed by their owners, who had virtually unlimited control over their organizations; they were not yet subject to significant intervention and constraints coming from government and unions.

Animate (Organismic) Models Applied to Social Systems

There were a number of developments between the two world wars that made deterministic modeling of social systems less and less appropriate. Business and government organizations took growth to be necessary in order to respond effectively to demand for an increasing amount and diversity of products and services. In addition, technological developments required workers with increasingly greater skills. The educational level of workers increased but so did union and government intervention.

However, the threat of financial destitution associated with unemployment decreased as social security emerged. Finally, as businesses went public in order to raise the capital required to fuel growth and technological improvements, management and ownership were separated. The publicly owned company became a *corporation* (derived from "corpus," meaning "body") and the chief executive became the "head" of the firm. Because of these developments organismic models were increasingly used when dealing with social systems.

Sloan's concept of an organization was essentially organismic, that of a single-minded biological entity. This provided a relatively effective way to manage organizational growth and increase the diversity of organizational outputs. In his (implicit) model, corporations, like the human bodies, were divided into two distinct parts: (1) management, the *brain* (Beer, 1972); and (2) the operating unit, the *body*.

The operating unit, the body, was considered to have no choice, no consciousness. It was restricted to reacting deterministically to instructions coming from management, the brain, and/or events in its environment. Ideally, an operating unit would be a robot programmed to carry out without deviation a set of procedures defined by headquarters. Military organizations, governmental bureaucracies, and autocratic corporations closely approximated the behavior of robots.

Social-Systemic Models Applied to Social Systems

As a result of World War II a large portion of the workforce in Western nations was drawn into the military. Replacements included Rosie the Riveter and Tillie the Toiler who were motivated at least as much by patriotism as by additional income. Such workers could not be treated as replaceable machine parts or organs of a body that only required consideration of the effects of their work on their health and safety. They had to be treated as human beings with purposes of their own. In addition, unions discovered that corporations working under cost-plus contracts or demands for increased production could easily be induced to make concessions to workers' interests. Work rules went through a profound transformation. Furthermore, because of the great increase in technological developments, the skills required of the workforce increased dramatically. The more skilled the workers, the harder they were to replace. Technological developments required a significant investment in specialized training of the workforce. Management had to obtain an adequate return on this investment. All this produced a need to treat employees as human beings with purposes of their own.

Children of the post–World War II workforce made up the permissive generation whose members were not about to be treated as other than purposeful entities. They expected their interests to be taken into account by their employers and, where they weren't, they were alienated from work and their productivity decreased (*Work in America,* 1973). The quality-of-work-life movement was an effort to correct this. In addition, protest groups formed outside organizations insisting that their interests be better served by the organization that affected them, for example, consumerists and environmentalists. Management's social responsibility and its work-related ethics emerged as major concerns.

By the end of the 1960s it was apparent that the West was experiencing both an accelerating rate of change largely due to technological developments, and increasing complexity produced by an explosion of interconnections resulting from continuously improving transportation and communications. The socio-economic environment became turbulent: one in which predictability of the future diminished significantly and the only equilibrium that could be obtained was dynamic, like that of an airplane flying through a storm. These changes undermined whatever effectiveness had been obtained by applying organismic models to social systems; centralized control and the treatment of subordinates as mindless parts were no longer good practices.

Increasingly, employees could do their jobs better than their bosses, but only if they were given the freedom to do so. Therefore, the mechanistic and organismic concept of management as command and control, or even softer supervision, became less and less appropriate. The functions of management became one of enabling and motivating subordinates to do as well as they know how, to develop them so they can do better in the future than the best they can do now, to manage their interactions, not actions, and manage the interactions of the unit managed with other internal and external organizations. This can only be done with a social systemic model in mind.

Furthermore, the unprecedented generation and distribution of both wealth and knowledge resulted in increasing choice and greater interdependency. This changed the nature of social settings and individual behavior. The greater the interactions and interdependencies, the more vulnerable social systems became to the actions of a few. The more knowledge available, the greater the value of communication and information. However, advances in information technology and communication did not yield the quality or quantity of control managers hoped for. Since it was assumed that members of organismically conceptualized organizations would behave like organs in a human body by reacting mechanistically to information provided by the brain, it appeared reasonable to conclude that malfunctioning of organizations was due either to the lack of information or noise in the communication channels. Therefore, more and more information and better and better communications were provided. Unfortunately, this mode of thinking is ineffective in dealing with the complexities of increasing social interactions and interdependencies. It fails to recognize that members of an organization, unlike the parts of an organism, have a choice and do not react passively to the information they receive. Imagine a thermostat that developed a mind of its own. When it received information about the temperature in the room that it did not like, it would not react to it. This would result in a chaotic air-conditioning system. The effectiveness of a servo-mechanism is based on the fact that it does not have a choice and can only react in a predefined manner to the events in its environment. Our organs—heart, lungs, and so on—cannot decide on their own not to work for us. Even when they are defective, we do not conclude that they "are out to get us."

Furthermore, increases in information eventually produces a condition Meier (1963) called "information overload." As the amount of information received increases beyond the amount its receivers can handle effectively, they use less and less of it. Not only do receivers become saturated with information—and therefore cannot receive any more—but they can and do become supersaturated—discard some of the information they already have.

An organization with purposeful parts almost inevitably generates internal conflict. Wherever there is choice, conflict is likely; without choice, there can be no conflict. In conflict situations, organismic thinking is ineffective because it tries to resolve conflict by increasing the flow of information between the conflicting parties. Unfortunately, when conflict is based on differing values or scarcity of resources, an increased flow of information, contrary to conventional wisdom, does not improve but aggravates the conflict. For example, the more information enemies at war have about each other, the more harm they can inflict on each other.

However, the biological mode of organization can be successful: in the short term, in the particular context of paternalistic cultures; where loyalty, conformity, and commitment are considered to be the core virtues. These virtues are reinforced by the security of belonging to a group which in turn protects and provides for its members. For example, Japan, an industrialized society, with a relatively strong paternalistic culture, closely approximates an organismic system. Therefore, it has been able to capitalize more effectively on the strength of the biological model of organization. In the context of a strong paternalistic culture, conflict can be resolved by the intervention of a strong father figure, whose command, "Give the apple to your sister," would be respected without much hard feelings. To appreciate the power of this type of leader, recall that such American corporate giants as Ford, DuPont, General Motors, and IBM owe much to their paternalistic founding fathers.

The nature of highly developed social systems is fundamentally different from that of a paternalistic culture. Members of societies that have matured past the secure and unifying umbrella of a paternalistic culture, insist on the right to make choices. But there is a price to be paid for this right; it can induce insecurity and conflict. Purposeful actors, individually or in groups, who pursue incompatible ends and/or employ conflicting means, generate conflict. Consequently, because of its organismic orientation, corporate America is ill equipped to deal effectively with internal and external conflict. Furthermore, it finds it almost impossible to make the changes required to flourish in its rapidly changing and increasingly complex environment. A significant part of its energy is wasted on futile efforts to deal with such conflict. The frustration that results reinforces its inability to change. This in turn creates a feeling of impotency and hopelessness that immobilizes Western governments, institutions, and organizations.

A conflict-free organization can be created by reducing choice, reducing members to robots. Fascist societies and autocratic organizations have attempted to approximate such a state. Such systems are dehumanizing and, over time, result in reduced productivity of the workforce and reduced quality of its outputs. This in turn produces a precipitous decline of an economy as is occurring in many Western nations. On the other hand, relying exclusively—as organismic modelers of organizations do—on an increasing flow of information and compromise to reduce conflict does not produce encouraging results. Witness the situation in the United Nations, which has dramatically increased the flow of information between nations and compromise among them.

Therefore, the challenge before us is to create a type of organization that is capable of continuously *dissolving* conflict while *increasing* choice. This requires an organizational concept that is not compatible with either a deterministic or animate model of organization. It requires application of social-systemic models to social systems.

THE SOCIAL SYSTEMIC ORGANIZATION

In other places we (Gharajedaghi, 1985, 1986; Ackoff, 1981, 1994) have proposed an organizational design that is based on a social-systemic model. It has the following features, none of which are compatible with other than a social-systemic model:

1. It is a *democratic organization,* one in which every individual who is affected by what that organization does has a voice in deciding what it does, and in which anyone who has authority over others taken individually, is subject to their collective authority.

2. It has an *internal market economy,* one in which every part of the organization can purchase the goods and/or services it requires from any internal or external source it chooses, and can sell its output to any buyer it wants. Both these types of decision, buying and selling, are subject to overrides by higher authorities who must, nevertheless, compensate the part of the organization affected for its loss of income or increased costs due to the higher-level intervention.

3. It has a *multidimensional organizational structure,* one in which units of three different types are located at each level of the organization: units defined by (a) their function (i.e., units whose output is primarily consumed internally), (b) their output (product or services primarily consumed externally), and (c) their users (markets, defined by type or location of customers). This type of organization eliminates the need for continual restructuring. Restructuring is replaced by reallocation of resources.

4. It uses *interactive planning* which involves idealized redesign of the organization, and determination of the closest approximation to that design that can be realized. Such planning then involves selection of the means by which the approximation is to be pursued; provision of the resources required by the pursuit; specifying the implementation steps to be taken, when and by whom; and finally,

design of monitoring and controls of both the implementation and the effects of the plan.

5. It contains a *decision support system* that facilitates learning and adaptation by (a) recording the expectations associated with each decision of significance, (b) the assumptions and information on which they are based, and (c) the process by which the decision was reached, and by whom. It then monitors the implementation, assumptions, and effects of every decision, corrects them where assumptions turn out to be wrong or expectations are not met, and retains in an easily accessible memory what has been learned. Finally, it carries out continuous surveillance of the environment to detect changes that have occurred or are about to occur that require adaptation by the organization.

Any one or subset of these changes can significantly improve organizational performance. However, when all are made together, there is a powerful multiplicative effect, one that is much greater than the sum of its parts.

CONCLUSION

We have argued that it is useful to cast systems and their models into one of three types: deterministic, animate, and social-systemic. The difference between them is a matter of "choice." Deterministic systems and their parts display no choice. Animate systems can display choice but their parts can't. Social–systemic systems display choice, their parts do as well, and they are part of larger systems that also display choice and contain other systems that do so as well.

Our point has been that when models of one type are applied to systems of a different type, at least as much harm is done as good. The amount of harm (hence good) that is done depends on the level of maturity that social systems have reached.

Our society and the principal private and public organizations and institutions that it contains have reached a level of maturity that eliminates whatever effectiveness applying deterministic and animalistic models to social systems may once have had. Finally, we showed five characteristics that we believe social systems designed as social systems should have in order to function as effectively as possible.

BIBLIOGRAPHY

Ackoff, R. L. (1981). *Creating the Corporate Future,* Wiley, New York.

Ackoff, R. L. (1994). *The Democratic Corporation,* Oxford University Press, New York.

Beer, S. (1972). *The Brain of the Firm,* Allen Lane/Penguin Press, London.

Flower, E. F. (1942). Two Applications of Logic to Biology. In Clarke, F. P., and Nahm, M. (Eds.), *Philosophical Essays in Honor of Edgar Arthur Singer, Jr.,* University of Pennsylvania Press, Philadelphia.

Forrester, J. W. (1961). *Industrial Dynamics,* Wright-Allen Press, Cambridge.

Forrester, J. W. (1971). *World Dynamics,* Wright-Allen Press, Cambridge.

Gharajedaghi, J. (1985). *Toward a Systems Theory of Organization,* Intersystems Publications, Seaside, CA.

Gharajedaghi, J. (1986). *A Prologue to National Development Planning,* Greenwood Press, New York.

Hussong, A. M. (1931). *An Analysis of the Group Mind,* Doctoral Dissertation, University of Pennsylvania.

Meier, R. L. (1963). Communication overload: proposals from the study of a university library. *Administrative Science Quarterly 7,* 521–544.

Sorokin, P. (1928). *Contemporary Sociological Theories,* Harper, New York.

Work in America: Report of a Special Task Force to the Secretary of Health, Education, and Welfare, MIT Press, Cambridge, MA (1973).

Zeleny, M. (Ed.). (1981). *Autopoiesis: A Theory of Living Organization,* Elsevier, New York.

CHAPTER 3

GROWTH VERSUS DEVELOPMENT

Growth and development are *not* the same thing. Neither is necessary for the other. A rubbish heap can grow but it doesn't develop. Artists can develop without growing. Nevertheless, many managers take development to be the same as growth. Most efforts directed at corporate development are actually directed at corporate growth.

To grow is to increase in size or number. *To develop is to increase one's ability and desire to satisfy one's own needs and legitimate desires and those of others.* A legitimate desire is one that, when satisfied, does not impede the development of anyone else.

Development is an increase in capability and competence.

Development of individuals and corporations is more a matter of learning than earning. It has less to do with how much one has than how much one can do with whatever one has. For this reason Robinson Crusoe is a better model of development than Jean Paul Getty.

Development is better reflected in quality of life than in standard of living. Therefore, the level of development of a corporation is better reflected in the quality of work life it provides its employees than in its profit-and-loss statement.

If an undeveloped country or corporation was flooded with money it would be richer but no more developed. On the other hand, if a well-developed country or corporation was suddenly deprived of wealth, it would not be less developed.

A well-developed country or corporation can do more with its resources than one that is less developed. This is *not* to say that the amount of resources available is irrelevant. Resources can be used to accelerate development and improve quality of life, but they can best be used for these purposes by those who are developed.

From *Management in Small Doses* (Wiley, 1986).

Growth and development do not have to conflict; they can reinforce each other. The best evidence that this is happening is a simultaneous increase in standard of living and quality of life. However, there is currently a widespread belief that quality of life is being sacrificed to increase standard of living. This belief is accompanied by a willingness to sacrifice standard of living to improve quality of life, a willingness that is reflected in the environmentalist movement.

A lack of resources can limit growth but not development. The more developed individuals, organizations, or societies becomes the less they depend on resources and the more they can do with whatever resources they have. They also have the ability and the desire to create or acquire the resources they need.

An individual can grow too much. Some people and many societies believe that a corporation can too. *But would anyone argue that individuals, corporations, or countries can develop too much?*

CHAPTER 4

TOWARD A SYSTEM OF SYSTEMS CONCEPTS

$\mathbf{T}$he concepts and terms commonly used to talk about systems have not themselves been organized into a system. An attempt to do so is made here. *System* and the most important types of systems are defined so that differences and similarities are made explicit. Particular attention is given to that type of system of most interest to management scientists: *organizations.* The relationship between a system and its parts is considered and a proposition is put forward that all systems are either variety-increasing or variety-decreasing relative to the behavior of its parts.

INTRODUCTION

The concept *system* has come to play a critical role in contemporary science.* This preoccupation of scientists in general is reflected among Management Scientists in particular for whom the *systems approach* to problems is fundamental and for whom *organizations,* a special type of system, are the principal subject of study.

The systems approach to problems focuses on systems taken as a whole, not on their parts taken separately. Such an approach is concerned with total-system performance even when a change in only one or a few of its parts is contemplated because there are some properties of systems that can only be treated adequately from a holistic point of view. These properties derive from the *relationships* between parts of systems: how the parts interact and fit together. In an imperfectly organized system, even if every

From "Toward a System of Systems Concepts," in *System Analysis Techniques,* by J. Daniel Couger and Robert W. Knapp (Eds.), pp. 27–38 (Wiley, 1974).
* For excellent extensive and intensive discussions of "systems thinking," see F. E. Emery, *Systems Thinking,* and C. W. Churchman, *The Systems Approach.*

part performs as well as possible relative to its own objectives, the total system will often not perform as well as possible relative to its objectives.

Despite the importance of systems concepts and the attention that they have received and are receiving, we do not yet have a unified or integrated set (i.e., a system) of such concepts. Different terms are used to refer to the same thing and the same term is used to refer to different things. This state is aggravated by the fact that the literature of systems research is widely dispersed and is therefore difficult to track. Researchers in a wide variety of disciplines are contributing to the conceptual development of the systems sciences, but these contributions are not as interactive and additive as they might be. Fred Emery has warned against too hasty an effort to remedy this situation:

> It is almost as if the pioneers [of systems thinking], while respectfully noting each other's existence, have felt it incumbent upon themselves to work out their intuitions in their own language, for fear of what might be lost in trying to work through the language of another. Whatever the reason, the results seem to justify the stand-offishness. In a short space of time there has been a considerable accumulation of insights into system dynamics that are readily translatable into different languages and with, as yet, little sign of divisive schools of thought that for instance marred psychology during the 1920s and 1930s. Perhaps this might happen if some influential group of scholars prematurely decide that the time has come for a common conceptual framework. (p. 12)

Although I sympathize with Emery's fear, a fear that is rooted in a research perspective, as a teacher I feel a great need to provide my students with a conceptual framework that will assist them in absorbing and synthesizing this large accumulation of insights to which Emery refers. My intent is not to preclude further conceptual exploration, but rather to encourage it and make it more interactive and additive. Despite Emery's warning I feel benefits will accrue to systems research from an evolutionary convergence of concepts into a generally accepted framework. At any rate, little harm is likely to come from my effort to provide the beginnings of such a framework since I can hardly claim to be, or to speak for, "an influential group of scholars."

The framework that follows does not include all concepts relevant to the systems sciences. I have made an effort, however, to include enough of the key concepts so that building on this framework will not be as difficult as construction of the framework itself has been.

One final word of introduction. I have not tried to identify the origin or trace the history of each conceptual idea that is presented in what follows. Hence few credits are provided. I can only compensate for this lack of bibliographic bird-dogging by claiming no credit for any of the elements in what follows, only for the resulting system into which they have been organized. I must, of course, accept responsibility for deficiencies in either the parts or the whole.

SYSTEMS

1. A *system* is a set of interrelated elements. Thus a system is an entity which is composed of at least two elements and a relation that holds between each of its elements and at least one other element in the set. Each of a system's elements is connected to every other element, directly or indirectly. Furthermore, no subset of elements is unrelated to any other subset.

2. An *abstract system* is one all of whose elements are concepts. Languages, philosophic systems, and number systems are examples. *Numbers* are concepts, but the symbols that represent them, *numerals,* are physical things. Numerals, however, are not the elements of a number system. The use of different numerals to represent the same numbers does not change the nature of the system.

In an abstract system the elements are created by defining and the relationships between them are created by assumptions (e.g., axioms and postulates). Such systems, therefore, are the subject of study of the so-called "formal sciences."

3. A *concrete system* is one at least two of whose elements are objects. It is only with such systems that we are concerned here. Unless otherwise noted, "system" will always be used to mean "concrete system."

In concrete systems, establishment of the existence and properties of elements and the nature of the relationships between them requires research with an empirical component in it. Such systems, therefore, are the subject of study of the so-called "nonformal sciences."

4. The *state of a system* at a moment of time is the set of relevant properties which that system has at that time. Any system has an unlimited number of properties. Only some of these are relevant to any particular research. Hence those which are relevant may change with changes in the purpose of the research. The values of the relevant properties constitute the state of the system. In some cases we may be interested in only two possible states (e.g., off and on, or awake and asleep). In other cases we may be interested in a large or unlimited number of possible states (e.g., a system's velocity or weight).

5. The *environment of a system* is a set of elements and their relevant properties, which elements are not part of the system but a change in any of which can produce* a change in the state of the system. Thus a system's environment consists of all variables that can affect its state. External elements that affect irrelevant properties of a system are not part of its environment.

6. The *state of a system's environment* at a moment of time is the set of its relevant properties at that time. The state of an element or subset of elements of a system or its environment may be similarly defined.

Although concrete systems and their environments are *objective* things, they are also *subjective* insofar as the particular configuration of elements that form both is dictated by the interests of the researcher. Different observers of the same phenomena may conceptualize them into different systems and environments. For example, an architect may consider a house together with its electrical, heating, and water systems as one large system. But a mechanical engineer may consider the heating system as a system and the house as its environment. To a social psychologist a house may be an environment of a family, the system with which he is concerned. To him the relationship between the heating and electrical systems may be irrelevant, but to the architect it may be very relevant.

The elements that form the environment of a system, and the environment itself, may be conceptualized as systems when they become the focus of attention. Every system can be conceptualized as part of another and larger system.

Even an abstract system can have an environment. For example, the meta-language in which we describe a formal system is the environment of that formal system. Therefore, logic is the environment of mathematics.

7. A *closed system* is one that has no environment. An *open system* is one that does. Thus a closed system is one which is conceptualized so that it has no interaction with any element not contained within it; it

---

* One thing *(x)* can be said to produce another *(y)* in a specified environment and time interval if *x* is a necessary but not a sufficient condition for *y* in that environment and time period. Thus a producer is a "probabilistic cause" of its product. Every producer, since it is not sufficient for its product, has a coproducer of that product (e.g., the producer's environment).

is completely self-contained. Because systems researchers have found such conceptualizations of relatively restricted use, their attention has increasingly focused on more complex and "realistic" open systems. "Openness" and "closedness" are simultaneously properties of systems and our conceptualizations of them.

Systems may or may not change over time.

8. A system (or environmental) *event* is a change in one or more structural properties of the system (or its environment) over a period of time of specified duration, that is, a change in the structural state of the system (or environment). For example, an event occurs to a house's lighting system when a fuse blows, and to its environment when night falls.

9. A *static (one-state) system* is one to which no events happen. A table, for example, can be conceptualized as a static concrete system consisting of four legs, top, screws, glue, and so on. Relative to most research purposes it displays no change of structural properties, no change of state. A compass may also be conceptualized as a static system because it virtually always points to the Magnetic North Pole.

10. A *dynamic (multi-state) system* is one to which events happen, whose state changes over time. An automobile which can move forward or backward and at different speeds is such a system, or a motor which can be either off or on. Such systems can be conceptualized as either open or closed; closed if its elements react or respond only to each other.

11. A *homeostatic system* is a static system whose elements and environment are dynamic. Thus a homeostatic system is one that retains its state in a changing environment by internal adjustments. A house that maintains a constant temperature during changing external temperatures is homeostatic. The behavior of its heating subsystem makes this possible.

Note that the same object may be conceptualized as either a static or dynamic system. For most of us a building would be thought of as static, but it might be taken as dynamic by a civil engineer who is interested in structural deformation.

SYSTEM CHANGES

12. A *reaction* of a system is a system event for which another event that happens to the same system or its environment is sufficient. Thus a reaction is a system event that is deterministically caused by another event. For example, if an operator's moving a motor's switch is sufficient to turn that motor off or on, then the change of state of the motor is a reaction to the movement of its switch. In this case, the turning of the switch may be necessary as well as sufficient for the state of the motor. But an event that is sufficient to bring about a change in a system's state may not be necessary for it. For example, sleep may be brought about by drugs administered to a person or it may be self-induced. Thus sleep may be determined by drugs but need not be.

13. A *response* of a system is a system event for which another event that happens to the same system or to its environment is necessary but not sufficient, that is, a system event produced by another system or environmental event (the *stimulus*). Thus a response is an event of which the system itself is a coproducer. A system does not have to respond to a stimulus, but it does have to react to its cause. Therefore, a person's turning on a light when it gets dark is a response to darkness, but the light's going on when the switch is turned is a reaction.

14. An *act* of a system is a system event for the occurrence of which no change in the system's environment is either necessary or sufficient. Acts, therefore, are self-determined events, autonomous changes. Internal changes—in the states of the system's elements—are both necessary and sufficient to bring about action. Much of the behavior of human beings is of this type, but such behavior is not restricted to humans. A computer, for example, may have its state changed or change the state of its environment because of its own program.

Systems all of whose changes are reactive, responsive, or autonomous (active) can be called reactive, responsive, or autonomous (active), respectively. Most systems, however, display some combination of these types of change.

The classification of systems into reactive, responsive, and autonomous is based on consideration of what brings about changes in them. Now let us consider systems with respect to the kind of changes in themselves and their environments their reactions, responses, and actions bring about.

15. A system's *behavior* is a system event(s) which is either necessary or sufficient for another event in that system or its environment. Thus behavior is a system change which initiates other events. Note that reactions, responses, and actions may themselves constitute behavior. Reactions, responses, and actions are system events *whose antecedents are of interest*. Behavior consists of system events *whose consequences are of* *interest*. We may, of course, be interested in both the antecedents and consequences of system events.

BEHAVIORAL CLASSIFICATION OF SYSTEMS

Understanding the nature of the classification that follows may be aided by Table 4.1 in which the basis for the classification is revealed.

16. A *state-maintaining system* is one that (1) can react in only one way to any one external or internal event; but (2) it reacts differently to different external or internal events; and (3) these different reactions produce the same external or internal state (outcome). Such a system reacts only to changes; it cannot respond because what it does is completely determined by the causing event. Nevertheless it can be said to have the *function* of maintaining the state it produces because it can produce this state in different ways under different conditions.

Thus a heating system whose internal controller turns it on when the room temperature is below a desired level, and turns it off when the temperature is above this level, is state-maintaining. The state it maintains is a room temperature that falls within a small range around its setting. Note that the temperature of the room which affects the system's behavior can be conceptualized as either part of the system or part of its environment. Hence a state-maintaining system may react to either internal or external changes.

In general, most systems with "stats" (e.g., thermostats and humidistats) are state-maintaining. Any system with a regulated output (e.g., the voltage of the output of a generator) is also state-maintaining.

A compass is also state-maintaining because in many different environments it points to the Magnetic North Pole.

Table 4.1
Behavioral Classification of Systems

Type of System	Behavior of System	Outcome of Behavior
State-maintaining	Variable but determined (reactive)	Fixed
Goal-seeking	Variable and chosen (responsive)	Fixed
Multi-goal-seeking and purposive	Variable and chosen	Variable but determined
Purposeful	Variable and chosen	Variable and chosen

A state-maintaining system must be able to *discriminate* between different internal or external states to changes in which it reacts. Furthermore, as we shall see below, such systems are necessarily *adaptive;* but unlike goal-seeking systems they are not capable of learning because they cannot choose their behavior. They cannot improve with experience.

17. A *goal-seeking system* is one that can respond differently to one or more different external or internal events in one or more different external or internal states and that can respond differently to a particular event in an unchanging environment until it produces a particular state (outcome). Production of this state is its goal. Thus such a system has a *choice* of behavior. A goal-seeking system's behavior is responsive, but not reactive. A state which is sufficient and thus deterministically causes a reaction cannot cause different reactions in the same environment.

Under constant conditions a goal-seeking system may be able to accomplish the same thing in different ways and it may be able to do so under different conditions. If it has *memory,* it can increase its efficiency over time in producing the outcome that is its goal.

For example, an electronic maze-solving rat is a goal-seeking system which, when it runs into a wall of a maze, turns right and if stopped again, goes in the opposite direction, and if stopped again, returns in the direction from which it came. In this way it can eventually solve any solvable maze. If, in addition, it has memory, it can take a "solution path" on subsequent trials in a familiar maze.

Systems with automatic "pilots" are goal-seeking. These and other goal-seeking systems may, of course, fail to attain their goals in some situations.

The sequence of behavior which a goal-seeking system carries out in quest of its goal is an example of a process.

18. A *process* is a sequence of behavior that constitutes a system and has a goal-producing function. In some well-definable sense each unit of behavior in the process brings the actor closer to the goal which it seeks. The sequence of behavior that is performed by the electronic rat constitutes a maze-solving process. After each move the rat is closer (i.e., has reduced the number of moves required) to solving the maze. The metabolic process in living things is a similar type of sequence the goal of which is acquisition of energy or, more generally, survival.

Production processes are a similar type of sequence whose goal is a particular type of product.

Process behavior displayed by a system may be either reactive, responsive, or active.

19. A *multi-goal-seeking* system is one that is goal-seeking in each of two or more different (initial) external or internal states, and which seeks different goals in at least two different states, the goal being determined by the initial state.

20. A *purposive system* is a multi-goal-seeking system, the different goals of which have a common property. Production of that common property is the system's purpose. These types of systems can pursue different goals, but they do not select the goal to be pursued. The goal is determined by the initiating event. But such a system does choose the means by which to pursue its goals.

A computer which is programmed to play more than one game (e.g., tic-tac-toe and checkers) is multi-goal-seeking. What game it plays is not a matter of its choice, however; it is usually determined by an instruction from an external source. Such a system is also purposive because "game winning" is a common property of the different goals which it seeks.

21. A *purposeful system* is one which can produce the same outcome in different ways in the same (internal or external) state and can produce different outcomes in the same and different states. Thus a purposeful system is one which can change its goals under constant conditions; it selects ends as well as means and thus displays *will*. Human beings are the most familiar examples of such systems.

Ideal-seeking systems form an important subclass of purposeful systems. Before making their nature explicit we must consider the differences between goals, objectives, and ideals, and some concepts related to them. The differences to be considered have relevance only to purposeful systems because only they can choose ends.

A system which can choose between different outcomes can place different values on different outcomes.

22. The *relative value of an outcome* that is a member of an exclusive and exhaustive set of outcomes, to a purposeful system, is the probability that the system will produce that outcome when each of the set of outcomes can be obtained with certainty. The relative value of an outcome can range from 0 to 1.0. That outcome with the highest relative value in a set can be said to be *preferred*.

23. The *goal* of a purposeful system in a particular situation is a preferred outcome that can be obtained within a specified time period.

24. The *objective* of a purposeful system in a particular situation is a preferred outcome that cannot be obtained within a specified period but which can be obtained over a longer time period. Consider a set of possible outcomes ordered along one or more scales (e.g., increasing speeds of travel). Then each outcome is closer to the final one than those which precede it. Each of these outcomes can be a goal in some time period after the "preceding" goal has been obtained, leading eventually to attainment of the last outcome, the objective. For example, a high-school freshman's goal in his first year is to be promoted to his second (sophomore) year. Passing his second year is a subsequent goal. And so on to graduation, which is his objective.

Pursuit of an objective requires an ability to change goals once a goal has been obtained. This is why such pursuit is possible only for a purposeful system.

25. An *ideal* is an objective which cannot be obtained in any time period but which can be approached without limit. Just as goals can be ordered with respect to objectives, objectives can be ordered with respect to ideals. But an ideal is an outcome which is unobtainable in practice, if not in principle. For example, an ideal of science is errorless observations. The amount of observer error can be reduced without limit but can never be reduced to zero. Omniscience is another such ideal.

26. An *ideal-seeking system* is a purposeful system which, on attainment of any of its goals or objectives, then seeks another goal and objective which more closely approximates its ideal. An ideal-seeking system is thus one which has a concept of "perfection" or the "ultimately desirable" and pursues it systematically, that is, in interrelated steps.

From the point of view of their output, six types of system have been identified: state-maintaining, goal-seeking, multi-goal-seeking, purposive, purposeful, and ideal-seeking. The elements of systems can be similarly classified. The relationship between (1) the behavior and type of a system and (2) the behavior and type of its elements is not apparent. We consider it next.

RELATIONSHIPS BETWEEN SYSTEMS AND THEIR ELEMENTS

Some systems can display a greater variety and higher level of behavior than can any of their elements. These can be called *variety increasing*. For example, consider two state-maintaining elements, A and B. Say A reacts to a decrease in room temperature by closing any open windows. If a short time after A has reacted the room temperature is still below a specified level, B reacts to this by turning on the furnace. Then the system consisting of A and B is goal-seeking.

Clearly, by combining two or more goal-seeking elements we can construct a multi-goal-seeking (and hence a purposive) system. It is less apparent that such elements can also be combined to form a purposeful system. Suppose one element A can pursue goal G_1 in environment E_1 and goal G_2 in another environment E_2; and the other element B can pursue G_2 in E_1 and G_1 in E_2. Then the system would be capable of pursuing G_1 and G_2 in both E_1 and E_2 if it could select between the elements in these environments. Suppose we add a third (controlling) element which responds to E_1 by "turning on" either A or B, but not both. Suppose further that it turns on A with probability P_A where $0 < P_A < 1.0$ and turns on B with probability P_B where $0 < P_B < 1.0$. (The controller could be a computer that employs random numbers for this purpose.) The resulting sytem could choose both ends and means in two environments and hence would be purposeful.

A system can also show less variety of behavior and operate at a lower level than at least some of its elements. Such a system is *variety reducing*. For example, consider a simple system with two elements one of which turns lights on in a room whenever the illumination in that room drops below a certain level. The other element turns the lights off whenever the illumination exceeds a level that is lower than that provided by the lights in the room. Then the lights will go off and on continuously. The system would not be state-maintaining even though its elements are.

A more familiar example of a variety-reducing sytem can be found in those groups of purposeful people (e.g., committees) which are incapable of reaching agreement and hence of taking any collective action.

A system must be either variety-increasing or variety-decreasing. A set of elements which collectively neither increase nor decrease variety would have to consist of identical elements, either only one of which can act at a time or in which similar action by multiple units is equivalent to action by only one. In the latter case the behavior is nonadditive and the behavior is redundant. The relationships between the elements would therefore be irrelevant. For example, a set of similar automobiles owned by one person does not constitute a system because he can drive only one at a time and which he drives makes no difference. On the other hand, a radio with two speakers can provide stereo sound; the speakers each do a different thing and together they do something that neither can do alone.

ADAPTATION AND LEARNING

In order to deal with the concepts "adaptation" and "learning" it is necessary first to consider the concepts "function" and "efficiency."

27. The *function(s)* of a system is production of the outcomes that define its goal(s) and objective(s). Put another way, suppose a system can display at least two structurally different types of behavior in the same or different environments and that these types of behavior produce the same kind of outcome. Then the system can be said to have the function of producing that outcome. To function, therefore, is to be able to produce the same outcome in different ways.

Let C_i ($1 \leq i \leq m$) represent the different actions available to a system in a specific environment. Let P_i represent the probabilities that the system will select these courses of action in that environment. If the courses of action are exclusive and exhaustive, then

$$\sum_{i=1}^{m} P_i = 1.0.$$

Let E_{ij} represent the probability that course of action C_i will produce a particular outcome O_j in that environment. Then:

28. The *efficiency* of the system with respect to an outcome O_j which it has the function of producing is

$$\sum_{i=1}^{m} P_i E_{ij}.$$

Now we can turn to "adaptation."

29. A system is *adaptive* if, when there is a change in its environmental and/or internal state which reduces its efficiency in pursuing one or more of the goals that define its function(s), it reacts or responds by changing its own state and/or that of its environment so as to increase its efficiency with respect to that goal or goals. Thus adaptiveness is the ability of a system to modify itself or its environment when either has changed to the system's disadvantage so as to regain at least some of its lost efficiency.

The definition of "adaptive" implies four types of adaptation:

29.1. *Other-other adaptation:* A system's reacting or responding to an external change by modifying the environment (e.g., when a person turns on an air conditioner in a room that has become too warm for him to continue to work in).

29.2. *Other-self adaptation:* A system's reacting or responding to an external change by modifying itself (e.g., when the person moves to another and cooler room).

29.3. *Self-other adaptation:* A system's reacting or responding to an internal change by modifying the environment (e.g., when a person who has chills due to a cold turns up the heat).

29.4. *Self-self adaptation:* A system's reacting or responding to an internal change by modifying itself (e.g., when that person takes medication to suppress the chills). Other-self adaptation is most commonly considered because it was this type with which Darwin was concerned in his studies of biological species as systems.

It should now be apparent why state-maintaining and higher systems are necessarily adaptive. Now let us consider why nothing lower than a goal-seeking system is capable of learning.

30. To *learn* is to increase one's efficiency in the pursuit of a goal under unchanging conditions. Thus if a person increases his ability to hit a target (his goal) with repeated shooting at it, he learns how to shoot better. Note that to do so requires an ability to modify one's behavior (i.e., to display choice) and memory.

Since learning can take place only when a system has a choice among alternative courses of action, only systems that are goal-seeking or higher can learn.

If a system is repeatedly subjected to the same environmental or internal change and increases its ability to maintain its efficiency under this type of change, then it *learns how to adapt*. Thus adaptation itself can be learned.

ORGANIZATIONS

Management Scientists are most concerned with that type of system called "organizations." Cyberneticians, on the other hand, are more concerned with that type of system called "organisms"; but they frequently treat organizations as though they were organisms. Although these two types of system have much in common, there is an important difference between them. This difference can be identified once "organization" has been defined. I will work up to its definition by considering separately each of what I consider to be its four essential characteristics.

(1) An organization is a purposeful system that contains at least two purposeful elements which have a common purpose.

We sometimes characterize a purely mechanical system as being well organized, but we would not refer to it as an "organization." This results from the fact that we use "organize" to mean, "to make a system of," or as one dictionary puts it, "to get into proper working order," and "to arrange or dispose systematically." Wires, poles, transformers, switchboards, and telephones may constitute a communication system; but they do not constitute an organization. The employees of a telephone company make up the organization that operates the telephone system. Organization of a system is an activity that can be carried out only by purposeful entities; to be an organization a system must contain such entities.

An aggregation of purposeful entities does not constitute an organization unless they have at least one common purpose: that is, unless there is some one or more things that they all want. An organization is always organized around this common purpose. It is the relationships between what the purposeful elements do and the pursuit of their common purpose that give unity and identity to their organization.

Without a common purpose the elements would not work together unless compelled to do so. A group of unwilling prisoners or slaves can be organized and forced to do something that they do not want to do, but they do not constitute an organization even though they may form a system. An organization consists of elements that have and can exercise their own wills.

(2) An organization has a functional division of labor in pursuit of the common purpose(s) of its elements that define it.

Each of two or more subsets of elements, each containing one or more purposeful elements, is responsible for choosing from among different courses of action. A choice from each subset is necessary for obtaining the common purpose. For example, if an automobile carrying two people stalls on a highway and one gets out and pushes while the other sits in the driver's seat trying to start it when it is in motion, then there is a functional division of labor and they constitute an organization. The car cannot be started (their common purpose) unless both functions are performed.

The classes of courses of action and (hence) the subsets of elements may be differentiated by a variety of types of characteristics; for example:

(a) by *function* (e.g., production, marketing, research, finance, and personnel, in the industrial context),

(b) by *space* (e.g., geography, as territories of sales offices),

(c) by *time* (e.g., waves of an invading force).

The classes of action may, of course, also be defined by combinations of these and other characteristics.

It should be noted that individuals or groups in an organization that *make* choices need not *take* them, that is, carry them out. The actions may be carried out by other persons, groups, or even machines that are controlled by the decision makers.

(3) The functionally distinct subsets (parts of the system) can respond to each other's behavior through observation or communication.*

In some laboratory experiments subjects are given interrelated tasks to perform but they are not permitted to observe or communicate with each other even though they are rewarded on the basis of an outcome determined by their collective choices. In such cases the subjects are *unorganized*. If they were allowed to observe each other or to communicate with each other, they could become an organization. The choices made by elements or subsets of an organization must be capable of influencing each other, otherwise they would not even constitute a system.

---

* In another place (Ackoff), I have given operational definitions of "observation" and "communication" that fit this conceptual system. Reproduction of these treatments would require more space than is available here.

(4) At lest one subset of the system has a system-control function.

This subset (or subsystem) compares achieved outcomes with desired outcomes and makes adjustments in the behavior of the system which are directed toward reducing the observed deficiencies. It also determines what the desired outcomes are. The control function is normally exercised by an executive body which operates on a feed-back principle. "Control" requires elucidation.

31. An element or a system *controls* another element or system (or itself) if its behavior is either necessary or sufficient for subsequent behavior of the other element or system (or itself), and the subsequent behavior is necessary or sufficient for the attainment of one or more of its goals. Summarizing, then, an "organization" can be defined as follows:

32. An *organization* is a purposeful system that contains at least two purposeful elements which have a common purpose relative to which the system has a functional division of labor; its functionally distinct subsets can respond to each other's behavior through observation or communication; and at least one subset has a system-control function.

Now the critical difference between organisms and organizations can be made explicit. Whereas both are purposeful systems, organisms do not contain purposeful elements. The elements of an organism may be state-maintaining, goal-seeking, multi-goal-seeking, or purposive; but not purposeful. Thus an organism must be variety increasing. An organization, on the other hand, may be either variety increasing or decreasing (e.g., the ineffective committee). In an organism only the whole can display will; none of the parts can.

Because an organism is a system that has a functional division of labor it is also said to be "organized." Its functionally distinct parts are called "organs." Their functioning is necessary but not sufficient for accomplishment of the organism's purpose(s).

CONCLUSION

Defining concepts is frequently treated by scientists as an annoying necessity to be completed as quickly and thoughtlessly as possible. A consequence of this disinclination to define often is research carried out like surgery performed with dull instruments. The surgeon has to work harder, the patient has to suffer more, and the chances for success are decreased.

Like surgical instruments, definitions become dull with use and require frequent sharpening and, eventually, replacement. Those I have offered here are not exceptions.

Research can seldom be played with a single concept; a matched set is usually required. Matching different researches requires matching the sets of concepts used in them. A scientific field can arise only on the base of a system of concepts. Systems science is not an exception. Systems thinking, if anything, should be carried out systematically.

BIBLIOGRAPHY

Ackoff, R. L., *Choice, Communication, and Conflict,* a report to the National Science Foundation under Grant GN-389, Management Science Center, University of Pennsylvania, Philadelphia, 1967.

Churchman, C. W., *The Systems Approach,* Delacorte Press, New York, 1968.

Emery, F. E., *Systems Thinking,* Penguin Books Ltd., Harmondsworth, Middlesex, England, 1969.

CHAPTER 5

BEATING THE SYSTEM

NOTES FROM AN ANTIBUREAUCRAT

If you're going to sin, sin against God, not the bureaucracy. God will forgive you but the bureaucracy won't.

Admiral Hyman G. Rickover

The British created a civil service job in 1803 calling for a man to stand on the Cliffs of Dover. The man was supposed to ring a bell if he saw Napoleon coming. The job was abolished in 1945.

Robert Townsend, *Up the Organization*

The only thing that saves us from bureaucracy is its inefficiency.

Eugene McCarthy

CHECK AND DOUBLE CHECK

Whenever Madge, a London housewife, went shopping, she would stop to cash a check at a large branch of a chain store that was located very near her flat. This saved her walking several blocks to the closest branch of her bank.

One day when Madge stopped at the store to cash her check, she was told that the store had a new policy: no check cashing. She was indignant, but not for long. She went to the dress department of the store and bought a dress priced at approximately the amount of the check she wanted to cash. The store accepted her check in payment for the dress. Madge then took the dress to the return desk and asked for a refund. They gave it to her in cash.

Moral: No system is as smart as some of the people it serves.

From *Ackoff's Fables* (Wiley, 1991).

SYSTEMS AND VARIETY

What we learn from experience is conditioned by the social systems with which we interact: family, schools, government and its institutions, communities, corporations, and so on. All effects on us of social systems fall into one of two classes: either they enable us to do or have something we could not otherwise do or have, or they prevent us from doing or having something we could otherwise do or have. In other words, the systems with which we interact may either increase or reduce the variety of behavior available to us.

Of course, a system may be enabling in some areas and obstructive in others. For example, a school may enable children to learn a subject they would not otherwise learn, but it may also prevent them from learning something they would learn if left to their own devices. However, most systems can be characterized as predominantly either variety-increasing or variety-decreasing. A prison, for example, is clearly variety-decreasing, while a library is variety-increasing.

BEATING BUREAUCRACY

The most variety-decreasing type of social system is one we call a *bureaucracy*. A bureaucracy is an organization whose principal objective is to keep people busy doing nothing. They are preoccupied with what we call make-work. For example, application for renewal of a driver's license, which takes only a few minutes to process in the state in which I reside, takes hours to process in Mexico. The output is identical in both cases: a card authorizing operation of an automobile. What is being done in the additional time required for the processing in Mexico? Nothing. It could be eliminated with no effect on the output.

The problem created by people who are busy doing nothing is that they frequently obstruct others who have real work to do. They impose unproductive requirements on others. For example, my application for renewal of my driver's license in Pennsylvania requires no signature but my own; in Mexico, I had to collect a large number of signatures of officials before I could submit my application. It sometimes required more than a day to do so.

Bureaucracies obstruct development. They retard improvement of quality of life. For these reasons most efforts directed at beating systems are directed at getting around bureaucracies, trying either to avoid doing what they needlessly require, or to do something that clearly needs doing but that they try to keep from being done.

Bureaucrats want all parts of an organization to conform to one set of rules and regulations. Exceptions to rules, no matter how justified they may be, are anathema to a bureaucracy. Conformity is treated as good in itself, an ultimate good. Because bureaucrats give more attention to obtaining conformity than to what is conformed to, they are sometimes vulnerable.

Equal What?

One of my university's faculty members, who exemplified the bureaucrat, was appointed by the provost to chair a committee to review compensation of graduate students employed to teach or do research. Under his leadership this committee conducted a survey that revealed significant differences in student compensation in different parts of the university. He and his committee learned that students employed in the research group that I directed were the highest paid in the university. The chairman then dedicated himself to "getting" me.

He asked me to appear before his committee. When I did he opened the session with a discourse on the desirability of equity in compensation of students regardless of where or on what they were working. He then asked what I thought about the position he had just formulated, clearly expecting me to disagree with it. However, I said that I agreed completely. This caught him by surprise. It took several minutes of hemming and hawing before he got back on course.

"Then," he said, "you will have no objection to reducing the salary paid to your students to a level equal to that of most other students."

"I certainly would," I said, again surprising him. "I agree to equity, but at the level of compensation that my students receive."

In the discussion that followed it became clear that equity was not the issue; the level of compensation was. I was asked to justify our high level of student compensation. I did so in a way that convinced at least a few on the committee. The chairman broke into the discussion to say that even if our compensation was justified, the National Science Foundation, the principal source of support of students on campus, would not tolerate such compensation as we provided.

He had not done his homework. I revealed that we had two contracts with that foundation and our students' compensation had never been questioned.

Nevertheless, the committee eventually recommended equalization of student compensation at a lower level than we used. The administration, however, decided not to implement it. The fact that a large portion of the overhead applied to our students' compensation went to the university's general fund may have influenced this decision.

Moral: In a bureaucracy, the only thing more important than conformity is income.

Bureaucracies tend to mechanize procedures, thereby reducing choice. They specify exactly what is to be done in situations that would otherwise require choice. Those who design these procedures assume they know and have taken into account all possible situations. This is not possible for even a smart person, let alone a bureaucrat.

When the assumption that all possible contingencies have been taken into account turns out to be false, those responsible for administering bureaucratic rules or regulations tend to deny the disconfirming evidence. A bureaucratic regulation, like many of the principles taught in school, can withstand any amount of disconfirming evidence.

He or She Shells

One of my classmates in graduate school was a biological taxonomist who was well known for having developed a widely used system of classifying seashells. I once asked him how he tested this system for its exhaustiveness. He told me that whenever he could, he would visit a beach that he had not previously visited, walk along the shore, and classify each shell he encountered. "Of course," he added, "occasionally I have to step on one."

Moral: To a bureaucrat, an exception to a rule can be a crushing defect.

I had a friend, Glen Camp, who dedicated himself to stepping on the bureaucracies that stepped on the shells that could not be classified. He was the most creative practitioner of this art I have ever known.

A Double Whammy

Glen Camp, now deceased, was a genius not only at beating systems but at keeping them beat. He was a brilliant and innovative operations researcher who worked on naval problems during World War II. His greatest system-bashing accomplishment occurred when he was assigned to find ways of decreasing the vulnerability of submarines to mines.

Glen went on a submarine mission in the Pacific in order to make observations and collect relevant data. He recorded his data on three-by-five-inch index cards. It was not long before he had a large collection of them. He went to the ship's store and asked for some rubber bands to help him organize his cards. The supply clerk told him there was a war going on and that no rubber bands were available. Glen patiently explained his urgent need for them, but the unsympathetic storekeeper told him to tie the cards together with string. Glen explained that this would be a bother because he had to get at the cards frequently. The storekeeper was unmoved. Glen had to settle for string.

When Glen's submarine returned to the West Coast and its naval base there, he immediately went to the base supply room and again asked for rubber bands. Once again he was told about the war and the shortages it created. Glen was so annoyed by all this that he decided to get even. He found a way to do so: at a five and dime he bought several pairs of women's elastic garters, which did not serve his purpose as well as rubber bands but served it better than string. Glen then turned in a request for reimbursement for the cost of the garters.

The naval officer who processed requests for reimbursement sent for Glen. He said he did not doubt that Glen had purchased several pairs of women's garters, even though he could not imagine what for. However, he said, whatever the reason, the request would never be approved by higher authorities; it was too irregular. He suggested that Glen make out a new request for the same amount, but for something conventional like food or transportation. Glen refused, pointing out that when he signed a request for reimbursement he swore to the truthfulness of the information provided. The frustrated officer reluctantly took Glen's request and passed it on. More than a year passed before Glen received payment for the garters. It had to be approved all the way up to an undersecretary of the navy.

When Glen received the payment, he sold the garters to his secretary for half their original price and prepared a new form returning to the navy the money he had received from this salvage operation.

Moral: A regulation upheld can hold up the regulated.

The inflexibility and intransigence of bureaucracies can sometimes be turned against them by treating them as unreasonably as they treat you. Clay Hollister, my departmental chairman at Case Institute of Technology, could match the stubbornness of any offending system.

More Than Expected

Clay did not habitually try to beat systems, but when he did . . . he did so with a vengeance. Sears was the target of one of his forays.

He was a dedicated do–it–yourselfer and user of Sears' catalogues. One such catalogue announced a sale. Among the items offered at significantly reduced prices were four-by-eight-foot sheets of quarter-inch Masonite. Although Clay had no immediate need for them, he thought he would eventually and therefore ordered four sheets of Masonite.

One day several weeks later, while Clay was at work, Sears delivered four dozen sheets of Masonite to his home, packed in four heavy wooden crates. Clay notified Sears almost immediately of its error, again by mail. Nevertheless, shortly thereafter and while he still had the entire shipment, he received a bill for four dozen sheets of Masonite. Clay returned the bill to Sears along with a copy of his earlier letter notifying the store of its error. In time he received a letter from Sears offering to credit him for the error if he would return the extra sheets of Masonite by parcel post. Clay wrote back pointing out that the sheets were much too large to send by parcel post and, furthermore, it was Sears' responsibility to pick them up, not his to return them.

Sears ignored Clay's second letter and continued to send bills to him monthly. Interest charges were added and increased with each successive bill because of his failure to pay on time. Eventually Sears threatened to turn the unpaid bill over to a collection agency. Clay retaliated by billing Sears for storage of the 44 sheets of Masonite he had not ordered. Both continued to bill the other over a number of months. Eventually Sears wrote to Clay offering to sell him the extra 44 sheets at a very reduced price. Clay pointed out to Sears that the amount it owed him for storage was now about equal to the price it wanted; he offered to call it even and keep the extra sheets of Masonite. Sears agreed.

Moral: The best system designer is one who knows how to beat any system that others design.

Bureaucracies, of course, expect complaints from those they victimize, but their responses to complaints tend to be as impersonal as the behavior that instigated the complaint.

A Dirty Word about Taxes

I once received a computer-prepared letter from a state agency informing me of my failure to pay a tax. I had paid that tax. I indicated this in a return letter in which I enclosed a copy of the check with which I had paid the tax. The state agency ignored my reply and returned another computer-generated letter, more ominous than the first, warning me of the dire consequences of my continuing default. I replied again, this time also enclosing a copy of my previous letter. The third letter I received was also computer generated and oblivious to what had preceded it.

I was no longer amused. The problem was: how to break through the computerized barrier and reach a human being. I did something I had never done before: I wrote a letter in which almost every other word was either profane or obscene. In a postscript to the letter, I explained that I had resorted to such offensive language in the hope that I might elicit a human response. I received a computerized admission of error from the agency, but no apology or sign of a human hand.

Moral: The worst thing to do about a bureaucracy's error may be not to.

SYSTEMS AND SERVICE

Service seems to have become a lost art. Systems that are supposed to serve seldom do, and when they do they often do so reluctantly. Employees of such systems become immune to the discomfort and inconvenience they and their systems cause. The only way service can be extracted from many such systems is by force, psychological or physical.

An Overnight Fray

One night I flew into New York City several hours later than my scheduled arrival time because of bad weather, but I had a late reservation (good until midnight) at a prominent hotel. I arrived there at 11:45 P.M.

There were about five men waiting in line to register, but only one clerk was on duty. I joined the line, which moved very slowly. I reached the clerk a few minutes after midnight. When I presented him with the confirmation of my reservation he told me that it was no longer valid because it was after midnight. I pointed out that I had arrived before midnight and had been waiting in line since then. Those waiting behind me confirmed my statement. The clerk listened impatiently and then repeated that my reservation was no longer valid, adding that no rooms were available anyhow.

I was infuriated and told the clerk that I would not move from my position in front of him until I had been given a room. He tried to persuade me to move out of the way. When this failed, he threatened to call the night manager and implied there would be dire consequences to me if he did so. I encouraged him to go ahead. He disappeared. (The several men waiting behind me continued their moral support.)

After an absence of about ten minutes the cleark reappeared with the night manager, who had apparently been awakened from a sound sleep. He directed a sequence of increasingly ominous threats at me. I did not budge. When he was convinced that I would not be persuaded to move, he said he was going to call the police. I encouraged him to do so. He and the clerk disappeared.

About ten minutes later they reappeared. The manager said that although he was under no obligation to provide me with a room he was going to do so in order to avoid a scene. He then registered me for a room whose sudden availability he did not explain. When he had finished he obviously expected an expression of gratitude from me. Instead he got an even angrier tirade because, I pointed out, the clerk could have given me that room in the beginning and saved all the subsequent unpleasantness. The manager did not reply. He left angrily and I went to my room.

Moral: Few services are good without reservations.

Why do so many service personnel treat those they are supposed to serve as nuisances, if not enemies? I have found this to be particularly true of airline ground personnel. On many airlines, poor service has been elevated to a fine art. My colleagues and I, all of whom travel by air several times each week, have concocted an imaginary Vice President of Customer Inconvenience to whom we have attributed unlimited ingenuity and perversity. And he trains his airline's personnel almost perfectly.

I recall an evening when I was flying an international airline for whose chief executive officer I was doing some research. I was erroneously bumped from a flight despite having reconfirmed my reservation earlier. The agent would not listen to my protests. I asked him for use of his phone. When he asked why, I said I wanted to call his chief executive officer. He looked at me disbelievingly. After I dialed the number and asked the secretary for the chief executive, the agent disconnected me and promptly put me back on the flight, but not without a great deal of disgruntled mumbling.

Very often when airline personnel are confronted with a customer's problem created by something the airline did, they absolve themselves of any responsibility for the mishap and try to get rid of the inconvenienced customer. They might be forgiven if they did nothing more than show some sympathy.

Of course there are exceptional airline personnel, I encountered one once, an employee of SAS.

Scandinavian Service

One night I arrived in Stockholm by air several hours late. The airport had been kept open to receive my flight. It began to close once we were off the plane and our baggage had been delivered. I was supposed to be met by a Swedish friend who was to have arranged a hotel for me. He was not there. I waited until the airport had emptied, but he had not appeared. All the airport's change bureaus had closed, so I could not get the coins needed to use the phone. Besides, I did not know his home phone number or his home address, and there were a large number of entries with the same name as his in the telephone directory. In addition, all the taxis had left. The airport appeared to be completely deserted; it was barely illuminated by a few night lights.

I wandered about the airport desperately looking for help. After some time I found an office with a light on. I knocked on the door and was invited in. A young SAS agent was closing shop. I explained my predicament to her. She asked me to sit down and relax. She assured me that she would solve my problem. Then she took a phone book and systematically began to call those with the same name as my friend's. She went through almost a dozen before she reached my friend's wife.

The wife explained that my friend had been called away on urgent business, but several days earlier he had wired me about it and instructed me not to come. I had not received his wire. Then the agent said she would arrange a hotel room for me, and did. She then called a cab, which came to the airport. She explained my situation to the driver and he agreed to wait for payment until I changed some money at the hotel. Off I went, forever grateful to that young lady.

Moral: No one hath greater love than a satisfied customer.

What a difference between this young lady's attitude and that of the New York hotel's registration clerk. The difference between them was the amount of empathy they had with those they served. The clerk could not see my situation from my point of view, only from his own. The SAS agent clearly identified with me and understood my problem. She treated me as she would like to have been treated in such a situation.

The word *service* derives from the Latin word meaning "slave": service was the work expected of slaves. The rise of Christianity, however, generated an opposing view of service as the highest form of human effort, as exemplified in "service to God." These opposing connotations of service still prevail. In most professions good service ranks as the highest possible accomplishment; it is admired and attracts respect and status. On the other hand, *domestic service* still carries much of its original Latin connotation: slave labor. It attracts little respect or status.

Practice of the arts or crafts contrasts sharply with service. It was and is the work of free people, and it results in tangible products; service produces only effects. In materialistic societies such as ours, the products of arts and crafts have a higher social standing than the effects of service. For these reasons, most forms of social service try to align themselves with such arts and crafts as law, medicine, engineering, and architecture.

What transforms slavelike labor into exalted service are the amount of skill required to provide it; the importance of the need or desire served; the relationship between the server and the served; and prevailing religious, moral, and social opinion. The esteem in which servers and their services are held by the served has a great effect on the quality of service rendered. Servers who view themselves and are viewed by others as necessary evils—or worse still, an unnecessary evils—are unlikely to show much empathy with those they serve. Most airline agents, and the long lines one must stand in to get to them, are viewed as unnecessary evils. (In some cases one's ticket must be shown four times before one can get on a plane.) Hostility to the server by those served generates hostility by the server to those served. This vicious cycle can only be broken by redesigning services so they are arranged for the convenience and comfort of the served and are perceived as such by both the served and the servers.

REMOVING SYSTEMICALLY IMPOSED OBSTRUCTIONS

Bureaucracies are almost always aware of their inefficiency, ineffectiveness, and inhumanity. Therefore, they try to keep out of the limelight. This makes them vulnerable to exposure, the threat of which can sometimes work wonders.

Jessie

The research group and academic department in The Wharton School, of which I was a part until 1986, were located on the fourth floor of a relatively new building, Vance Hall. One of our graduate students employed by the center, Bill Roth, had a wonderful male Labrador retriever, Jessie, who came to work and class with him every day. Every morning Jessie called on each of us in our offices to say hello and collect the treats inevitably provided. When he wanted to go outdoors, he would walk to the bank of elevators at the end of our hall and wait patiently until someone took him down to the ground floor. He reversed the procedure when he wanted to return. He was the most attentive student, and the quietest, in the many seminars he attended.

Jessie was a very important part of our fourth-floor society.

One day, Jessie mistakenly got off the elevator on the third floor and wandered around in a confused state. The professor who directed the center that occupied that floor was very much annoyed by Jessie's presence. He called the university's director of buildings and grounds and told him to remove the dog and prevent his reentering the building. Fortunately, a passing student who knew Jessie retrieved him and returned him to the fourth floor. Nevertheless, a directive was issued by the university prohibiting the admission of pets to our building. A No Pets Allowed sign was posted at each of its entrances.

Jessie, of course, could not read. He continued coming up to the fourth floor, but he was now equipped with a letter I wrote and conspicuously attached to his collar. It read:

To whom it may or may not concern:

Jessie, a black, male Labrador retriever who is not my pet but is my friend, and who has been the mascot of the Social Systems Sciences Unit for the last three years, is hereby authorized to enter and work on the fourth floor of Vance Hall.

If anyone has any objections to this authorization, please contact the undersigned.

(Signed by me.)

Unfortunately, on one of Jessie's subsequent trips he got on an elevator occupied by the third-floor director. Shortly thereafter I received a call from the vice president of the university in charge of facilities telling me how sorry he was to have to do this, but that he had to prohibit Jessie's entering our building.

I told him I would comply. However, I invited him to attend a press conference that I intended to call that afternoon in which I planned to tell the story of Jessie. I intended to use it as an example of the insidious dehumanization of the higher educational process. I said I would welcome the vice president's giving the university's view of the matter at that time. His response was profane. Nevertheless, he withdrew his insistence that Jessie be exiled. I don't know how he handled the third-floor director, but I heard no more about it.

Moral: The power of the press lies more in the threat of publication than in publication itself.

Jessie and his owner, Bill Roth, eventually graduated and went on to their first academic job at Moravian College. Unfortunately, Jessie has since died of old age.

COUNTERMEASURES

There is a technique developed by the military either to beat a system or to design a system that would be difficult to beat. It consists of forming a "countermeasure team" to represent those who want to beat the system—the enemy, in the military case. This team is given all the information available to the good guys, including tentative designs of the system involved. The task of the countermeasure team is to develop ways of beating the system. When it has determined how to do so, the good guys are given this information to use in redesigning their system. After they have done so, the countermeasure team goes at it again. This process continues until the enemy either cannot find an effective countermeasure, or the time required to do so is long enough to justify introduction of the system. The idea behind this procedure is that when a team of intelligent people who have perfect information about a system—something real enemies seldom have—can no longer beat that system quickly enough to make it valueless, that system can be built with little chance of its being beaten.

Note that such a procedure does not reduce the number of choices available to the enemy, but it does reduce their effectiveness. For example, a major national accounting firm once employed the research group of which I was a part to find effective ways of embezzling money from banks so that it could improve its auditing procedures. We found better ways of embezzling than the auditors had dreamed of, but we were able to design new auditing procedures that made our discoveries ineffective. Much to our amazement, the accounting-auditing firm did not adopt these procedures. Its executives said that as long as they used their current procedures, which were approved by the profession, they could not be held legally responsible for thefts they failed to detect. However, if they departed from standardized procedures and failed to detect an embezzlement, they would be legally liable for it. They chose to minimize their risks rather than those of their clients.

In another case, a company that wanted to buy a factory from one of its minor competitors that was going out of business knew that its major competitor was anxious to prevent such a purchase. Acquisition of that factory would increase the competitiveness of the purchaser in a region in which the principal competitor had an advantage. The would-be purchaser employed the research group of which I was a part to act as a countermeasure team while an internal group developed a strategy for obtaining the factory. It took four iterations of the internal group developing an offer and our countermeasure team developing a way of obstructing it before we could no longer find a way of preventing the purchase. Subsequently, when the offer to purchase was made, the principal competitor followed exactly the steps the countermeasure team had taken. The would-be purchaser got the plant.

A smart system can use knowledge of how it can be beat to redesign itself to reduce or eliminate that kind of beating.

Smoke Smuggling

In the middle 1970s I was asked by a department of the United Nations to visit (prerevolutionary) Iran, to talk with some of its officials about recent developments in the management sciences. I was also asked to help the government with any specific problems it had and to which my experience had some relevance. Several problems were put to me, but the one I remember best involved the purchase and sale of American-made cigarettes.

The minister in charge of consumer affairs told me that the sale of cigarettes in Iran was the second largest source of income to the government, second only to the sale of oil. The government had a monopoly on the *legal* production, distribution, and sale of cigarettes in Iran. A large and previously increasing portion of the income generated by this business came from the sale of cigarettes imported from the United States, then distributed to and sold through government-licensed retail stores.

In the last few years an illicit trade in American cigarettes had developed, significantly reducing the government's income. Smugglers were buying American cigarettes in Kuwait, where they could be obtained tax-free, and bringing them to Iran in small boats. They were then distributed to unlicensed street vendors who sold them at a price significantly lower then that at which they were sold in government-licensed outlets. The number of vendors and their share of the market were increasing rapidly.

The minister wanted to know what could be done to eliminate or reduce the smuggled-cigarette business. At my request a small team was set up to deal with the problem. All members of the team except me were familiar with both the legal and illegal cigarette businesses. First, we identified each step in the illicit business and estimated its cost. We were also able to estimate the profit earned by each of the parties involved along the way: the purchaser in Kuwait, the fisherman who brought the cigarettes to Iran, the distributors in Iran, and, finally, the street vendors. Adding the profits obtained by each, we determined the total profit generated by the illegal trade in American cigarettes. Then we did the same for the government's importing, distribution, and sale of American cigarettes. We found that the total profit generated by the government's system was less than that of the illicit system, even though the illicitly sold cigarettes were priced lower.

Therefore, we proposed that the government reorganize its imported cigarette business so as to use the same method of procurement, distribution, and sale the smugglers used. The team pointed out that if the government did so, its profits would probably be even greater than the smugglers', because the government was more likely than the smugglers to avoid having to bribe custom officials and the police.

It is my understanding that these recommendations were followed after I left Iran.

Moral: If you can't beat a system, join it.

CORRUPTION

Because bureaucracies tend to be inefficient and obstruct development, they invite and encourage corruption. Bribes are required to make them operate less inefficiently and obstructively. Bureaucracies create obstructions for the purpose of eliciting bribes.

On Getting In by Handing Out

In 1975 my wife and I loaded my VW minivan and, with our dog and cat, headed for Mexico. I had arranged to spend a year as a visiting professor at the National Autonomous University (UNAM) in Mexico City.

I had previously done some work for a Mexican firm located in Monterrey, which was near my planned point of entry into Mexico. That firm offered to send one of its expediters to meet me at the border and help with my entry. I welcomed the offer because it had taken one of my colleagues and his family two days to enter Mexico at that same point.

We were met at the point of entry, Nuevo Loredo, by the expediter, who began the admission process with us. Even with his help it took us eight hours to get cleared for entry. When we were finally permitted to enter, I asked our facilitator how many bribes he had paid. He said, "Sixteen." When I asked him how long it would have taken had he refused to pay any bribes, he said, "Infinity."

Moral: The shortest distance between some countries is a crooked line.

I had no help in handling most of my subsequent contacts with Mexican varieties of corruption. As a result, I learned that corruption is a way systems have of beating people that people can seldom beat. This was demonstrated to me on my first working day in Mexico City, when I drove from the house I occupied to the university.

On Unlimited Limits

I drove to work in our VW bus with U.S. license tags on it. A short way from our house I was stopped by two policemen who spoke to me in Spanish, which I could not understand. My lack of understanding did not seem to bother them at all, but it bothered me a great deal because I did not know what was going on. A young man who happened to be passing volunteered to interpret for me. He said the police claimed that I had exceeded the speed limit. I said I had seen no posting of a speed limit. Nevertheless, they told me, I had passed one that established the limit at 35 kilometers per hour. I could not recall having seen such a sign, but there clearly was no use arguing. I told the police to go ahead and make out a ticket for me. They were reluctant to do so; they said they could save me a lot of trouble by collecting the fine right there. I said I preferred to have a ticket. After some dispute about this, one of the policemen asked for my wallet. When I handed it to him he emptied it of all but a few pesos. He then returned it to me and told me to get going.

I went back over the route I had taken before being stopped by the police and looked for the posting of the speed limit to which they had referred. I could not find it.

When I returned home that evening, I warned my wife about the place at which I had been stopped. The next day, when she was driving the same car through the same area, she was stopped by the same policemen. Unlike me, she could manage a bit in Spanish. The police told her she had been exceeding the speed limit. She said she hadn't because I had warned her about the 35 kilometer limit. They told her that the limit had been lowered the previous night to 25 kilometers, and proceeded to extract their bribe from her.

Moral: The more corrupt a culture, the greater are the out-of-pocket expenses required to live in it.

Corruption occurred at all levels in and out of the Mexican government. However, Mexicans appeared to me to be less bothered by it than North Americans. Their attitude toward it was very different from that of gringos. A Mexican friend explained it to me as follows: In the United

States we tip those who serve us after being served, and the amount of our tip reflects our evaluation of the service received. In Mexico the steps are the same but their order is changed: One tips in advance, and the size of the tip determines the quality of service received. In Mexico, the "tip-in-advance" is called a *mordida,* a bite.

I realize, of course, that there is a great deal of corruption in the United States. How can any American be unaware of this? However, in the United States corruption once exposed is seldom tolerated or left unpunished. In Mexico it is taken for granted, treated as a fact of life.

I spent a good deal of time reflecting on the nature and causes of corruption while in Mexico. Later, after I had returned to the States, an agency of the Mexican government sponsored the preparation of a monograph on the subject by my university colleagues and me. We concluded that corruption occurs when one party, A (for example, a policeman), who has an obligation to a second party, B (for example, the government), to provide service to a third party, C (for example, a member of the public), serves C in such a way as to benefit A more than he or she is supposed to. In addition, anyone who induces another to behave corruptly is corrupt. Therefore, corruption is the exploitation for one's personal benefit of a position in which one is expected to serve others.

The immorality of corruption is not nearly as bothersome to me as is its obstructiveness to development. It is a special kind of obstruction, a meta-obstruction, because it is a response to the existence of other obstructions to development. If development were not obstructed, as it is even in the most developed countries, there would be no corruption, because there would be no need for it. To remove the obstructions to a society's development not only promotes development but it also reduces corruption.

The three principal obstructions to societal development, and hence the three principal producers of corruption, are *scarcity of resources, maldistribution of resources,* and *insecurity.* By a resource I mean anything, physical or mental, that can be used to obtain something else that one needs or desires. Therefore, information, knowledge, and understanding are resources as much as is money.

Scarcity of resources is an obvious obstruction to development. Those who have little or none of a resource they need are more easily corrupted than those who have what they need. For example, peasants who wanted the money, seeds, fertilizers, and equipment necessary to grow crops and who approached a branch of Mexico's rural development bank were told they could have what they wanted if they applied for more than they needed. When they received more than they needed they had to give the difference back to the loan officer. He, in turn, released them from an obligation to repay their loan to the bank. Compliance was the most effective way for peasants to get the resources they needed. This practice obviously reduced the amount of resources available for distribution to peasants and therefore retarded rural development. (It is my understanding that this practice has been eliminated since my extended stay in Mexico.)

Even where there is enough of a resource to go around, many may not have enough of it because it is distributed inequitably. Those who do not have enough want more and may be disposed to corruption to obtain it. Those who have more than they want are inclined to protect themselves against a possible future shortage by hoarding it, and through corruption to increase their security. It is commonplace, particularly in countries in which entertainment is a scarcity, for people to pay bribes to obtain tickets from those who hoard them. Those who hoard them often solicit bribes from those who want them. Tickets to special events, artistic or athletic, are made available at a cost considerably greater than their face value.

Where there is a scarcity of resources and maldistribution of what is available, those who have some or even enough resources often feel insecure, threatened. They want to protect what they have against possible loss or appropriation. This is often most easily accomplished through corruption. For example, employees who feel insecure about their jobs where employment is hard to get may give a portion of their salaries to their bosses in order to increase their job security.

LAWS, RULES, AND REGULATIONS

In some cases a system can be beaten by rigorously following its rules and regulations. English workers know this when they "work to rule." Employee adherence to rules is often more harmful to an employing organization than is a strike. Moreover, those who work to rule do not have to give up their income to make their points. Similarly, most managers know that the easiest way to bring an organization to its knees is to interpret its budget literally. Most organizations survive only because their managers have learned how to cheat with respect to their budgets.

There is something diabolically satisfying in beating a system by adhering to its rules. Here are a few such cases.

On Pants That Don't Suit

In the early 1950s my wife and I lived in Washington, D.C., where I spent six months as a consultant to the U.S. Bureau of the Census. One evening, together with a census colleague and his wife, we went out to dinner. We had selected a popular seafood restaurant located on the riverfront. Both wives were attractively dressed in pantsuits, which were then just coming into vogue.

When we approached the restaurant's hostess to be seated, she informed us that women wearing pantsuits were not allowed in the restaurant; they were not considered to be properly dressed. When we asked why, she told us, in effect, that hers was not to reason why but to do or die. She was simply following orders.

Our wives were not upset by their exclusion. They excused themselves and mysteriously disappeared. They went to the ladies' room, took off their pants, and reappeared wearing only the tunics that formed the upper parts of their suits. The tunics were about the length of miniskirts. The hostess was satisfied and seated us.

Moral: Taking off one's pants may skirt the issue.

Beating a system by taking it literally is wonderfully illustrated by the story of the Yale freshman who, when he appeared at the freshman dining hall on his first day, saw a sign at its entrance reading Jacket and Tie Required. On the next day he appeared wearing a jacket and tie—and nothing else.

Systems would much rather be told lies that preserve their conventions than truths that shake them up.

On Disjoint Authorship

When I was getting ready to start work on my doctoral dissertation, I learned of an obscure and very infrequently used university rule that permitted dissertations to be written jointly by the degree candidate and his or her supervisor. I had not known this and no one I knew at the university was aware of it. Nevertheless, I approached my supervisor,

Professor C. West Churchman, with the suggestion that he coauthor my thesis. Much to my surprise and delight, he agreed. (This began a collaboration that lasted almost 20 years.)

Over the next several years, including the four I spent in the army during World War II, West and I produced a document of about 600 single-spaced typed pages. I submitted it to the chairman of the graduate faculty in philosophy. He returned it to me almost immediately, saying that jointly authored theses were not permitted. I was prepared for such a response. I showed the chairman a copy of the relevant university regulation. It shocked him. He didn't believe it, so he checked and found the rule to be valid. He treated me as though I had committed a sin in discovering its validity.

The chairman informed me that the examining committee would have to know which portions of the thesis I had written alone, so I could be examined on them. I explained that Churchman and I had written every part of that thesis collaboratively. Nevertheless, he said, the committee would be unwilling to examine me unless I could provide an example of my independent contribution to the work.

West and I discussed this requirement and decided to designate a particular section. Like all other sections, it had been jointly written, but I did not so inform the committee, which was satisfied. It examined me on that section and reluctantly accepted the thesis as a whole.

Moral: The best response to an arbitrary requirement is one that is itself as arbitrary as the requirement.

Law and lawyers can be very effective allies of bureaucracies that want to keep anything from happening, but they can be double-edged swords.

On Laws and Lawyers

After a fruitful day of collaborative problem-solving, a corporation's top executives and academic consultants were relaxing over a few after-dinner drinks. The chief executive officer of the corporation turned to one of the consultants, Tom Cowan, a retired professor of jurisprudence, and asked, "Tom, how come whenever I ask our lawyers whether I can try something new, they always say, 'No'?"

Tom replied, "You deserve that kind of reply because you're asking the wrong kind of question."

"I don't understand," the executive said.

"Let me explain," Tom said. "Why do you consult lawyers?"

The executive looked puzzled, shrugged his shoulders, and replied, "For the obvious reasons: to advise me on legal matters and to represent us in suits that either we initiate against others or they initiate against us."

Tom snapped back, "Come on, you're not testifying in court now. I'm not asking how you use lawyers, but *what you use them for.* What is the principal reason for surrounding yourself with lawyers?"

The executive thought for a moment and then replied, "I suppose you mean: to avoid legal problems, *to keep me out of jail.*"

"Right! Now, consider: When you consult a lawyer, you're not in jail. Then you ask him if you can do something other than what you have been doing. The one thing he knows for sure is that you have not gotten into trouble for not doing what you propose doing. Therefore, to make sure you stay out of trouble, he says, 'No.' He is paid not to take risks, but to minimize them. It's your job to take them."

"Okay," the executive said. "I get your point. Then what *should* I ask the lawyer?"

"Don't ask him anything; tell him: 'I'm going to do so-and-so. Now you tell me how to do it without getting into trouble.' And he probably will. You see, most decision-makers do not use lawyers to enable them to do what they want to do, but to keep them from doing what they don't want to do."

> **Moral:** Lawyers keep those who employ them from doing many illegal or stupid things, but not from using lawyers.

Laws, rules, and regulations are often written by lawyers. The one thing no lawyer will do, and few other than lawyers can do, is write a law, rule, or regulation that deprives other lawyers of possible work. A better lawyer than the one who wrote a law, rule, or regulation can usually find a way around it, and there is always a better lawyer around.

Obscured Clearance

Many years ago the university-based research group that I directed negotiated a large contract with the U.S. Arms Control and Disarmament Agency (ACDA). About a week after the contract had been signed, sealed, and delivered, I received a carton full of clearance-application forms that every member of my group was supposed to fill out and submit.

The requirement for clearances had never been discussed during contract negotiations; it came as a complete surprise to me. I called the agency's contracting officer and told him that we would not fill out the applications because we saw no reason for doing so. I explained that the work we had agreed to do was not classified, hence would not require access to classified information. Moreover, only a few members of my group would be involved in the research; most would not. A number of the group's members were not citizens of the United States, and I was not about to put them through the extended indignity of clearance procedures, particularly ones that served no useful purpose.

The contracting officer told me that the law that created ACDA required that it use the same security measures as were required of the Atomic Energy Commission, and these required clearance of all members of my group.

I told the contracting officer that we were not willing to comply with that requirement, whatever its source. He then said that he had no alternative but to cancel the contract. I told him that cancellation was not the only alternative: the agency could engage a good lawyer who would figure out how to get around the law. He dismissed my suggestion as facetious. The contract was cancelled.

A few weeks later I received a call from the agency telling me the contract was being reinstated and that clearance would not be required of any member of my group. No explanation was provided.

I had a similar experience when I agreed to address a group of army generals who were going to meet at Duke University. Subsequently, I received a clearance-application form and a request from the army to fill it out. I called the officer who had invited me to the meeting and told him I would not comply because my talk would contain no classified material and I did not intend to stay to hear any other talks; my schedule did not permit it. He told me that the place of the meeting was classified and, therefore, entrance to it required clearance. I replied that since it was the army that wanted me to be cleared, not me, the army should apply for my clearance, not me.

The officer then asked if I had ever been cleared by any military organization. I told him I had. He asked for details, which I provided. He then said he would get the information from the previous source of clearance, fill out the application form, and send it to me for my signature. I told him I would not sign it because doing so would make it *my* request for clearance, and it should be the army's. He assured me that the application had to have my signature. I said I would not provide it and again suggested he consult a good lawyer. Not surprisingly, the invitation to speak was withdrawn.

A few weeks later I was informed by telegram that I had been cleared to attend the meeting and asked if I would do so. I said I would. Again, no explanation for the change was provided.

Moral: Clearance is not a way of clearing the way; it is a way of obstructing it.

Laws, rules, and regulations are frequently misused. They are much more likely to be used as an excuse for not doing something than for doing it.

SYSTEMS AND DRESS
Bureaucratic systems try to deal with the unexpected in ways that preserve their images of reality and concepts of propriety.

On Coding Dress at Work

One day while working in my office at Case Institute of Technology, I received a phone call from the vice president of finance of the Chesapeake and Ohio (C&O) Railroad asking me to come to his company's headquarters at once. He wanted me to make a presentation to a board meeting that was already in progress. He wanted me to explain the approach we were taking to one of the railroad's major operating problems.

Although C&O's headquarters were less than half an hour away by car, I said I could not come immediately; I would have to go home and dress properly for the meeting. He said time was critical; dress was not. Therefore, I should come as I was. I explained that I was wearing a sweat suit and sneakers. Nevertheless, he insisted I come at once. I did. When I arrived at the executive floor I was immediately taken to the meeting in the boardroom.

Although I was on first-name terms with most of the members of the board, that day not one of them addressed me by my first name; they addressed me as "Professor Ackoff." It was apparent that doing so was their way of justifying my inappropriate dress.

Moral: We tend to respect uniforms more than those who wear them.

I learned something from this experience that has been useful to me ever since. There are times in my interactions with an organization's personnel when I want to be taken as one of them, and other times when I want to be kept distinct from them. I find that to a large extent I can control their perceptions of me by the way I dress. When I want to be perceived as one of them, I dress as one of them. When I want to be perceived as a university professor, I wear less formal clothing—but usually not a sweat suit; a sport coat and slacks does the trick.

I also learned that when corporate personnel come to my office for a working session, they like to dress informally, like university professors. It is a relief from their usual business attire, but more importantly it symbolizes a day devoted to thought rather than action. Whatever our reasons for informal dress in our offices, it is perfectly clear that it makes our visitors relax and feel more at home.

It is not surprising that the higher the tech of an organization—that is, the more thinking involved in its work—the less formally its members tend to dress. In addition, there has been a trend toward informal dress at work since the end of World War II. I suspect this is the product of both more permissive upbringing of the young and increased intellectual content of a good deal of white-collar work.

Dress obviously can be used as a way of symbolizing rank, as it is, for example, in the military. The need for such symbolism decreases the more that rank depends on competence and the more conspicuous that competence is.

BUREAUCRATIC ERRORS

Bureaucracies seldom admit to making an error. My good friend Merrill Kilby took great delight in forcing them to own up to their mistakes. It took a great deal of creativity for him to succeed.

Infallibility

For many years Merrill served as the administrative officer of the research group I directed in The Wharton School. He was one of the most dedicated antibureaucrats I have ever known. His antibureaucratic career within the university appeared to come to an end when he reached the age of compulsory retirement in the early 1980s. However, the Fates gave him one more shot at the university's bureaucracy.

Among the benefits due Merrill after his retirement was his full salary for three consecutive months. About six months after his retirement he appeared in my office and asked me to come with him to visit the university's benefits office. When I asked why, he said, "To have some fun." Knowing I would, I joined him.

When we appeared at the benefits office, a young woman came to the counter to help us. Merrill began by saying he had retired a few months earlier and that he was due his salary for three months after retirement, but that the university had made a mistake. At this point the woman interrupted and assured Merrill that the university does not make mistakes in administration of retirement benefits. Merrill said he was glad to hear that and asked if she would please put this in writing.

The request for the document took her by surprise and made her suspicious. She asked Merrill to wait while she consulted her supervisor. She left us for a few moments and returned with her supervisor in tow. He reiterated the infallibility of his office. Merrill said he did not doubt it, but he would like a letter to this effect so as to be absolved of responsibility for any error the university might have made.

At this point the supervisor also became suspicious and for the first time asked Merrill what he thought the university might have done incorrectly. Merrill then explained that he was continuing to receive monthly salary checks after the three that were due him. He produced the checks and showed them to the supervisor. The supervisor and the clerk were suitably embarrassed and apologized for their behavior. This, however, did not keep Merrill from rubbing it in a bit.

Moral: The assumption of infallibility is best left to God, and He ought to think twice before making it.

Antibureaucrats extract great satisfaction from cases in which bureaucracies cut off their noses to spite their faces. This occurs when they solve one problem in a way that creates another as bad as or worse than the first.

The Aborted Report

The Case Institute of Technology research group of which I was a part had contracted with the Transportation Corps of the U.S. Army to study possible improvements in its vehicle-maintenance procedures. The contract required that, when the work was completed, a draft report be prepared and submitted to the contracting officer. He would circulate that report to responsible authorities and collect the changes they desired. These were then to be communicated to us for incorporation into the final version of the report.

Our research yielded an unexpected finding: The principal cause of failure of the types of equipment we studied was maintenance. This finding and its support were treated in detail in the draft report we submitted.

Coincidentally, when our submission was made Congress was conducting hearings on the defense budget and was clearly looking for ways to reduce it. Officials in the Transportation Corps were worried when they saw our report because they thought it could be used by Congress to reduce the funds made available to the corps. Therefore, our report was classified as "secret." This deprived Congress of access to it, but, although this was not intended, it also deprived us of access to it. We could not prepare the required final version of the report because it was classified and we were not cleared to work with classified material at that time. The final version of that report never was prepared.

Moral: One is very likely to cut off one's own nose when spiting another's face.

On Turning Systems Inside Out

All of us tend to rationalize our unwillingness to do something by invoking restrictions or constraints that we imagine are imposed on us by a system that we cannot control. This process is seldom conscious and, therefore, is very difficult to correct. When another tries to do so, we resist, refusing to accept the fact that the constraints are self-imposed.

As part of a university's faculty I often proposed to its administration some action for which there was no precedent. These proposals were almost always rejected with the explanation that they violated some rule or regulation. In such cases I always asked to see the relevant rule or regulation. It was very seldom produced. All sorts of excuses were used for this. The fact was that most of the alleged rules and regulations were fabrications of bureaucratic minds. After the alleged rule or regulation could not be produced, opposition to my proposals not only persisted but intensified, as though to punish me for claiming that there was a systemic deficiency. Rejection of my proposals continued to be attributed to externally imposed constraints.

PROPOSALS AND PROPOSITIONING

Bureaucracies are prone to forming habits, repetitive ways of doing things. For example, they usually require proposals from competitive suppliers of services that they, the bureaucracies, want to acquire. Laws or regulations frequently require that such proposals be submitted and that the choice of a supplier be based on them. Nevertheless, in my opinion, selecting a supplier on the basis of submitted proposals is about as reasonable as selecting an automobile on the basis of its manufacturer's advertising.

Personally, I am unwilling to work for a client who selects a supplier on the basis of an unpaid-for proposal. Contrary to what may appear to be the case, my attitude toward proposals and those who act on them has not been a serious handicap in my consulting and research career. Quite the opposite: it has been responsible for some very important learning experiences. Here are a few of them:

On Pro- and Con-Posals

Back in my Case Institute days, I received a request for a proposal (an RFP) from a unit of the air force. It involved a study to determine how to communicate effectively in the presence of an intelligent source of noise. Translated, this meant: How do you communicate to someone when someone else is trying to prevent it? For example, how can an airplane's pilot and a ground controller communicate when an enemy is trying to jam their channel of communication?

The RFP went on to say that it wanted the researchers to use Game Theory in their quest for a solution. This struck me as ridiculous. I could see no possible connection between Game Theory and the communication problem. In my opinion, whoever wrote the RFP did not understand either Game Theory or communication. I wrote a letter to this effect to the relevant air force officer, using it to explain why we would not submit a proposal. I indicated very briefly what kinds of technology I thought were applicable to the problem.

Several weeks later I received a letter from the air force saying we had been awarded the contract on the strength of my letter. No proposal was required.

It was a proposal of a very different color that brought the Ford Foundation and me together, briefly. I received a phone call from a vice president of the foundation, an old acquaintance, saying he had a project he would like to have us do for Ford. Two Middle East countries, traditional enemies, had agreed to a joint scientific effort directed at finding a peaceful solution to their differences. The vice president wanted us to facilitate and guide such an effort. I told him we were very much interested in doing so. "Fine," he said, "then prepare and submit a proposal to that effect."

I told him that his request made no sense. He had all the relevant information; we didn't. Therefore, why didn't he write the proposal he would like to receive, send it to us, and, after modifying it if necessary, we would sign and submit it to him. Much to my surprise, he agreed.

Several weeks later we received the proposal he had drafted. We made only a few minor changes, of which he approved. Then we signed and submitted the proposal. We heard nothing about it for about six months. Then we received a form letter from another vice president of the Ford Foundation thanking us for having submitted our proposal, but turning it down on the grounds that it did not fall into an area of current interest to the foundation.

The danger of acting on the basis of a proposal was revealed to me in an incident involving the U.S. Department of the Interior. I received a request for a proposal from that department on a subject of great interest to me. The department wanted to determine how to locate facilities and services of the federal government so as to contribute to equalization of opportunity for (1) employment to minorities and (2) development to communities. The RFP specified the maximum amount that the government was willing to pay to have the work done. This amount struck me as ridiculously low. I did not see how the required work could possibly be done for that amount of money. Although I did not submit a proposal, I wrote to the department to this effect.

The contracting officer called me and we discussed my letter at length. He told me the department had received a number of proposals, all involving amounts no more than the maximum stated in the RFP. I told him that, in my opinion, those who submitted such proposals were either ignorant or deceitful. He did not agree, but we parted as friends.

About a year later he called me to say that a year earlier they had awarded the contract to a major consulting firm. He told me that the report it produced failed completely to address the problem the department had formulated. It addressed a lesser, not totally unrelated problem, that could be treated with the amount of resources made available. The contracting officer then told me he was sorry he had not taken my skepticism more seriously.

I had a contrary experience with a request for a proposal issued by AT&T. When this company was deregulated and forced to break up, I was asked to submit a letter-length proposal for a study to determine how the new AT&T should be organized. Since my research group had done a good deal of work for AT&T and several of its subsidiaries, the prospect of working on this very large and very complex problem was exciting to us. Because of this and the fact that only a letter-length proposal was required, I prepared one and submitted it.

A short while later I received a phone call from one of the AT&T officials handling the matter. He told me he liked our proposal but his colleagues and company officials did not believe we could do what we said we would for the amount of money we quoted. He said the second-lowest bid they had received was several times larger than ours. Then he asked if we were sure we had estimated our cost correctly. I told him we were. He said he had to have a higher estimate of cost for the work we proposed in order to make it more believable to AT&T personnel. He asked if we would be willing to double it. I said no. The contract was awarded to someone else at eight times *the cost* we had estimated.

Moral: It is better to put your money where your mouth is than to put it where someone else's mouth is.

CONTRACTS

Contracts are often as irrational as proposals and as obstructive to choice and development.

Pro- and Con-Tracting

In the late 1950s I bought a plot in a heavily wooded rural area just outside Cleveland, Ohio. I then spent about six months in a labor of love, designing the house my wife and I wanted to build there. When the design was complete I gave it to four contractors for bids. While waiting for the bids, by sheer chance I was visited by a friend's father, John Rinkema, who was a retired building contractor from Chicago. He knew about my intention to build a house and asked if he could see my drawings. The two of us spent most of the evening going over them in detail. He suggested several valuable modifications.

John told me that of the many houses he had built, none had a design as modern as mine. He then said that his retirement bored him and that he would like to build my house. He asked if he could bid on it. I saw this as an opportunity to build my house under a rational contractual arrangement. In most building contracts, the contractor is paid a percentage of the total cost of the building, and is therefore motivated to make the building as expensive as possible. I wanted to put the contractor on my side, not against me.

When I explained my attitude toward building contracts to John, he was as interested as I in developing one that was sensible. After some discussion, John and I agreed that he would build the house for a price no greater than the lowest bid I received from the other contractors. In addition, he would calculate how much profit he would make on building the house at that price, and I would pay him that amount in advance. Subsequently, I would pay all bills. Finally, we agreed to divide equally each dollar less than the estimated cost for which he built the house.

This contract made the builder's interests and mind compatible. I wanted a reduction of my cost to be in his interest. It clearly turned out this way. John did a great job of building my house and he did so for $2,000 under the estimated cost. We split that saving.

Not much later, my close friend and collaborator, C. West Churchman, who had moved to the San Francisco area about the time I built my house, bought land in Mill Valley and hired a young architect to design a house for him and his family. West gave the architect a set of carefully prepared specifications of the properties he wanted his house to have. Among these was a statement of the maximum price he was willing to pay for it.

I happened to visit West when he received the first design his architect had prepared. I examined the drawings carefully and told West that the house designed could not be built within the cost limits he had set.

West assured me that he had discussed cost with the architect and that the architect has assured him that the house could be built within his cost restriction. I could not convince West to the contrary. Shortly thereafter he put the design out for bids. The lowest bid he received was far above the upper limit he had set.

West was devastated. He and his wife had fallen in love with the architect's design, but they could not afford it. In order to reduce the cost of the house, features would have to be eliminated that they were now unwilling to give up. Therefore, when they went to work with the architect on reducing cost they never got it down to the originally stated maximum. West eventually built that house, but at a cost well above the maximum amount he had intended to spend.

Moral: The principal objective of a contract should be to ensure terminal satisfaction of both parties.

In my opinion, West's architect should not have been paid his fee. Architects are supposed to know the cost of building various types of structures, and they should adhere to a client's specification of a maximum expenditure. But since the architect's fee is usually a percentage of the total cost of the structure, it is in his or her interest to raise the cost of the structure as high as the client will go. The typical contract between client and architect puts the two in conflict.

The same type of conflict is apparent in contracts most corporations have with their advertising agencies. The agencies are paid a percentage of the amount their clients spend on advertising. This induces the agency to try to maximize its client's advertising expenditures; it is an agent to advertising media, not of its client.

Agencies need not be compensated in the traditional way. A number of years ago Anheuser-Busch established a very different kind of relationship with its agency, D'Arcy. D'Arcy's fee was set so that if the amount of advertising was reduced without a reduction of sales, or sales were increased without an increase in advertising, its fee would increase. However, if things went the other way, its fee would decrease.

Protection of the interests of the server, not the served, is the primary focus of most contracts for service. Those served usually do not know enough to ensure protection of their interests. This ignorance is exploited by servers who usually know more than enough to protect their interests.

BUREAUCRATIC MONOPOLIES

If development is to be accelerated in any social environment, many of the systems that it contains must be debureaucratized and demonopolized. The only way a bureaucratic monopoly can survive is to be subsidized, and to be subsidized in a way that is independent of its performance. This relieves it of any responsibility for effective service to those it is supposed to serve.

Government is full of such organizations, but so are corporations. Internal service units—for example, finance, personnel, research, and development units—are among those that in most corporations are bureaucratic monopolies. They are subsidized by a higher level unit, receive no financial support from their users, and their users have no alternative but to use their services. This situation constitutes a paradox.

We are committed to a market economy at the national (macro) level and to a nonmarket, centrally planned, hierarchically managed (micro) economy within most corporations and other types of organizations in our society. Our macro and micro economies are not consistent. They can be; market economies can be introduced within corporations and even government. In Chapter Two we saw how a market economy could work in the public school system by use of the voucher system.

Creation of a market economy within a firm requires that the following characteristics be designed into it.

1. Each unit in the organization, including the executive office, operates as a profit center.
2. Each unit also operates as an investment bank and government for its immediately subordinate units: It taxes their profits and receives payment (in the form of interest or dividends) for the capital it provides them. As a government, each unit can enact laws that preclude specified activities of subordinate units. For example, it may preclude outsourcing of products that involve a "secret" formula or production process. Such preclusions should be kept to a minimum.
3. Each unit is free either to supply itself with whatever goods and services it wants or to buy them internally or externally at a price acceptable to it. (This freedom is subject to an override, discussed in paragraph 6 below.)
4. Each unit is also free to sell its services or products internally or externally to whomever it wants at a price it establishes (subject to the same override).
5. Each unit can retain up to a specified amount of its profit for use as it sees fit. Any amount above this must be turned over to the next-higher level of management. In return, the unit is paid interest on this amount by the higher receiving unit.
6. Any manager can override a subordinate unit's decision to make, buy, or sell, but that manager must compensate that unit for any additional cost or loss of profit that it incurs because of that override.

The fact that every unit operates as a profit center does not imply that its principal objective is to maximize annual profit or return on investment. What is implied is that profitability be taken into account in evaluating each unit's performance, but this need not be annual profitability. Nor does this requirement imply that every unit must be profitable. An organization may maintain an unprofitable unit for nonfinancial reasons—for example, for the prestige it brings. Nevertheless, repeatedly unprofitable units should be reviewed periodically for possible discontinuation or divestment.

Note that this type of internal economy eliminates subsidized monopolies operating within an organization. All internal units that supply goods or services and for which there are alternative external sources of supply must compete with them even for internal business. This makes them more responsive and efficient suppliers.

An internal market economy is as applicable to a not-for-profit or governmental organization as it is to one for profit. Even though an organization as a whole is subsidized by an external source, it can distribute funds internally solely for services rendered or products supplied. For example, as I mentioned earlier, students can be given freedom to choose their schools, and the income of publicly supported schools can be restricted to a payment for each student enrolled.

CONCLUSION

Beating a system that obstructs or constrains development is a challenge. Succeeding is fun. It brings with it the joy of victory over a huge, impersonal, and inflexible machine-like mind. Beating a system is a creative act, like solving a puzzle or designing something new. It involves overcoming self-imposed constraints. Trying to beat a system requires exercise of all the mental functions: thinking, sensing, feeling, and intuition. It contrasts with passive acceptance of what is. It occupies our mind with what might be, imagining a future that would be better than the present.

Significant personal and cultural development is not possible without beating systems. In some cases, systems are beaten, even destroyed, by use of force. However, it is much better to beat them by use of ideas. Force is directed at getting rid of what we don't want; ideas are directed at getting what we do want. They are not equivalent: getting rid of what we don't want does not assure us of getting what we want. For example, changing TV channels to get rid of a program we don't want does not assure us of getting a program we do want.

When we beat a system, we make it do something it did not intend to do and, in the case of a bureaucratic system, something it proscribed. Beating a system not only removes constraints imposed on us by the system, but also removes constraints imposed on the system by itself. This extends its range of choices and enables it to develop. Without choice there are no mistakes; without mistakes there is no learning, and without learning there is no development.

Most systems, like recalcitrant children, do not appreciate being beaten, even when the beating is good for them. This is especially true of bureaucracies. They find choice unsettling; they prefer a static equilibrium produced by complete conformity to rule in an unchanging environment: continuous repetition of the expected. Whatever else creativity implies, it implies production of the unexpected. It is the unexpected that produces the quantum leaps in development and quality of life.

PART II

PLANNING

In this section I first make the distinction between tactical and strategic planning. Then the two conventional types (styles) of planning, reactive and preactive, are described along with their deficiencies. Out of these deficiencies emerges a radically new type of planning: interactive. Its target is an idealized design the designers would have right now if they could have any system they wanted, subject only to a few minor constraints. Then the closest feasible approximation is developed and addressed by the remainder of the planning process.

The characteristics, requirements, and effects of interactive planning are discussed.

My comprehensive treatment of this subject can be found in *Creating the Corporate Future*.

CHAPTER 6

THE NATURE OF PLANNING

Wisdom is the ability to see the long-run consequences of current actions, the willingness to sacrifice short-run gains for larger long-run benefits, and the ability to control what is controllable and not to fret over what is not. Therefore the essence of wisdom is concern with the future. It is not the type of concern with the future that the fortune teller has; he only tries to predict it. The wise man tries to *control* it.

Planning is the design of a desired future and of effective ways of bringing it about. It is an instrument that is used by the wise, but not by the wise alone. When conducted by lesser men it often becomes an irrelevant ritual that produces short-run peace of mind, but not the future that is longed for.

Recently I asked three corporate executives what decisions they had made in the last year that they would not have made were it not for their corporate plans. All had difficulty in identifying one such decision. Since each of their plans were marked "secret" or "confidential," I also asked them how their competitors might benefit from the possession of their plans. Each answered with embarrassment that their competitors would not benefit. Yet these executives were strong advocates of corporate planning.

The need for corporate planning is so obvious and so great that it is hard for anyone to be against it. But it is even harder to make such planning useful. Planning is one of the most complex and difficult intellectual activities in which man can engage. Not to do it well is not a sin, but to settle for doing it less than well is.

We do not yet understand corporate planning well enough to prepare a handbook on it. At present, and for some time to come, planning will have to be tailored to the unique characteristics of the organization and situation in which it is carried out. Nevertheless some guidance at a fairly

---

From *A Concept of Corporate Planning* (Wiley, 1970).

general level is possible. We can strive for an appreciation of what planning can do, a philosophy with which it can be approached, a concept of how it can be organized and systematized, and an awareness of the best methods, techniques, and tools that can be incorporated into it.

The science relevant to planning has developed rapidly in the recent past. However, even the best planning of which we are capable requires at least as much art as it does science. I am as interested in improving the art as I am in improving the science. Nowhere is the successful blending of the two more critical than it is here.

The principal contribution of scientists to planning may not lie in the development and use of relevant techniques and tools but rather in their systematization and organization of the planning process, and in the increased awareness and evaluation of this process that their presence produces.

Planning is clearly a decision-making process; but equally clearly not all decision making is planning. Not so clear, however, are the characteristics that make it a special kind of decision making. It is special in three ways.

1. Planning is something we do in advance of taking action; that is, it is *anticipatory decision-making*. It is a process of deciding what to do and how to do it before action is required. If we desire a certain state of affairs at some future time and it takes time to decide what to do and how to do it, we must make the necessary decisions before taking action. If these decisions could be taken quickly without loss of efficiency, planning would not be required.

2. Planning is required when the future state that we desire involves a set of interdependent decisions; that is, a *system of decisions.* A set of decisions forms a system if the effect of each decision in the set on the relevant outcome depends on at least one other decision in the set. Some of the decisions in the set may be complex, others simple. But the principal complexity in planning derives from the interrelatedness of the decisions rather than from the decisions themselves; for example, in planning a house, a decision to place the living room in a particular corner has an effect on the location of every other room and hence on the "performance" of the house as a whole.

    Sets of decisions that require planning have the following important characteristics:

a. They are too large to handle all at once. Therefore planning must be divided into stages or phases that are performed either sequentially by one decision-making body, or simultaneously by different bodies, or by some combination of sequential and simultaneous efforts. Planning must be staged or, put another way, it must itself be planned.

b. The set of necessary decisions cannot be subdivided into independent subsets. Hence a planning problem cannot be broken down into independent subplanning problems. The subplanning problems must be interrelated. This means that decisions made early in the planning process must be taken into account when making decisions later on in the process and *the earlier decisions must be received in light of the decisions made subsequent to them.* This is why planning must be carried out before action is required.

These two systemic properties of planning make clear why planning is not an act but a *process,* a process that has no natural conclusion or end point. It is a process that (it is to be hoped) approaches a "solution," but it never quite gets there, for two reasons. First, there is no limit to the amount of reviewing of previous decisions that is possible. The fact that action is eventually required, however, makes it necessary to settle for what one has at some point in time. Second, both the system being planned for and its environment change during the planning process, and it is therefore never quite possible to take all such changes into account. The need to continuously update and "maintain" a plan derives in part from this fact.

3. Planning is a process that is directed toward producing one or more future states which are desired and which are not expected to occur unless something is done. Planning is thus concerned both with avoiding incorrect actions and with reducing the frequency of failure to exploit opportunities. Obviously, if one believes that the natural course of events will bring about all that is desired, there is no need to plan. Thus planning always has both a pessimistic and an optimistic component. The pessimism lies in the belief that unless something is done a desired future state is not likely to occur. The optimism lies in the belief that something can be done to increase the chance that the desired state will occur.

Summarizing, we can say that planning is a process that involves making and evaluating each of a set of interrelated decisions before action is required, in a situation in which it is believed that unless action is taken a desired future state is not likely to occur, and that, if appropriate action is taken, the likelihood of a favorable outcome can be increased.

TACTICAL AND STRATEGIC PLANNING

The distinction between tactical and strategic planning is often made but is seldom made clear. Decisions that appear to be strategic to one person may appear to be tactical to another. This suggests that the distinction is relative rather than absolute. Indeed this is the case. Much of the confusion and apparent ambiguity derive from the fact that the difference between strategic and tactical planning is three dimensional.

1. The longer the effect of a plan and the more difficult it is to reverse, the more strategic it is. Therefore strategic planning is concerned with decisions that have enduring effects that are difficult to reverse; for example, next week's production planning is more tactical and less strategic than planning a new plant or distribution system. Strategic planning is long-range planning. Tactical planning is of shorter range. But "long" and "short" are relative terms and therefore so are "strategic" and "tactical." In general strategic planning is concerned with the longest period worth considering; tactical planning is concerned with the shortest period worth considering. Both types of planning are necessary. They complement each other. They are like the head and tail of a coin: we can look at them separately, even discuss them separately, but we cannot separate them in fact.

2. The more functions of an organization's activities are affected by a plan, the more strategic it is. That is, strategic planning is broad in scope. Tactical planning is narrower. "Broad" and "narrow" are also relative concepts thus adding to the relativity of "strategic" and "tactical." A strategic plan for a department may be a tactical plan from the point of view of a division. Other things being equal, planning at the corporate level is generally more strategic than planning at any organizational level below it.

3. Tactical planning is concerned with selecting means by which to pursue specified goals. The goals are normally supplied by a higher

level in the organization. Strategic planning is concerned with both formulation of the goals and selection of the means by which they are to be attained. Thus strategic planning is oriented to ends as well as to means. However, "means" and "ends" are also relative concepts; for example, "advertising a product" is a means to the end of "selling it." "Selling it," however, is a means to the end of "profit," and profit is itself a means to many other ends.

Put briefly, strategic planning is long-range corporate planning that is ends oriented (but not exclusively so). It should be apparent that both strategic and tactical planning are required in order to maximize progress.

CHAPTER 7

ALTERNATIVE TYPES
OF PLANNING

*Interactive planning differs significantly from two more commonly
used types of planning: reactive and preactive.*

REACTIVE PLANNING

Reactive planning is bottom-up tactically oriented planning. What strategy it contains is implicit, a consequence of numerous independently made tactical decisions. It begins with the lowest or low-level units of an organization identifying the deficiencies and threats they face. Then they attempt to return to a preferred earlier state by designing projects intended to reveal the causes of these deficiencies and threats and to remove or suppress them. Next, using cost-benefit analyses, priorities are assigned to projects. Finally, using an estimate of the amount of resources that will be available for work on projects, a set of them is selected starting at the top of the priority list, working down until all the expected resources have been allocated. The set of projects thus selected constitutes the unit's plan.

Unit plans are passed up to the next higher-level unit, where they are edited and coordinated and integrated with a plan similarly prepared at that unit. This process is continued until the accumulated plans reach the top of the organization, where again they are edited, coordinated, and integrated with projects designed at that level. This, then, is the corporate plan.

Reactive planning has two major deficiencies. First, it is based on the mistaken assumption that if one gets rid of what one does not want, one gets what one wants. This assumption can be seen as false by anyone who turns on a television set and gets a program he or she does not want.

From *A Guide to Controlling Your Corporation's Future,* with Elsa Vergara Finnel and Jamshid Gharajedaghi (Wiley, 1984).

The viewer can get rid of it by changing to another channel, but this does not necessarily result in something better.

Second, reactive planning is carried out in parts of an organization independently of other parts at the same and higher levels. An organization, however, is a system whose major deficiencies arise from the ways its parts *interact,* not from their actions taken separately. Therefore, it is possible and even likely that improvement of the performance of each part of an organization considered separately will result in a deterioration of the performance of the organization as a whole.

PREACTIVE PLANNING

Preactive planning is top-down strategically oriented planning. Objectives are explicitly set but tactics are left to the discretion of individual units. Such planning has two parts, *prediction* and *preparation,* of which prediction is the more important. If a prediction is in error, even good preparation for what it predicts may be in vain.

The preactive planning process begins at the top of an organization with preparation of one or more forecasts of the future. These are analyzed for the threats and opportunities they present. Then a broad statement of overall organizational strategies for dealing with these threats and opportunities is prepared. The predicted future(s) and the strategic "white paper" are then passed down through the organization. Each level adjusts the forecast and the analysis to its own specific environmental conditions, and selects objectives and goals that are compatible with those of the organization as a whole. Programs to pursue these objectives and goals are formulated in general terms.

The accumulation of forecasts, objectives to which commitments are made, and programs for their pursuit constitute unit plans that are reviewed at one or more higher levels. In these reviews plans prepared at different levels are integrated, and those prepared at the same level are coordinated.

The effectiveness of preactive planning clearly depends on the accuracy of the forecasts for which it prepares. Unfortunately, such forecasts are chronically in error. The reason is that the only things we can predict accurately (in principle as well as practice) are aspects of the future that will not be affected by what we and others do (for example, the weather). But preactive planning is based on forecasts of supplier, consumer, and competitive behavior as well as economic, social, and political conditions, all of which are affected by what is done by organizations that plan and those that do not. This logically requires an endless repetition of the prediction–preparation cycle. Since this is not possible, whatever predictions are used do not take into account the effects of the plans based on them. For this reason, among others, significant portions of the forecast are bound to be in error.

Moreover, even those aspects of an organization's future that are not affected by what it and others do (e.g., the weather) cannot be forecasted well for more than a short period. As in the case of the weather, however, the need to forecast it can be eliminated by bringing it *under control*, as we do by building structures within which work can proceed whatever the external weather may be.

INTERACTIVE PLANNING

Interactive planning is directed at gaining control of the future. It is based on the belief that an organization's future depends at least as much on what it does between now and then as on what is done to it. Therefore, this type of planning consists of *the design of a desirable future and the selection or invention of ways of bringing it about as closely as possible.*

DEALING WITH THE FUTURE

Our knowledge of the future can be classified into three types: certainty, uncertainty, and ignorance; each requires a different kind of planning: commitment, contingency, and responsiveness.

a. First, there are certain aspects of the future about which we can be virtually certain. There are some future changes that may be virtually inevitable and there are some "unchanges" that may be also; that is, aspects of the environment that will remain stable. To take some trivial examples, the percentage of males and females in the population may not change, but the number of twenty-one-year-olds in the United States may change from now to 1980. However, this number can be estimated with virtual certainty. The relatively certain aspects of the future may (and frequently are) difficult to identify. A good deal of research may be required to uncover them. They often become obvious only retrospectively; for example, only now is it becoming obvious that there will be a large demand for metering emissions of pollutants into air and water.

With respect to those aspects of the future about which we can be virtually certain, we can carry out *commitment* planning. But even here the possibility of error should be taken into account by providing appropriate controls. Continuous updating of estimates of what is inevitable or unchanging is required. Furthermore prudence dictates that commitments be made not any sooner than necessary to accomplish the desired objective. It is not always best to be the first to try to exploit a perceived opportunity.

With tongue partly in cheek we can say that successful long-range planning involves, among other things, (1) uncovering the inevitable, (2) determining how to exploit it, and (3) taking credit for having brought it about.

b. Second, there are certain aspects of the future about which we cannot be relatively certain, but we can be reasonably sure of what the possibilities are; for example, we may not know what type of motor power will eventually replace the internal combustion engine in automobiles, but we can be reasonably sure that it will be either a "cleaned up" engine of the same type or one that is powered by steam or electrically, by a battery or fuel cell. In such cases *contingency* planning is required; that is, we should prepare a plan for each eventuality so that we can quickly exploit the opportunities that are presented when "the future makes up its mind."

Contingency planning is old hat in the military but is relatively rare in business; for example, in planning for a military invasion, consideration is always given to each possible outcome of an operation and plans are made for each. Military planners do not wait to see what happens before planning what to do about it. They try to cover every possibility in advance, because time is "of the essence" once a possibility has become a reality.

c. Finally there are aspects of the future that we cannot anticipate; for example, natural or political catastrophes, or technological breakthroughs. We cannot prepare for these directly, but we can do so indirectly through *responsiveness (interactive)* planning. Such planning is directed toward designing an organization and a system for managing it that can quickly detect deviations from the expected and respond to them effectively. Hence responsiveness (interactive) planning consists of building responsiveness and flexibility into an organization.

The Nature of Adaptation

Adaptation is a response to a change (stimulus) that actually or potentially reduces the efficiency of a system's behavior, a response which prevents that reduction from occurring. The change may be either internal (within the system itself) or external (in its environment); for example, change in managerial personnel that reduces corporate efficiency would be an internal stimulus, but a change in a competitor's pricing policy would be an external one.

Adaptive responses are also of two types. In the first, *passive* adaption, the system changes its behavior so as to perform more efficiently in a changing environment (e.g., a person putting on a sweater when he gets cold or a company reducing its costs and prices when the competition does). In the second, *active* adaptation, the system changes its environment so that its own present or future behavior is more efficient (e.g., turning up the heat when one gets cold in a house or bringing about legislation to prevent price cutting by competitors). . . . These two types of adaptation can of course be combined.

Changes in the environment may be rapid and of short duration (e.g., changes in demand for a product from day to day), or slow and of long duration (e.g., introduction of a new product by a competitor). An adaptive organization should be capable of coping with both. Consider what is required to do so.

We obviously require flexibility of plant, equipment, and personnel. For example, the direction of traffic flow in the third Lincoln Tunnel connecting New Jersey and New York City can be reversed, depending on the change in demand from morning to evening. The same can be done to the two center lanes of an expressway in Chicago. Such flexibility can be planned for, frequently with considerable economies. Three tunnels, one of which is reversible, can carry the same load as four one-way tunnels because of the asymmetry of automobile traffic into and out of New York in the morning and evening. Ideally we would like to have facilities that can be used to serve any purpose and can expand and contract depending on demand. Such flexibility is possible only to a limited extent. Therefore demand itself must be at least partially controlled.

Control of demand in the short run and in the long run usually requires different approaches. Consider the long-run problem first.

A manufacturer of machine tools was subject to fluctuations in demand as great as two to one in successive years. This prevented effective use of facilities and personnel. The company looked for another highly cyclical, but counter-cyclical, product line that required the same technology as it was already using. It found such a class of products in highway construction equipment and entered the business. By so doing it reduced variations in annual production loads to only a small fraction of what they had been previously.

Thus one way of obtaining control over the future is to reduce the variations one might expect in the behavior of essential parts of the system or its environment.

Consider another company that produces a raw material used in more than 3000 different forms. Of these about 10 percent accounted for all of the profits and most of the volume of business. Small orders for the remaining large number of small-volume unprofitable items led to frequent disruptions of production schedules, which were geared for long, continuous production runs of the high-volume profitable items. Marketing management refused to drop the small-volume unprofitable items from the company's product line or to raise their prices even to cover cost because—it argued—this would antagonize those customers who were also heavy consumers of the high-volume profitable items and would run the risk of losing them.

An optimizer's (preactive planner's) approach to this problem consisted of constructing a model of the production-inventory-sales system and deriving from it a way of scheduling the production line to meet the demand on it—a way that minimized the sum of the production, inventory, and shortage costs. The improvements yielded were significant but small.

An adaptivizer (interactive planner) took a different approach. He found that by eliminating 4 percent of the least profitable items from the product line, he could reduce production costs and increase profits by an amount equal to the improvement the optimizer had obtained. Therefore he concentrated on the marketing, not the production, system. He found that salesmen were given a base salary plus a percentage of the dollar value of their sales. This led him to design a new salesman incentive plan. It was profit (rather than volume) oriented; it paid no commission on sales of unprofitable items and higher commissions than before on profitable ones. The plan was so designed that, if salesmen continued to sell the same mix of items as they had before, their earnings would not change.

In the first year of this plan's operation sales of about half the unprofitable items in the product line virtually stopped, and sales of the profitable items increased significantly. The optimizing planner generally takes the system structure for granted and seeks a course of action that best solves the problem. The adaptive planner, on the other hand, tries to change the system in such a way that more efficient behavior follows "naturally."

The principle of control used in the last example is one of the most important in adaptive (interactive) planning because it provides an effective way of handling short- as well as long-range variations in the system. It involves motivating participants in the system to act in a way that is compatible with the interests of the organization as a whole, and it does this by providing incentives that make individual and organizational objectives more compatible.

Consider this principle in the realm of traffic control and how it might be used to induce people to use transportation facilities in such a way as to serve their own and their community's interests more effectively. First, the tolls for bridges, tunnels, and turnpikes, at least during periods of heavy demand, could be made inversely proportional to the number of passengers in a car. More specifically tolls would be based on the number of empty seats in an automobile. Thus a two-seat car with two passengers would have a lower toll than a six-seater with two, three, four, or five passengers. A six-seater with three passengers would have a lower toll than one with only two. This would encourage better occupancy of all cars and more use of smaller cars.

Second, tolls might be varied with demand. The heavier the demand for a facility, the higher the charges. Thus charges would be increased during peak hours and decreased during off hours. This would produce a more even use of facilities.

Adaptive thinking of course is not new. But planning that is primarily and systematically committed to producing more adaptive organizations is. We have only begun to exploit the possibilities of such planning. Those who do so most effectively are most likely to develop and exploit the potentialities of their organizations.

REACTIVE, PREACTIVE, AND INTERACTIVE PLANNERS

Reactive planners focus on increasing their ability to undo changes that have already occurred. Preactive planners focus on increasing their ability to forecast changes that will occur. Interactive planners focus on increasing their ability to control or influence change or its effects, and to respond rapidly and effectively to changes they cannot control, thereby decreasing their need to forecast.

Reactive planning is primarily concerned with removal of threats; preactive planning is concerned with exploitation of opportunities. Interactive planning is concerned with both equally but it assumes that threats and opportunities are created by what an organization does as well as by what is done to it.

Reactive planners try to do well enough, to "satisfice," to enable the organization planned for to *survive*. Preactive planners try to do as well as possible, to "optimize," to enable the organization planned for to *grow*. Interactive planners try to do better in the future than the best that is currently possible, to "idealize," to enable the organization planned for to *develop*. An organization develops when it increases its ability and desire to satisfy the needs and desires of those who depend on it, its stakeholders.

We now consider the characteristics of interactive planning in more detail by focusing on what might be called its "operating principles."

OPERATING PRINCIPLES OF INTERACTIVE PLANNING

There are three such principles: *the participative principle, the principle of continuity,* and *the holistic principle.*

The Participative Principle

The most important (but not the only) benefit of planning is not derived from use of its product, a plan, but from engaging in its production. In interactive planning, process is the most important product. By engaging in this process its participants come to understand their organization and its environment, and how their behavior can improve performance of the whole, not just their part of it. It is this increase in the ability of each part of an organization to contribute to improvement of overall performance that is the principal benefit of planning.

Effective planning cannot be done *to* or *for* an organization; it must be done *by* it. Therefore, the proper role of the professional planner, whether inside or outside an organization, is not to plan for others, but to encourage and facilitate their planning for themselves. All those who are part of an organization and all those external to it who are affected by it (except competitors) should be given an opportunity to participate in its planning. The professional planner should provide all these stakeholders with the information, knowledge, understanding, and motivation that can enable them to plan more effectively than they would otherwise.

The Principle of Continuity

All plans are based on a large number of assumptions. An assumption is a proposition that we treat as though it were true; we act on it. It differs from a forecast; for example, we carry a spare tire in our cars because we assume we may have a flat tire but we do not predict that we will have one. Nevertheless, an assumption may be based on a forecast, as when we assume it will rain tomorrow because that is the forecast. On the other hand, we can (and often do) assume that a forecast is wrong.

Because organizations and their environments change continually over time, planners should explicitly formulate as many as possible of their relevant assumptions about what will, will not, can, and cannot change. They should monitor these assumptions continually. When they are found to be in error, plans should be modified appropriately, that is, adapted to changing assumptions. Such adaptation must be continuous if the effectiveness of plans is to be maintained or, more important, increased.

To maximize the learning and adaptation of planners, planning decisions should be implemented experimentally, that is, in as controlled a way as possible. This facilitates frequent comparisons of a plan's actual performance with explicitly formulated expectations. Where actual and expected performance differ significantly, the causes of the deviations should be identified and appropriate corrective action taken.

The Holistic Principle

This principle has two parts: the *principle of coordination* and the *principle of integration*. Each has to do with a different dimension of organization. Organizations are divided into levels, and each level (except possibly the top) is divided into units that are differentiated by function, type of output, market, or some combination of these. Coordination has to do with the interactions of units at the same level, integration with interactions of units at different levels.

The Principle of Coordination.   The principle of coordination asserts that all parts of an organization at the same level should be planned for simultaneously and interdependently. This follows from the fact that the sources of threats and opportunities frequently are not located where their symptoms appear. Therefore, no part or aspect of a particular level of an organization can be planned for effectively if planned for independently of any other part or aspect of that level. For example, reduction of the cost of production may require redesign of products or changes in the mix of sales; a change in the sales mix may require a change in the way salesmen are compensated. In planning, breadth is more important than depth, and interactions are more important than actions.

The Principle of Integration.   The principle of integration asserts that planning done independently at any level of an organization cannot be effective; all levels should be planned for simultaneously and interdependently. It is commonplace for a practice or policy established at one level of an organization to create problems at another level. Therefore, the solution of a problem that appears at one level may best be obtained by changing a policy or a practice established at another level.

When the principles of coordination and integration are combined the *holistic principle* is obtained: every part of an organization at every level should plan simultaneously and interdependently. The concept of all-over-at-once planning differs significantly from both reactive bottom-up and preactive top-down planning.

THE FIVE PHASES OF INTERACTIVE PLANNING

1. *Formulation of the mess.* Determination of what problems and opportunities face the organization planned for, how they interact, and what obstructs or constrains the organization's doing something about them. The output of this phase takes the form of a *reference scenario.*
2. *Ends planning.* Determination of what is wanted by means of an *idealized redesign* of the system planned for. Goals, objectives, and ideals are extracted from this design. Comparison of the reference scenario and the idealized redesign identifies the gaps to be closed or narrowed by the planning process.

3. *Means planning.* Determination of what should be done to close or narrow the gaps. This requires selecting or inventing appropriate courses of action, practices, projects, programs, and policies.
4. *Resource planning.* Determination of what types of resource and how much of each will be required by the means chosen, when they will be required, and how they are to be acquired or generated.
5. *Implementation and Control.* Determination of who is to do what, when it is to be done, and how to assure that these assignments and schedules are carried out as expected and produce the desired effects on performance.

These five phases of interactive planning . . . usually interact; they all can take place simultaneously. The order in which they are presented is the one in which they are usually, but not invariably, initiated. In continuous planning, none of them is ever completed.

CHAPTER 8

PROBLEM TREATMENTS

There are four ways of treating problems: *absolution, resolution, solution,* and *dissolution.*

1. To *absolve* a problem is to ignore it and hope it will go away or solve itself.
2. To *resolve* a problem is to do something that yields an outcome that is good enough, that *satisfies.* Problem resolvers take a *clinical* approach to problems; they rely heavily on experience, trial and error, qualitative judgments, and common sense. They try to identify the cause of a problem, remove or suppress it, and thereby return to a previous state.
3. To *solve* a problem is to do something that yields the best possible outcome, that *optimizes.* Problem solvers take a *research* approach to problems. They rely heavily on experimentation and quantitative analysis.
4. To *dissolve* a problem is to eliminate it by *redesigning* the system that has it. Problem dissolvers try to *idealize,* to approximate an ideal system and thereby do better in the future than the best that can be done now.

The differences between these approaches is illustrated by the following case. A large city in Europe uses double-decker buses for public transportation. Each bus has a driver and a conductor. The driver is seated in a compartment separated from the passengers. The closer the driver keeps to schedule, the more he is paid. The conductor collects zoned fares from boarding passengers, issues receipts, collects these receipts from disembarking passengers, and checks them to see that the correct fare has been paid. He also signals the driver when the bus is ready to move on after

From *Management in Small Doses* (Wiley, 1986).

stopping to receive or discharge passengers. Undercover inspectors ride the buses periodically to determine whether conductors collect all the fares and check all the receipts. The fewer misses they observe the more the conductors are paid.

To avoid delays during rush hours, conductors usually let passengers board without collecting their fares and try to collect them between stops. Because of crowded conditions on the bus they cannot always return to the entrance in time to signal the driver to move on. This causes delays that are costly to the driver. As a result hostility has grown between drivers and conductors which has resulted in a number of violent episodes.

Management of the system first tried to ignore the problem, hoping that if it were left alone it would absolve itself. This effort at absolution did not work; the situation got worse.

Management then tried to resolve the problem by proposing a return to an earlier state by eliminating incentive payments and accepting less on-schedule performance. The drivers and the conductors rejected this proposal because it would have reduced their earnings.

Next management tried to solve the problem by having the drivers and conductors on each bus share equally the sum of the incentive payments due each. This proposal was also rejected by drivers and conductors; they were opposed to cooperating in any way.

Finally, a problem dissolver was employed by management to deal with the situation. Instead of trying to compromise the conflicting interests of the drivers and conductors, he decided to take a broader view of the system. He found that during rush hours there were more buses in operation than there were stops in the system. Therefore, at his suggestion, conductors were moved off the buses at peak hours and placed at the stops. This reduced the number of conductors required at peak hours and made it possible to improve the distribution of their working hours. Under the new system conductors collected fares during peak hours from people waiting for buses and were always at the rear entrance to signal drivers to move on. At off-peak hours, when the number of buses in operation was fewer than the number of stops, conductors returned to the buses.

The problem was dissolved.

To problem dissolvers problems are opportunities, not threats. By redesigning the systems with the problems, a better performance than the best currently possible can be obtained.

CHAPTER 9

MESS MANAGEMENT

Problems are to reality what atoms are to tables. We experience tables, not atoms. Problems are abstracted from experience by analysis. We do not experience individual problems but complex systems of those that are strongly interacting. I call them *messes.*

Because *messes* are *systems* of problems, they lose their essential properties when they are taken apart. Therefore, if a mess is disassembled, it loses its essential properties. Furthermore, as in any system, if each part taken separately is treated as well as possible, the whole is *not* treated as well as possible. A system is more than the sum of its parts; it is the product of their interactions. If taken apart, it simply disappears. Then how can we formulate a mess without taking it apart?

It can be done by the use of *reference projections.* These are projections of the performance of an enterprise that are based on two *false* assumptions. First, it is assumed that the organization involved will not change any of its current plans, policies, or practices. If this were true, the orig-inization would not be trying to formulate its mess. Second, it is assumed that the organization's environment will change only as expected; this is obviously false. Under these assumptions the performance of the organization is projected into the future. These projections reveal the future implied by the organization's current plans, policies, and practices: *the future it is in.*

No matter how successful an organization is, reference projections taken collectively reveal how it would destroy itself if it were not to change. These projections reveal the Achilles heel of the organization. They do this because the no-change assumption implies no adaptation even to a predictably changing environment; for example, projections were made in 1959 which revealed the impending crisis of the American automotive industry. By using data from the preceding 40 years

---

From *Management in Small Doses* (Wiley, 1986).

projections were made of (1) the number of people of driving age in the United States in the year 2000, (2) the number of cars per person of driving age, (3) the number of miles driven per car per year, and (4) the percentage of these miles driven within cities. By combining these projections an estimate was prepared of the number of urban automobile miles that would be driven in the United States in the year 2000 if the industry continued on its then current path and its environment changed only as expected.

Next, by using these projections an estimate was made of the additional parking space and lane-miles of streets and highways that would be needed in the year 2000 to maintain 1960 levels of congestion. Then the cost of their construction, estimated by using projected construction costs, revealed that more than 12 times the maximum amount ever spent per year in the United States for such construction would be required for each of the next 40 years. Although these expenditures were unlikely, they were, in fact, implicitly assumed in the plans then in force in the industry.

This was not the mess facing the industry, however. The mess was revealed by assuming that these large expenditures would be made. If they were, 117 percent of the surfaces of American cities would be covered by streets, highways, and parking lots by the year 2000. This, of course, could not happen. Therefore, continued growth of the automotive industry as it had been was not possible. This was the mess.

What would prevent cities from being covered by streets, highways, and parking lots? The answer rested in decisions still to be made. Studies showed that one way to avoid the mess would be to reduce the size of automobiles. The American automotive industry chose not to do so at that time. It waited for more than a decade before the cost of oil, foreign competition, and government requirements forced it to move slightly in that direction. The consequences of the industry's failure to pay attention to its mess are well known.

We have to know where we are headed before we can take action to avoid getting there. Such redirection of an enterprise requires *mess management,* not problem solving, and mess management requires creative and comprehensive planning.

CHAPTER 10

ENDS PLANNING

Ends planning consists of designing a desired future and extracting from it those ends that the rest of the planning process is addressed to pursuing.

Ends are desired outcomes and are of three types:

1. *Goals.* Ends that are expected to be obtained within the period covered by the plan.
2. *Objectives.* Ends that are not expected to be obtained until after the period planned for, but toward which progress is expected during this period.
3. *Ideals.* Ends that are believed to be unattainable, but toward which continuous progress is thought to be possible and is expected.

Therefore, goals can be considered to be means with respect to objectives, and objectives can be similarly considered with respect to ideals.

Ends planning involves four steps:

1. Selecting a mission.
2. Specifying desired properties of the system planned for.
3. Idealized redesign of that system.
4. Selecting the gaps between this design and the reference scenario which planning will try to close.

Each of these steps is now considered in turn.

SELECTING A MISSION

A mission is an overriding purpose that can unify and mobilize all parts of the organization planned for. The formulation of the mission should

---

From *Creating the Corporate Future* (Wiley, 1981).

be challenging and exciting to virtually all of an organization's stakeholders. It should also provide a focus for the planning process that follows.

A mission statement should identify the business in which the organization wants to be. This may differ from the business it is in. The statement should also specify what effects it wants to have on each class of its stakeholders.

SPECIFYING DESIRED PROPERTIES

The desired properties of a system can usually be identified in brainstorming sessions. Such sessions should not be constrained by considerations of feasibility. The properties specified should be those that the participants believe the organization planned for should ideally have now. A distinction should be made between those properties on which a consensus is reached and those on which there is a significant difference of opinion.

The following are a few of the specifications once prepared for an idealized telephone system:

1. There would be no wrong numbers.
2. You would know who is calling before answering the phone.
3. The phone could be used without hands.
4. You would not have to go to the phone; it would come to you.
5. You could arrange to receive calls placed to your home or office even when you are not there.
6. When you are on the phone and someone is trying to reach you, you would know who it is and would be able to deliver a message to them without interrupting the current call.

Specification of desired properties can be facilitated by using the following checklist of aspects of the organization or unit planned for. The list may have to be modified to fit some organizations:

1. *Inputs.*

   Five types of resource should be considered: plants and equipment, materials and energy, people, information, and money. For each of these the following questions should be asked:

   a. What is required?

   b. Should it be acquired from an external or internal source?

    c. For those resources to be acquired, from what sources should they be acquired and how? (The possibility of vertical integration should be considered.)

2. *The corporate process.*

    a. Who should own the organization and what should their role be?

    b. Which functions necessary for organizational activity should be provided by the organization itself and which should be acquired from external sources?

    c. How should the organization be structured and managed?

    d. In particular, what policies and practices should apply to personnel with respect to recruiting, hiring, orientation, compensation and incentives, benefits, promotions, career development, retirement, and severance?

    e. What should be the nature of the production processes and how should they be designed and organized?

3. *Products and services.*

    a. What products or services should the corporation offer and what special characteristics, if any, should they have?

    b. How should internal development of products or services be organized and carried out?

    c. How should acquisition be organized and carried out?

4. *Markets and customers.*

    a. What types of customer should the corporation seek?

    b. In which market areas?

    c. How should its products or services be distributed and sold?

    d. How should its products or services be marketed and, in the case of products, be serviced?

5. *The environment.*

    a. How should the organization relate to its stakeholders (including government and unions) and the communities in which it operates?

    b. How should information on stakeholders' perceptions of the organization be obtained and used?

c. How should the organization relate to environmental, consumer, and other special interest groups?

IDEALIZED REDESIGN OF THE SYSTEM

An ideally redesigned system is one with which the designers would now replace the existing system if they were free to replace it with any system they wanted. Such redesign is subject to only two constraints:

1. The design must be technologically feasible; that is, it cannot incorporate any technology that is not known to be feasible at the time the design is produced.
2. The design must be operationally viable; that is, it must be capable of operating in the current environment of the system planned for. However, no consideration should be given to the feasibility of implementing the ideally redesigned system because doing this constrains creativity. Moreover, the total design may be feasible even though it contains parts that are infeasible when considered separately.

Three principles should be followed in the idealized design process:

1. Where there is no objective basis for making a design decision, the system should be designed so that it can determine experimentally which of the available alternatives is the best. This applies to properties on which consensus is not reached. For example, if the designers have no basis for deciding which of two possible new practices to include in their design, they should incorporate an experimental comparison of both.
2. The system should be designed so it can continuously evaluate features that have been designed into it and decisions that are made within it. This enables it to learn efficiently.
3. Since any design incorporates assumptions about the future, the system should be designed to monitor these assumptions and to modify itself appropriately when an assumption turns out to be false. This enables it to adapt effectively.

The first two of these principles assure the design of a system that is capable of effective learning. The third assures its ability to adapt well to changing conditions. Therefore, the product of an idealized design is an adaptive-learning system. The output is neither utopian nor ideal because it is subject to improvement. It is the best ideal-seeking system that its designers can conceptualize now, but not necessarily later.

The idealized design process is initiated by producing "bits of design" around the properties identified in the second step of ends planning. Several procedures can be used to stimulate the generation of innovative ideas: brainstorming, synectics, dialectics, and so on. (See Ackoff and Vergara.)

Once the design elements have been completed, they should be checked for their technological, but no other kind of, feasibility. Where such feasibility is not apparent, experts should be consulted.

Now the various design elements can be assembled into a scenario, a comprehensive and coordinated picture of the desired whole. Note that whether or not the organization or unit being designed is autonomous, its design is constrained by the nature of the system that contains it. Therefore, it is desirable to prepare two separate but interrelated designs: one that accepts the constraints imposed by the containing system and one that does not. In preparing the unconstrained design any aspect of the containing system that affects the design of the contained system can be changed. Discussion of these two designs with managers of the containing system often can induce some of the changes desired. It is preferable to prepare the constrained design first, then to improve it by eliminating any undesirable constraints.

COMPARING THE REFERENCE SCENARIO AND THE IDEALIZED DESIGN

Once a consensus version of the constrained idealized design is obtained it can be compared with the reference scenario. This comparison will yield a set of differences that constitute the gaps between what would happen if things were to continue as they are and what the organization would most like. These gaps should be listed using the classification scheme given in the section on specifying desired properties of the system planned for.

Selecting the Gaps to Be Filled

The gaps listed should be classified as goals, objectives, and ideals. This classification may later have to be revised because of information subsequently obtained. Once this classification has been completed, means planning can be initiated.

BIBLIOGRAPHY

Ackoff, R. L., and E. Vergara, "Creativity in Problem Solving and Planning," *European Journal of Operational Research,* 7 (1981). pp. 1–13.

CHAPTER 11

MISSION STATEMENTS

Most corporate mission statements are worthless. They consist largely of pious platitudes such as: "We will hold ourselves to the highest standards of professionalism and ethical behavior." They often formulate necessities as objectives; for example, "to achieve sufficient profit." This is like a person saying his mission is to breathe sufficiently. A mission statement should not commit a firm to what it *must* do in order to survive but to what it *chooses* to do in order to thrive. Nor should it be filled with operationally meaningless superlatives such as *biggest, best, optimum,* and *maximum;* for example, one company says it wants to "maximize its growth potential," another "to provide products of the highest quality." How in the world can a company determine whether it has attained its maximum growth potential or highest quality?

To test for the appropriateness of an assertion in a mission statement, determine whether it can be disagreed with reasonably. If not, it should be excluded. Can you imagine any company disagreeing with the objective "to provide the best value for the money." If you can't, it's not worth saying.

What characteristics should a mission statement have? First, *it should contain a formulation of the firm's objectives that enables progress toward them to be measured.* To state objectives that cannot be used to evaluate performance by hypocrisy. Unless the adoption of a mission statement changes the behavior of the firm that makes it, it has no value.

The behavior of a Mexican firm was profoundly affected by the following passage from its mission statement:

> To create a wholesome, varied, pluralistic, multiclass recreational area incorporating tourist facilities and permanent residences, and to produce locally as much of the goods and services required by the area as possible, so as to improve the standard of living and quality of life of its inhabitants.

From *Management in Small Doses* (Wiley, 1986).

Second, *a company's mission statement should differentiate it from other companies.* It should establish the individuality, if not the uniqueness, of the firm. A company that wants only what most other companies want—for example, "to manufacture products in an efficient manner, at costs that help yield adequate profits"—wastes its time in formulating a mission statement. Individuality can be attained in many ways, including that in which a company's business is identified.

Third, *a mission statement should define the business that the company* wants *to be in, not necessarily* is *in.* However diverse its current businesses, it should try to find a unifying concept that enlarges its view of itself and brings it into focus; for example, a company that produces beverages, snacks, and baked goods and operates a variety of dining, recreational, and entertainment facilities identified its business as "increasing the satisfaction people derive from use of their discretionary time." This suggested completely new directions for its diversification and growth. The same was true of a company that said it was in the "sticking" business, enabling objects and materials to stick together.

Fourth, *a mission statement should be relevant to all the firm's stakeholders.* These include its customers, suppliers, the public, shareholders, and employees. The mission should state how the company intends to serve each of them; for example, one company committed itself "to providing all its employees with adequate and fair compensation, safe working conditions, stable employment, challenging work, opportunities for personal development, and a satisfying quality of working life." It also wanted "to provide those who supply the material used in the business with continuing, if not expanding, sources of business, and with incentives to improve their products and services and their use through research and development."

Most mission statements address only shareholders and managers. Their most serious deficiency is their failure to motivate nonmanagerial employees. Without their commitment, a company's mission has little chance of being fulfilled, whatever its managers and shareholders do.

Finally, and of greatest importance, *a mission statement should be exciting and inspiring.* It should motivate all those whose participation in its pursuit is sought; for example, one Latin American company committed itself to being "an active force for economic and social development, fostering economic integration of Latin America and, within each country, collaboration between government, industry, labor and the public." A mission should play the same role in a company that the Holy Grail did in the Crusades. It does *not* have to appear to be feasible: it only has to be *desirable:*

> . . . man has been able to grow enthusiastic over his vision of . . . unconvincing enterprises. He has put himself to work for the sake of an idea, seeking by magnificent exertions to arrive at the incredible. And in the end he has arrived there. Beyond all doubt it is one of the vital sources of man's power, to be thus able to kindle enthusiasm from the mere glimmer of something improbable, difficult, remote. (José Ortega y Gasset, *Mission of the University,* New York: Norton, 1966, p. 1)

If your firm has a mission statement, test it against these five criteria. If it fails to meet any of them, it should be redone.

If your firm has no mission statement, one should be prepared and as participatively as possible. An organization without a *shared vision* of what it wants to be is like a traveler without a destination. It has no way of determining whether it is making progress.

CHAPTER 12

CREATIVITY AND CONSTRAINTS

Most managers and management educators have a list of what they consider the essential properties of good management. I am no exception. My list, however, is unique because all the characteristics, properly enough, begin with C:

Competence

Communicativeness

Concern

Courage

Creativity

The greatest of these is creativity.

Without creativity a manager may do a good job, but he cannot do an outstanding one. At best he can preside over the progressive evolution of the organization he manages; he cannot lead it to a quantum jump—a radical leap forward. Such leaps are required if an organization is to "pull away from the pack" and "stay out in front." Those who lack creativity must either settle for doing well enough or wait for the breaks and hope they will be astute enough to recognize and take advantage of them. *The creative manager makes his own breaks.*

Educators generally attempt only to develop competence, communicativeness, and (sometimes) concern for others in their students. Most of them never try to develop courage or creativity. Their rationalization is that these are innate characteristics and hence can be neither taught nor learned.

That creativity can be acquired seems to follow from the fact that it tends to get lost in the process of growing up. Adults recognize that

From *The Art of Problem Solving* (Wiley, 1978).

Figure 12.1

young children, particularly preschoolers, are full of it. I recall a dramatic illustration of this point given by an eminent student of creativity, Edward de Bono, in a lecture to an audience consisting of managers and management scientists. He drew a picture on the blackboard of a wheelbarrow with an elliptical wheel (Figure 12.1) and asked the audience why it had been designed that way. There was a good deal of squirming, murmuring, and embarrassed tittering, but no answer. De Bono waited, letting the discomfort grow. He then told his audience that he had recently asked the same question of a group of children and almost immediately one of them had rushed to the board and drawn a squiggly line such as that shown in Figure 12.2. "The wheelbarrow is for a bumpy road," the child had said. The audience blushed and laughed self-consciously.

Most of us take for granted both the creativity of children and its subsequent loss. We do not try to understand, let alone prevent, this loss. Yet the disappearance of creativity is not a mystery; the explanation lies in a query that Jules Henry (1963), an American anthropologist, once made: What would happen, he asked,

> . . . if all through school the young were provoked to question the Ten Commandments, the sanctity of revealed religion, the foundations of patriotism,

Figure 12.2

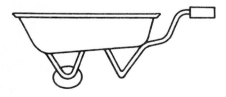

the profit motive, the two party system, monogomy, the laws of incest, and so on . . . . (p. 288)

The answer to Henry's question is clear: society, its institutions, and the organizations operating within it would be radically transformed by the inquisitive generation thus produced. Herein lies the rub: most of the affluent do not want to transform society or its parts. They would rather sacrifice what future social progress creative minds might bring about than run the risk of losing the products of previous progress that less creative minds are managing to preserve. The principal beneficiaries of contemporary society do not want to risk the loss of the benefits they now enjoy. Therefore, they, and the educational institutions they control, suppress creativity before children acquire the competence that, together with creativity, would enable them to bring about radical social transformations. Most adults fear that the current form and functioning of our society, its institutions, and the organizations within it could not survive the simultaneous onslaught of youthful creativity and competence. Student behavior in the 1960s convinced them of this.

The creativity of children is suppressed at home and at school where, Jules Henry (1963) remarked, "What we see is the pathetic surrender of babies" (p. 291). The eminent British psychiatrist Dr. Ronald Laing (1967) reinforced this observation: "What schools must do is induce children to want to think the way schools want them to think" (p. 71). Schools want them to think the way parents want them to think: conservatively, not creatively.

It is easy to see how schools suppress creativity in children. For example, when one of my daughters was in her early teens she came into my study one night with an extra-credit problem that her mathematics teacher had assigned for homework. On a sheet of paper distributed by the teacher were nine dots that formed a square (see Figure 12.3). The instructions below the figure said that a pen or pencil was to be placed on one of the dots and then four straight lines were to be drawn without lifting the pen or pencil from the paper so that all nine dots were covered by the lines.

My daughter had tried to solve the problem, with no success. She asked me for help, assuring me she would not claim the solution as her own. I recognized the problem, but I was unable to recall or find its solution. Impatient to get back to the work she had interrupted, I told her to forget about the problem. "It's not that important," I said. She left unconvinced and with an obviously lowered opinion of my problem-solving ability.

Figure 12.3

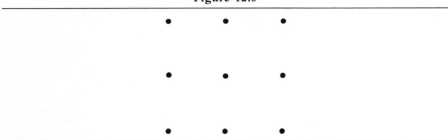

A short while later I heard her sobbing in the next room. I went in to see what was wrong. She told me she was ashamed to go to school without a solution to the problem. I invited her into my study and said that this time I would make a "real try." She came skeptically.

I knew, for reasons considered later, that a puzzle is a problem that we usually cannot solve because we make an incorrect assumption that precludes a solution. Therefore, I looked for such an assumption. The first one that occurred to me was that the paper had to remain flat on a surface while the lines were drawn. Once this assumption came to mind and I put it aside, a solution came quickly. I folded the sheet "in" across the middle line of dots and "out" across the bottom line so that the bottom dots fell on top of the dots of the top line (see Figure 12.4). Then, using a felt-tipped pen I drew a line through the top line of dots, holding the pen against the folded edge on which the bottom dots were located. Keeping my pen on the last dot, I unfolded the paper and flattened it.

Figure 12.4

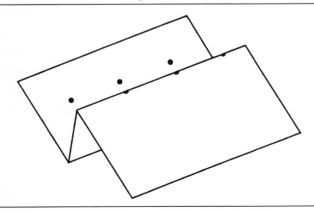

Figure 12.5

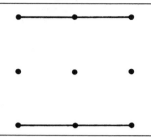

There was a line through the top and bottom rows of dots (see Figure 12.5). With three lines left it was easy to cover the remaining dots (see Figure 12.6).

My daughter was delighted with the solution, and her faith in me was partially restored. I returned to my work with more than a little self-satisfaction.

When I returned from work the next day I could hardly wait to hear what had happened in my daughter's class. She returned my greeting as I entered with her usual "Hi" but nothing more. I waited a few moments and then asked, "Well, what happened in your math class?"

"It doesn't matter," she replied, not looking at me.

"Yes it does," I countered. "Now come on, tell me."

"It will only get you mad," she said.

"Maybe it will, but if it does, I will not be mad at you. So tell me."

"Well," she said, "the teacher asked the class who had solved the problem. About five of us raised our hands. She called on another girl who had her hand up and asked her to go to the board and show her solution.

Figure 12.6

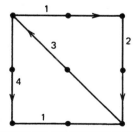

She did." My daughter then drew the solution shown in Figure 12.7 on a sheet of paper. It was the solution I had once known but forgotten.

"Then what happened?" I asked.

"The teacher congratulated the girl, told her to return to her seat, and started to talk about something else. I raised my hand. She stopped and asked me what I wanted. I told her I had a different solution to the problem, one you had given me. She was annoyed but asked me to go to the board and show it to the class. I told her I couldn't show it on the blackboard and needed to use the large pad on the easel in the corner of the room. She told me to go ahead. I drew the nine dots on a blank sheet and started to fold it when she asked what I was doing. I told her I was folding the paper. She told me I couldn't do that. I told her that the instructions didn't say I couldn't. Then she told me she didn't care what the instructions said; that was what she meant. She told me to sit down, so I never got to finish showing the solution."

This is how creativity is suppressed, although usually not so overtly. The teacher made it clear to her class that the objective of the assignment was not to find a solution to the problem, but to find the solution *she knew* and could pretend to have discovered on her own. She had no interest in any other solution.

Is it any wonder that students become more concerned with what a teacher expects of them in an examination than with what are the best answers to the questions asked?

Imagine what a teacher interested in promoting creativity could have done with the situation involving my daughter. She could have revealed the common property of both solutions: *they broke an assumption that the solver imposed on the problem.* In the teacher's solution the broken assumption was that the lines drawn had to lie within the perimeter of the square formed by the dots. She could then have gone on to encourage the students to find other solutions. Had she done so, one of the students might have discovered how to fold the paper so that one line drawn with a felt-tipped pen can cover all the dots (see Figure 12.8).

A puzzle is a problem that one cannot solve because of a *self-imposed constraint.* Creativity is shackled by self-imposed constraints. Therefore, the key to freeing it lies in developing an ability to identify such constraints and deliberately removing them.

It is not enough to become aware of the fact that self-imposed constraints are what obstruct creative problem solving. For example, now that you are aware of this fact, consider this problem.

Figure 12.7

Figure 12.8

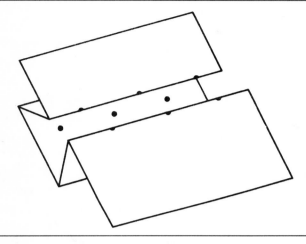

If you have a balance scale, what is the minimum number of weights required to weigh objects of any number of pounds from one to forty?

Stop here and try to find the solution.

If you are like most people you reasoned somewhat as follows. It is obvious that a one-pound weight is needed to weigh a one-pound object. A two-pound weight is needed to weigh a two-pound object. A three-pound weight is not needed because the one- and two-pound weights can be added. A four-pound weight is needed but not a five $(4 + 1 = 5)$, six $(4 + 2 = 6)$, or seven $(4 + 2 + 1 = 7)$. An eight-pound weight is needed. This will get us up to fifteen pounds. A sixteen-pound weight is needed. This will get us up to thirty-one pounds. Finally, a thirty-two-pound weight is needed, and this will get us up to sixty-three pounds, more than the forty required. Therefore, the answer is six weights (1, 2, 4, 8, 16, and 32).

Wrong! The answer is four weights. Even after giving the right answer, most people cannot see what they missed. In the six-weight solution it was assumed that the object to be weighed must be placed on one side of the balance and the weights on the other, but this is a self-imposed constraint. Objects and weights can be placed on the same side of the scale. Once we "see" this, we find that only one-, three-, nine-, and twenty-seven-pound weights are necessary. For example, to weigh a two-pound object, we place the object and a one-pound weight on one side and the three-pound weight on the other. Similarly, if we put a seven-pound object and a three-pound weight on one side, we can put a nine- and a one-pound weight on the other.

Principles that guide our searches for self-imposed constraints are obviously helpful, but it has been my experience that they do not provide sufficient guidance to creative problem solving. It often takes a bigger push than a principle can provide to get over the hump of a self-imposed constraint. I have found that *examples,* real ones drawn from life, are often more effective because they are likely to be remembered better and longer. Therefore, I use them throughout the book.

The guides to creative problem solving that I suggest are based on an analysis of the nature of problems and an extended experience with management-oriented research projects. Therefore, it may be helpful to reveal the analysis of problem solving from which the suggestions I make are partially derived.

A problem, as I conceptualize it, has five types of component.

1. The one(s) faced with the problem, the *decision maker(s).*

The decision maker may be a group, large or small, or an individual.

2. Those aspects of the problem situation the decision maker can control: *the controllable variables.*

For example, in buying an automobile, the buyer can control such things as the make and model he buys, which accessories he adds, how he finances the purchase, and so on. These variables may be either quantitative (e.g., the number of doors) or qualitative (e.g., the color).

Choice or decision making consists of taking a course of action defined by values of one or more controlled variables. There must be at least two courses of action available, otherwise there is no choice and therefore no problem. There may, of course, be an unlimited number of courses of action available.

3. Those aspects of the problem situation the decision maker cannot control but those which, together with the controlled variables, can affect the outcome of his choice: the *uncontrolled variables.*

These may also be either quantitative or qualitative. Together they constitute the *problem environment.*

For example, the sales taxes on the purchase price of an automobile and the cost of licensing it are not controlled by the purchaser, but they affect the outcome, the cost of the purchase. Note that *un*controlled variables are not necessarily uncontroll*able;* they may be controlled by others. Sales taxes are controllable by legislators. Some uncontrolled variables such as the weather are not subject to anyone's control. Orders for products received by a production department may be out of the control of the production manager, but under the control of the marketing manager. Furthermore, in a hierarchical organization each level controls something that lower levels cannot.

4. *Constraints* imposed from within or without on the possible values of the controlled and uncontrolled variables.

For example, the purchaser of an automobile may place a limit on how much he is willing to spend. He may also decide that he will not buy a used car. His choices may also be constrained by what is available at the time of purchase.

5. *The possible outcomes* produced jointly by the decision maker's choice and the uncontrolled variables.

For example, he may get either a good car or a "lemon." Note that there must be at least two possible outcomes. If this were not the case, the decision maker's choice would have no effect on the outcome; therefore, his choice would not be a "real" or "meaningful" one. Furthermore, the two or more possible outcomes must be *un*equally desirable; their values to him must be different, otherwise it would not matter to him which outcome occurred.

To one individual there may be no significant difference between the values of two automobiles of the same make and model but of different colors. To another this difference may be of great significance, in fact, critical.

A decision maker tries to select a course of action that produces an outcome he desires, one that is *efficient* relative to what he *values.* Such courses of action are said to be *effective.* Effectiveness is the product of efficiency and value. One who seeks the best, the most effective, course of action is said to *optimize.* One who seeks a solution that is good enough is said to *satisfice.*

In summary, choice exists only (1) when there are at least two possible courses of action available to the decision maker, (2) where there are at least two possible outcomes of unequal value to him, and (3) where the different courses of action have different effectiveness. In other words, choice exists when the action of the decision maker makes a difference in the value of the outcome.

Not every choice situation is a problem situation, but every problem involves a choice. A problem arises when the decision maker has some *doubt* about the relative effectiveness of the alternative courses of action. The solution process is directed at dispelling doubt.

It is apparent that a choice situation that presents a problem to one person may not do so to another because of a difference in their doubts. This is what makes for consultants, experts, advisors, and so on.

In dealing with a problematic situation, a decision maker must develop a *concept*—a representation or a model—of it. He attempts to solve the problem as *he conceives it*. Thus if his conception is wrong, the solution to the problem as conceived may not solve the problem as it exists. A common example is a formulation of a problem that leads to the suppression of symptoms rather than the removal of the cause of a deficiency that creates the problem. Because of such errors of conceptualization, it has often been observed that we more frequently fail to face the right problem than fail to solve the problem we face.

The conception of a problem that I have presented has a general form that can be represented by the equation:

The value of the outcome = A specified relationship between the controlled variables and the uncontrolled variables.

This equation may be subject to constraints on the controlled and uncontrolled variables.

Now to the question, What is the meaning of "art" in "the art of problem solving"? Normally, "art" used in this way has nothing to do with aesthetics. For most people aesthetics has no relevance to problem solving. The "art of problem solving" usually refers to both our inability to understand problem solving completely and our ability to make decisions despite this deficiency. This is not the sense in which I use the concept; I use it in its aesthetic sense. To make sense of this I must go back in history.

The philosophers of ancient Greece divided the pursuits of man into four major categories:

1. The scientific—the pursuit of truth
2. The political-economic—the pursuit of power and plenty
3. The ethical-moral—the pursuit of goodness and virtue
4. The aesthetic—the pursuit of beauty

These categories were refined out of the philosophical thought of centuries; they were not the products of a deliberate effort to divide man's activities into exclusive and exhaustive categories. Obviously they are not exclusive, since two or more can be pursued simultaneously. Nevertheless, I believe these categories are exhaustive for reasons discussed later.

It is not surprising that we fail to reflect sufficiently on or fully understand the meaning of "aesthetics of problem solving." Over the last twenty-five centuries very few philosophers have been able to incorporate aesthetics into a comprehensive philosophical system, and there has been little systematic development of aesthetics. On the other hand, aestheticians tend to give the other three categories of man's activities short shrift. As a result, we understand aesthetics much less than science-technology, political economy, or ethics-morality. It is safe to say that most of us have some idea of the way each of these three aspects of our activity relates to the others, but no idea of how any of them relates to aesthetics.

Thoughtful persons would agree that considerable progress has been made in science and technology. Some, but perhaps fewer, would also agree that progress has been made in the domains of political economy and ethics-morality. However, one would be surprised to hear it argued that mankind has made aesthetic progress—that the products of our art are better than those of the ancients or even those of more recent eras.

It has become traditional for affluent people to separate work from play and hence from pleasure. They are conscious of aesthetics—or at least they know of the interaction of beauty, play, and pleasure—in their homes and their recreational and social activities. However, their attitudes toward business and work have been dominated by the Puritan ethic. This ethic contrasts work with play. It conceptualizes work as an *ascetic,* not an aesthetic, activity. Work—and problem solving is considered to be work—is widely thought of as both necessary and necessarily unpleasant. The dissatisfaction it has produced is rationalized by many apologists of the Industrial Revolution who argue that it should be accepted, if not embraced, as a kind of earthly purgatory in which sin is expiated and virtue is gradually accumulated.

It is hardly necessary to point out that, just as fun has been taken out of the work most adults do, it has also been taken out of the learning most children are forced to do. There is little that is beautiful in education.

A principal objective of my effort here is to put beauty and fun back into at least that aspect of work and education we call problem solving.

To understand the meaning of the aesthetics or art of problem solving, we must understand the effort made by philosophers throughout recorded history to find one desire that is both universal and ultimate in terms of which progress can be measured. This has been a search for an ideal shared by all men and women, past, present, and future. Searches for such an ideal failed, ironically, because those conducting the search were too sophisticated. Let me explain.

Once upon a time there was a young man who was granted three wishes. We all know that with the first two he managed to get himself into such a mess that he had to use his last wish to get back to his initial state. On hearing any one of the many versions of this story, most bright children tell us they could do better with only one wish: *they would wish that all their wishes would come true.* My teacher, the much-too-little recognized philosopher Edgar Arthur Singer, Jr. (1948) systematized this childlike wisdom by identifying a desire so universal that it unifies all men at all times. It is the desire for the ability to satisfy desires whatever they may be, even the desire for nothing, Nirvana. It is in the nature of purposeful systems—and people are purposeful systems—to desire, and one can desire nothing without desiring the ability to satisfy it. The ability to satisfy all desires is an ideal necessarily shared by all men at all times. It is called *omnipotence.* Its ideal character is reflected in the fact that virtually every religion ascribes it to deity.

Omnipotence is an ideal that, if it could be attained, would assure fulfillment of all other desires and therefore of all other ideals. Consequently, it is what might be called a *meta-ideal.*

There are four conditions that are necessary and sufficient for the continuous and simultaneous progress of every person toward omnipotence.

First, such progress requires a continual increase in the efficiency of the means by which we can pursue our ends and, therefore, a continual increase in our information, knowledge, and understanding—an increase in our grasp of truth. It is the function of science to provide such an increase, and the function of technology to provide an ability to use the products of science effectively.

Second, progress toward omnipotence requires a continuous increase in the availability of and access to those resources needed to employ the most efficient means available. Availability implies a state of plenty and access implies a state of power. To provide these is the function of the political economy.

Third, it requires continuous reduction of conflict within and between individuals, because conflict means that the satisfaction of one (or one's) desire precludes the satisfaction of another (or another's) desire. Therefore, we pursue both peace of mind and peace on earth, a state of goodness and virtue. This pursuit is ethical-moral.

Finally, it requires the aesthetic function. This is the most difficult to understand.

If man is to continually pursue the ideal of omnipotence, he must never be willing to settle for anything less; that is, he must never be either permanently discouraged or completely satisfied. Whenever he attains one objective, he must then start after another that is even more valuable to him, and he must seek a continual increase in his ability to satisfy his desires. Therefore, he must always be able to find new possibilities for improvement and satisfaction. He must always be able to generate visions of a more desirable state than the one he is in.

E. A. Singer, Jr. (1948) showed that it is the function of art to provide such visions and to *inspire* us to their pursuit: to create the creator of visions of the better and to give this creature the courage to pursue his visions no matter what short-run sacrifices are required. Inspiration and aspiration go hand in hand. *Beauty* is that property of the works and workings of man and Nature that stimulates new aspirations and commitments to their pursuit. No wonder we say of a solution to a problem that inspires us, "it is beautiful."

Long before Singer, Plato conceived of art as a stimulant that was potentially dangerous to society because it could threaten society's stability. His conception of the disquieting function of art is the same as that put forward here, but his conception of utopia, his *Republic,* as a stable state is not. There is at least as much satisfaction to be derived from the pursuit of objectives as in attaining them, and from the pursuit of solutions to problems as in attaining them. Therefore, in an ideal state, as I conceive it, man would not be problem free, but he would be capable of solving a continual flow of increasingly challenging problems.

Of greater importance is the fact that an ideal state is not attainable whatever its characteristics; therefore, in all less-than-ideal states such disquiet as Plato sought to control is required if continual progress toward the ideal is to be made.

In contrast to Plato, Aristotle viewed art as carthartic, a palliative for dissatisfaction, a producer of stability and contentment. Whereas Plato saw art as a producer of dissatisfaction with the present state of affairs that leads to efforts to create a different future, Aristotle saw it as a producer of satisfaction with what has already been accomplished. Plato saw art as *creative* and Aristotle saw it as *recreative*.

These are not different things but two aspects of the same thing. Art is both creative and recreative. These aspects of it can be viewed and discussed separately, but they cannot be separated. Recreation is the extraction of pleasure here and now, a reward for past efforts. It provides "the pause that refreshes" and by so doing *recreates the creator*. Art also produces an unwillingness to settle for what we have. It pulls us from the past and pushes us into the future.

Thus, to make problem solving creative (inspiring) and fun (recreative) is to put art into it. To do so is to reunite work, play, and learning and therefore to reunify man, at least in his problem-solving activities.

So much for my concept of the nature of problem solving and the art on which this guide is based.

BIBLIOGRAPHY

Henry, J., *Culture against Man,* New York: Random House, 1963.

Laing, R. D., *The Politics of Experience,* New York: Ballantine Books, 1967.

Singer, E. A., Jr., *In Search of a Way of Life,* New York: Columbia University Press, 1948.

PART III

APPLICATIONS

Part III includes a variety of applications of the concepts and methods covered in the preceding sections of the book. Consumer design (Chapter 13) shows how idealized design can be used to provide a corporation with a real customer focus. The next three chapters on eduction and crime provide applications of systemic thinking and idealized design in the public sector. Chapters 17 and 19 provide an application to advertising. Chapter 18 discusses the development of the theory on which the second of the two selections on advertising was based. The design of an internal (to a corporation) market economy (presented in Chapter 20) has been used to reduce, convert, or eliminate internal bureaucratic monopolies for which corporations pay dearly by excessive costs of services and excess personnel. Finally, the design of a system to support management's decision-making, learning, and adaptation is presented in Chapter 21.

CHAPTER 13

CONSUMER DESIGN

$\mathbf{P}$roducers often try to find out what consumers want by asking them. This seldom yields useful information because consumers either don't know what they want or they try to provide (or avoid) answers they think are expected of them. In many cases a better way consists of using the consumer to *design* products or services; for example, a chain of men's stores, although successful, failed to attract the type of customer its owner wanted. He wanted to reach upwardly mobile professionals and businessmen by offering high-quality designer clothing at discount prices. But this method failed; rather it drew bargain hunters from lower income segments of the population. Repeated questionnaires addressed to potential buyers the firm wanted to attract yielded results that, when applied, failed to bring them into the stores.

The owner and his executives sought help from a research group with a reputation for unconventional approaches to marketing problems. This group selected 15 representatives of the targeted customer population and invited them to spend a Saturday designing their ideal men's store. The identity of the sponsoring firm was not revealed but several of its executives took part incognito.

The representatives of the targeted population produced a very creative design of a men's store. Once done, the identity of the sponsor was revealed and a comparison was made of the sponsor's stores with the one newly designed. The principal differences were wide and had not been revealed by any of the earlier research.

Here are a few of the differences. First, the designers made it known that they always decided how much to spend for articles of clothing before shopping. What they were looking for was a store that offered the highest quality at their predetermined price. Put another way: they did

From *Management in Small Doses* (Wiley, 1986).

not want to minimize price for a predetermined quality; they wanted to *maximize quality* for a predetermined price. Discount prices, the chain's advertising message, turned them off.

Second, they wanted different articles of clothing of the same size to be segregated. They did not want grouping by type, which requires hunting all around the store.

Third, they wanted to examine clothing without a salesman hovering over them. They wanted call buttons installed in each size-organized area for summoning a salesman when *they* wanted one.

Fourth, they did not want items for women in the store—not even gifts. They preferred to shop for women in stores that specialize in products suitable to them, just as they preferred to buy their own clothing in stores that specialize in supplying men. But they did want a lounge in which women could pass their time pleasantly and comfortably and be available for consultation. They thought a mixture of male and female salespersons would be desirable.

They wanted alternation costs included in the price of the clothing and delivery of all altered clothing. They also wanted more informative labels with complete information on the material used, where the clothing was made, and by whom. They said they were uninterested in the designer's name; they didn't believe that the designer identified on men's clothing had designed it anyhow.

As regular customers of a store they wanted access to its sales before the general public. They thought that there should be only two sales a year, presummer and prewinter, to occur at the same time each year. They also wanted the store to maintain and refer to records of their sizes and style preferences.

Similar consumer design groups have been used for other types of product and service, and even to write advertising copy. They have always been creative and informative.

It is harder for a market researcher to get inside a consumer's mind than it is for a consumer to turn his mind inside out.

CHAPTER 14

EDUCATION

Most schools appear to put a lid on children's minds. Curiosity and creativity are suppressed. Learning is equated to memorization, thus converting it into work and differentiating it from play. Only a relatively few are ever able to reunite work, play, and learning in later life.

Most children who perform well in school do so to "beat the system," to please their parents, or because it takes too much effort for them to do otherwise. To many, school is a maze one must go through in order to reach freedom, including freedom to learn. Those who do well in school are more likely to be stimulated to do so at home than in school. The successful products of our educational system are normally those who would have succeeded even without it. On the other hand, those who are not motivated to learn at home are unlikely to be so motivated at school.

MACHINE AGE EDUCATION

Most of our schools are industrialized disseminators of information and instruction using materials and methods that were appropriate when students—like factory workers—were thought of in machinelike terms, particularly as black boxes whose output would hopefully exactly match what was put into them.

The simple fact is that what the education system expects of students can be done better by computers and other "mental machines," and students know this. Computers can remember more and recall, compare, and calculate more quickly and precisely than human beings can. Teachers forget that forgetting what is irrelevant is one of man's most important abilities. The young do not want to be put into competition with machines; they want to learn to do what a machine cannot do and they want to know how to use and control these machines. They cannot learn

---

Adapted from *Redesigning the Future* (Wiley, 1974).

how to do so in a system that treats them like a product to be worked on and put together on an assembly line, a precisely scheduled process in which they are passed from one discrete operation to another. The processing itself is increasingly performed by machines, as are grading papers, registration, and computer-assisted instruction. Think of the damage to one's concept of *self* that results from being taught by a machine that has no self or by a teacher who has been taught to act like one.

Today's school is modeled after a factory. The incoming student is treated like raw material coming onto a production line that converts him into a finished product. Each step in the process is planned and scheduled, including work breaks and meals. Few concessions are made to the animated state of the material thus processed; it is lined up alphabetically, marched in step, silenced unless spoken to, seated in rows, periodically inspected and examined, and so on. The material worked on varies widely in quality but the treatment is uniform. The system tries to minimize the number of different kinds of product it turns out because the greater the variety of product, the greater is the production cost. The educational process is considered to be successful if the final product can be sold at a high price. The system even puts brand names and model numbers on its products.

Educators have reduced education to a large number of discrete and disconnected parts. They have dissected education into schools, curricula, grades, subjects, courses, lectures, lessons, and exercises. A system of quantification and qualification has been developed to reflect this atomistic concept of education: examination grades, course grades and credits, grade-point averages, diplomas, and degrees. Formal education is never treated as a whole, nor is it appropriately conceptualized as a part of a process much of which takes place out of school.

Unlike the young of earlier generations, today's students come armed with concerns about the world and concepts of relevance, concerns and concepts that are largely ignored in school. They are overinstructed in what they can better do alone: take things and concepts apart; and they are underinstructed in what is very difficult to do alone: put what they have learned together into an understanding of the world and their role in it. They are given answers to questions they do not ask and denied answers to those they do ask. They are taught to answer questions, not to ask them—despite the fact that progress depends at least as much on the questions we ask as it does on the answers given to us.

Educators make little or no effort to relate the bits and pieces of information they dispense. Subjects matters are kept apart. A course in one subject seldom uses or even refers to the content of another. A student's writing ability, for example, is only evaluated in an English course but not, say, in a history course. An English teacher seldom asks a student to write about something he has learned in history or another course, and if he does, the content is not evaluated. Such compartmentalization reinforces the concept that knowledge is made up of many unrelated parts. But it is only by grasping the relationships between these parts that information can be transformed into knowledge, knowledge into understanding, and understanding into wisdom.

For example, children (and most adults) are never made aware of the fact that mathematics is a language and therefore has many characteristics in common with English, and that there are fields of study concerned with the common properties of all languages (logic and semiotic). Nor do they learn that the uniqueness of mathematics derives from the fact that it deals with the *form* of experience abstracted for *its content,* nor what the difference between form and content is. Mathematics is known but not understood by most who teach it to children. One can know something without understanding it, but one cannot understand something without knowing it.

Emphasis on separateness of subjects was characteristic of the Machine Age. Emphasis on relationships and interactions is characteristic of the Systems Age. Machine Age education is disintegrating; that of the Systems Age should be integrating.

The mechanistic input-output orientation of Machine Age education results in treatment of students as though they were machines with the combined properties of tape recorders, cameras, and computers. The student is evaluated with respect to his ability to reproduce what he has been told or shown. Most examinations are tests of the ability to reproduce material previously presented to the one tested. Examinations are designed to serve the system's purposes, not the student's.

Cheating is more a consequence of the characteristics of examinations than it is of the characteristics of students. Otherwise why would teachers also cheat? They do where they too are evaluated by the performance of their students on examinations. Examinations invite corruption of the learning and teaching process. Teachers cheat to stay in the system; students, to get out of it. (I have more to say about examinations below.)

More "advanced" Machine Age teaching is based on the Pavlovian concept of the student as an input-output organism. Harvard psychologist B. F. Skinner modernized the language used to describe this concept, but he left the concept itself unchanged.) Students are taken to be organisms that can be conditioned to respond as desired by rewarding correct responses and punishing incorrect ones. Therefore, they are repeatedly exposed to the same stimulus until the correct response is given automatically. This method of teaching is further "advanced" by mechanizing the instructor's role in it. The result is called "computer-assisted instruction" or "programmed learning." The student and his friendly computer are placed in an isolation chamber in which the computer can dispassionately try to make the student know as much as it does. If Machine Age educators knew how to program the student directly—and some have tried to do so through subliminal suggestion—they would undoubtedly do so.

Computers and other new technologies can play a constructive role in education. Later I will consider how they can be used.

SYSTEMS AGE EDUCATION

Understanding the failure of formal education must begin with recognition of the fact that it is less efficient than at least some informal education. Evidence of this is plentiful. Children learn their first language at home more easily than they learn a second language at school. Most adults forget much more of what they were taught in schools than of what they learned out of them. The bulk of what they use at work and play they learned at work and play. This is even true of teachers. They learn more about teaching by doing it than by being taught how to do it. Most university professors teach subjects they were never taught. In more than twenty-five years of university teaching I have never taught a subject I was taught. The subjects I teach did not exist when I was a student. Most professional school graduates cannot practice the profession they were taught in school until they have practiced it out of school in some type of internship. Most of what they subsequently use in their work they learned during their internship, not in class.

Formal education denies the effectiveness of learning processes that take place out of class or school. These processes should be used and augmented in school. Most learning takes place *without teaching,* but schools are founded on teaching, not learning. As Edgar Z. Friedenberg put it: ". . . schools have a prior commitment to teach rather than help people learn. . . . " Teaching, unlike learning, can be industrialized and mechanized; it can be controlled, scheduled, timed, measured, and observed. But teaching is at most an *input* to the learning process, not an output.

Nevertheless, our current educational system operates as though an ounce of teaching produces at least an ounce of learning. Nothing could be farther from the truth.

Therefore, *Systems Age education should focus on the learning process, not the teaching process.*

Learning outside of school is not organized into subjects, semesters, courses, or other discrete units. A child's learning of a language, for example, is not separated from its learning of other subjects but is intimately bound up with it. A child learns a great deal without any concept of subjects and disciplines, and without being pushed into learning by examinations and grades. One might argue that this is only true for things the child wants to learn. But school, one might continue, *must* teach a child what he should know whether he wants to or not. This is a Machine Age argument. In the Systems Age school children should be motivated to learn whatever they ought to learn but never forced to learn what they do not want to. To impose learning is to take the fun out of it, and this is much more harmful to the child than is his failure to learn any particular subject.

It is widely recognized that we learn well what we want to learn and learn poorly what we do not. Formal education should try to *induce* students to want to learn more things than they would without it. When students want to learn something or the need for learning it becomes apparent to them, they will learn it.

Therefore, *Systems Age education should not be organized around rigidly scheduled quantized units of classified subject matter, but rather around development of the desire to learn and the ability to satisfy this desire.*

Even where rigid entrance requirements and long lists of prerequisites are imposed on students, they vary in ability, interests, and what they have already learned. Therefore, the same input to each student will not, and does not, produce the same output. Schools based on the industrial model ignore or minimize the differences between students and thus require them to adapt to educational production methods. The methods should be adapted to students. Individuality should be preserved at all costs. Uniformity and conformity are anathema to progress.

Therefore, *Systems Age education should individualize students and preserve their uniqueness by tailoring itself to fit them, not by requiring them to fit it.*

Learning is not restricted to part of one's life. It takes place continuously. In the past, when relatively little was known and it was added to or changed slowly, formal education could be completed in a few years. As knowledge accumulated, more and more formal education was required to absorb it. Because of the increasing rate at which knowledge increased, the problem of keeping up with additions to, and changes of, knowledge also grew. Refresher courses of many types and durations have become commonplace. "Continuing education"—education after departure from school—is now an integral part of our culture.

As the rate of acquisition of knowledge continues to accelerate—and it will—formal education will continue to be extended and thus will occupy more and more of a lifetime and will approach a continuous process. As it does, it will become apparent that the separation of play, formal education, and work is artificial and counterproductive.

Therefore, *Systems Age education should be organized as a continuing, if not a continuous, process.*

What solves an educational problem or even a system of educational problems at any one time and place is not likely to do so at another time and place. Hence we must give up the search for a best educational system, one that operates optimally regardless of time and place, not to mention students.

Therefore, *Systems Age education should be carried out by educational systems that can and do learn and adapt.*

An educational system should (1) facilitate a student's learning what he wants and needs to learn, (2) enable him to learn how to learn more efficiently, and (3) motivate him to want to learn, particularly those things he needs in order to satisfy his own desires and to be socially useful. A major objective of learning should be to facilitate the selection and pursuit of objectives. Objectives are valued outcomes. As previously noted, value is of two types: extrinsic and intrinsic. An extrinsic objective is one that is sought as a means to a still farther objective; for example, one may want to learn how to drive a car in order to go from one place to another. An intrinsic objective is one that is sought for its own sake, only for the satisfaction its attainment brings; for example, in learning how to play a musical instrument for one's own entertainment. Objectives may have both intrinsic and extrinsic value. Driving an automobile may be a source of pleasure to the young, and playing an instrument may be a source of income to an adult.

Learning has both intrinsic and extrinsic value. We seek to learn something just because of the satisfaction that doing so brings. We learn some things for their own sake, and others because of what doing so enables us to obtain. If learning has no intrinsic value to a person—that is, if it brings him no pleasure—it becomes a burden. If one is forced to learn something he does not want to learn, doing so will lack intrinsic value and what is learned is not likely to be learned well. The quality of one's life depends at least as much on what one has learned for its own sake as it does on what is learned for the sake of something else. Hence education should involve a great deal of free choice as to what is learned, how it is learned, and when it is learned.

Learning for dominantly extrinsic reasons should be directed as increasing the ability to use its products in pursuit of those objectives for which it was intended, not to increasing the ability to regurgitate it during examinations. If a student wants to learn calculus, for example, in order to design structures, he should be evaluated for his ability to design structures using the calculus, not for his knowledge of the calculus in the abstract. He is more likely to become interested in calculus if he learns it in order to do something else he wants to do than if he is forced to learn it for its own sake.

Educators simply do not know what the students of today will need to know tomorrow. Therefore, they should not impose their conception of requirements on students. This is even true for students in professional schools. Educators of professionals do not know what most of their students will be doing after graduation. For example, in a report prepared for the Carnegie Foundation in 1959, W. G. Ireson noted:

> The most important fact brought out by . . . surveys over a period of thirty years is that more than 60 percent of those persons who earned [engineering] degrees in the United States, either became managers of some kind within ten to fifteen years or left the engineering profession entirely to enter various kinds of business ventures . . ." (p. 507)

In an editorial in *Science,* Dael Wolfle noted that one-fifth of Americans awarded doctorates move out of the field in which they received their degree within five years after receiving it, and 35 percent do so within fifteen years.

Even if graduates stay in the field in which they were educated, they must replace and supplement much of their school-acquired knowledge to remain effective. Therefore, it is essential that graduates be as flexible as possible, that they want to continue their learning, and that they know how to do so.

The previously noted ability of college professors to learn new subjects to teach to others is much more important than their ability to teach. They should be preoccupied with transmitting their ability to learn, not with teaching what they have learned.

Today the principal instrument of education is a teacher lecturing to a class. A student may learn by being lectured to, but there are alternative ways of learning. Their relative effectiveness varies by time, place, subject, and student. Hence each student should have maximum freedom to experiment with and select the way in which he will learn a subject, as well as freedom to select the subjects he will learn. Consider some of the alternatives:

1. *Some subjects are best learned by teaching them to oneself.* This is particularly true for subjects that one is highly motivated to learn. Such learning may involve using others as resources, but in the way the learner, not the teacher, sees fit. The option of learning a subject on one's own—independent study, as it is called—should always be open to every student for any subject at any time.

2. *Some subjects are best learned by teaching them to others.* This is common knowledge among those who have taught. When a teacher teaches material that is new to him he invariably learns it better than do any of his students. Therefore, many bodies of knowledge, particularly those that are well organized and recorded in books, can be learned effectively by teaching them to others.

Small groups of three to five students can be organized into *learning cells* in which they teach each other different subjects or different parts of the same subject. Experiments with such cells have been carried out successfully with students at a variety of educational levels in several different countries.

Faculty members can help such learning cells in several ways. First, they can prepare a specification of the material that they believe should be learned and the principal sources that can be used. Secondly, they can serve as tutors when asked to. Some questions that arise in a student's mind while learning a subject are not answered in the sources available to him, or answers may be difficult to find. Faculty members or more advanced students can help in this regard.

Students at one level who have already learned a subject can teach it to others at a more junior level, or help them learn it on their own. It is already commonplace to use graduate students to instruct undergraduates in college, but it is not common to use more advanced students in this way in lower-level schools. It should be. It enables the senior student to consolidate and augment his previous learning.

I was recently involved in a course given by seventeen graduate students to six faculty members. The course was on planning in less-developed countries. Most of the students were from such countries and all of the faculty members had worked in them. Whatever the faculty members had written on the subject was made available to the students who then tried to educate the faculty further. It was an exciting and fruitful learning experience for both students and faculty.

3. *Some skills are best learned through demonstration and instruction by one who already has the skill.* Examples are sports, surveying, drafting, fine arts, and use of laboratory equipment and computers, driving a car, and playing a musical instrument. In some cases a student may learn such skills more easily from another student than from a faculty member. He should have the freedom to select his instructor.

4. *Awareness of questions that have either not been asked or answered and synthesis of those answers that are available are best attained in seminar discussions guided by one steeped in the relevant area.* Education should be devoted as much to raising questions as to learning answers. [Recall that] the American anthropologist Jules Henry once asked what would follow "if all through school the young were provoked to question the Ten Commandments, the sanctity of revealed religion, the foundations of patriotism, the profit motive, the two party system, monogamy, the laws of incest, and so on . . ." (p. 288). [Recall also that] the British psychiatrist R. D. Laing replied that there would be more creativity than society could currently handle, but not more than it should be capable of handling (pp. 71–72). The conversion from the kind of society we have to the kind we should have requires just such creativity.

Education should also be concerned with a continuing synthesis of what has already been learned and with the extraction of a *weltanschauung,* a world view, from it. Such a view makes it possible to convert information and knowledge into understanding.

5. *Many students are best motivated to learn and best learn how to do so in attempting to solve real problems under real conditions with the guidance of one* *who is already so motivated and who knows how to learn.* Therefore, students should work on research or service projects with faculty members or others with relevant knowledge and experience. Apprenticeship and internship are two of the most effective ways of learning (1) how to use what one knows, (2) what one does not know, (3) how to learn it, and being motivated to do so.

Such "practice" may well take place off campus.

Student members of such learning, be if out-of-the-classroom experiences or work-study project teams, should be at different stages of their education so that they can best learn from and teach one another.

Traditional lectures should be available to those who want them but students should have a choice of lecturers. Not all teachers can lecture well. A good lecturer on television or film may be preferable to a poor one in person. The technology of communication can be used to facilitate seminar-type discussions between students and faculty members who are at other schools. Exciting lectures, seminars, and even tutorials should be recorded so that other students can see and hear them at their convenience. The recordings (visual and/or auditory) should be kept in a library that is easily accessible to students. In time, any student in any school should have access to any faculty member of any school by means of such recordings. They would even enable us to keep active those who have retired or died.

FLEXIBLE LEARNING SYSTEM

A major deficiency of current formal education lies in its formality. The process is almost completely inflexible and unresponsive to individual differences among students and therefore requires students to adapt to it. Effective education should be flexible enough to enable the student to select the form and content of his education. He should have the opportunity to design and try his own ways of learning so that he can learn how to learn and adapt his methods of doing so to the nature of the subject at hand.

Such informal education, in a more open classroom setting, has always had its critics. They say it sacrifices the learning of basic skills necessary for success in the workplace and also for rigorous academic achievement. These criticisms reveal two important points. First, revolution in part of the educational system is not enough. Unless the methods used in all parts of the system are coordinated and integrated, old criteria will continue to be used by parts of the system to evaluate the output of new educational processes employed in other parts of the system. Academically oriented examinations that determine college admissions are widely used even though they have never been demonstrated to be strongly related to performance in college. Until college admission criteria are changed they will act as a yoke on experimentation in schools at a lower level.

Entrance requirements are used to assure uniformity of the raw material that colleges receive. Such uniformity is only relevant to educational processes that are carried out like mass production. If education were modified in the ways suggested here, there would be no need for entrance requirements. Only exit requirements would be needed and these would consist of demonstrated ability to do well what graduates want to do on leaving school.

Parents' concern with their childrens' slowness in acquiring basic skills in informal schools is based on an acceptance of an educational schedule appropriate only to formal schools. (They overlook the fact that among students in such schools the percentage of functional illiterates is rising alarmingly.) Basic skills are those needed to learn other things that are also needed. They are normally taken to be reading, writing, and arithmetic. It is worth noting that *talking* is omitted despite the fact that it is more basic still. It is omitted because it is assumed to have been learned before entering school. There is a moral here to which I will return.

Most children who have trouble learning how to read well are not strongly motivated to do so. They live with adults who seldom read to themselves let alone their children. It is difficult to convince a child to learn something that he seldom observes those he most admires using. Children who enjoy being read to and who see others enjoy reading to themselves are usually anxious to learn how to read in order to decrease their dependence on others for it. They also want skills they see adults enjoying. To take a child whose home life has produced no desire to read and force him to learn how to do so because an arbitrary schedule dictates it, is to assure his disenchantment with the process. There are many who have learned to read well but who have never learned to enjoy it. On the other hand, it is hard to believe that one who enjoys reading or being read to will not eventually learn to do it well. Motivation should precede instruction. If this delays a child's learning how to read—or similarly, to write or do arithmetic—then the fault lies at home and in scheduled expectations, not at school.

It is not at all unlikely that before long children will enter school with the ability to read and perhaps even to write and do elementary arithmetic. Television and parents can easily combine to make this possible. The popular children's television program, "Sesame Street," has already made strides in this direction. I have the strong feeling that we deliberately restrain many of our preschoolers from learning to read, write, and do arithmetic before entering school because we do not want them to be out of step when they do. Education that can easily take place at home is being constrained by the ignorance expected of children when they enter school. The desire of elementary schools to receive uniformly ignorant raw material is more responsible for delayed learning of basic skills than anything that is done in school, formal or informal.

In the early 1950s, my academic colleagues and I decided that knowledge of computer programming should be required of all those students in the graduate program for which we were responsible. Operating in the traditional mode, we initiated a required course on the subject. Over the next few years we received an increasing number of requests from students for the substitution of an examination on the course's content for the course. We responded by making the course optional and requiring the examination. The course had to be canceled shortly thereafter for lack of enrollment. So few failed the examination that we subsequently discontinued it and listed knowledge of computer programming as a prerequisite for admission to the program. This prerequisite was later dropped because it was realized those who entered the program without the required knowledge quickly acquired it and did so without course work.

There are basic skills in specific fields as well as in life in general. When students want to do that which requires a basic skill they learn it and do so efficiently, and usually on their own. The ability to read, write, and do elementary arithmetic ought to be expected of children entering school. (Think of what this would do to our concept of parental responsibility and how much it would contribute to the education of adults.) If children enter without such skills, the fact that others of their age have them is likely to motivate them to want to acquire them. Once they want to do so they may learn more easily from their contemporaries than they do now from teachers. They should, of course, have adult guidance or instruction available when *they* want it.

COMPUTER-ASSISTED LEARNING

I have already expressed my reservations about the use of computers as *teachers*. However, I do believe that they can be used effectively to facilitate *learning*. One cannot program a computer to perform a task that one cannot do oneself. The computer will only do what it is told to do, nothing more, nothing less. Therefore, the computer is, in the Machine Age sense, a perfect student; it remembers whatever it is told and only what it is told, and it does whatever and only what it is told to do. This makes it possible for students to learn a subject—for example, arithmetic—by trying to teach it to a computer. To do so requires ability to use a language that a computer understands, but such languages are now very simple and children have less difficulty in learning languages than do adults. I was once involved in an experiment in which seven-year-olds were taught to program a large computer to do their arithmetic homework. In teaching the computer how to do their homework they learned with great enthusiasm how to do it themselves.

Computerized instruction should not place the student and computer in splendid isolation. It should be used instead to facilitate students working together in social situations, interacting, and learning from and teaching each other. They can be so used, as the following example shows.

Three consoles with cathode-ray tubes (television screens), typewriters, and light-pen inputs were arranged in a triangle so that each of three students could see the other two and talk with them, but none could see the screens of the others. (See Figure 14.1.) The computer addressed the same question to each of the students in writing on their screens. They answered either by use of the light pen or typewriter. The computer then told them how many had given the correct answer, and no more. If all answers were not correct the students had to find out by discussion who had been in error and attempt to correct him. They then put their modified answers into the computer. The computer returned the same type of output. This process continued until all the answers were correct and then moved to another question. Between questions the students were free to consult any material they desired, at or away from the console. The computer did not teach in this situation but it did facilitate students' learning from one another.

In this triangular situation the student provided answers to questions asked by the computer. Education is even better served if these roles are reversed. This becomes possible if computers are used to confront students with relatively realistic situations in which they must determine whether there is a problem and, if there is, how to solve it and test their solution. Let me describe briefly one such use of the computer at the college level, one that was reported in detail by J. C. Porter et al.

Figure 14.1
A Computer-Assisted Learning Setup

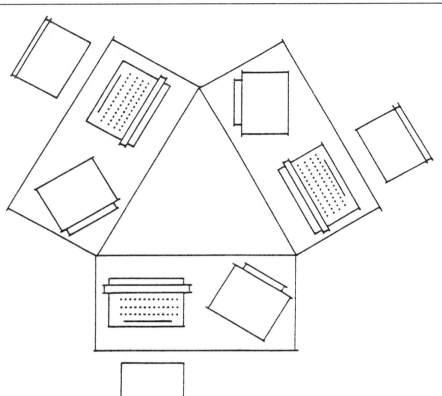

A computerized simulation of a production-distribution process whose characteristics could be completely controlled by the instructor was designed. The instructor could manipulate such characteristics as the number of products involved, the number and capacity of both production and storage facilities, the nature of customer demand, processing times, and costs. In brief, he could play God and control this small simulated industrial world at will. The simulator produced reports of a type common to many industrial firms. These reports were given to students working separately or in teams, as they saw fit. They had to analyze the data to determine if the system had a problem, and if it did, what it was. Once they had formulated and solved whatever problem they saw in whatever way they chose, using any resources to which they had access, they could design and carry out an experimental evaluation of their solution's performance in the simulator. They could then adjust and modify their solution in light of the results obtained. Different students and teams compared their results. The instructor would then reveal his solution based on complete knowledge of the system and compare it with those obtained by the students.

In some cases the students were able to do as well or nearly as well as the instructor by using approaches that differed significantly from his. This enabled the instructor to learn from what the students were doing. Both he and the students became increasingly aware that there are many different ways of solving the same problem, and that the same situation can be converted into many different problems.

These examples show how the computer can be used to humanize and increase the effectiveness of the educational process. Once we get over the desire to mechanize the teacher whose current function, in general, is better eliminated, many effective educational uses of the computer suggest themselves. In none of them should the student and computer be pitted against each other. The computer should be used as an instrument *of* the learner, not as an instrument of others *on* the learner.

EVALUATION OF STUDENTS

Closed-book examinations—the type most frequently used—are poor tests of knowledge or understanding because they are not like real-life situations in which a person's knowledge and understanding are tested or evaluated. They are primarily tests of memory. In real life we are evaluated by how well we get jobs done. We are expected to use all the resources we can bring to bear on the task. In closed-book examinations, on the other hand, the student is deprived of the use of readily available resources. This would be appropriate only if we were training him to survive, as Robinson Crusoe did, on a deserted island.

If examinations must be used to test students they should be modeled on evaluation processes used in the real world. Open-book, take-home, and oral examinations are far superior to closed-book examinations for judging a student's knowledge and understanding, and, of no little importance, they are learning experiences in themselves.

An examination in which the student prepares all or some of the questions as well as the answers reveals much more of his grasp of a subject than does a conventional examination. It enables him to indicate what aspects of a subject he considers to be important and why.

For years I have given my students take-home examinations in which they prepare the questions as well as the answers. They are evaluated on both. Their only complaint is that these examinations are too hard. But they are always a learning experience for students and me. When feasible, I let students grade one another's papers. I have systematically compared their grading with my own and have never found a significant difference.

On occasion I have let two students examine each other orally in my presence. Such examinations are usually more revealing of their grasp of a subject than are those that I prepare.

Such examinations as I have suggested are not easy to administer because they consume more time than do those of the conventional type. Most examinations are designed to minimize the work of the teacher. Such examinations minimize the learning that can be derived from them by the student *and* the teacher.

Many examinations claim to test a student's ability to solve problems, but few do so because their authors do not understand the difference between a *problem* and an *exercise*. A problem, as previously noted, is abstracted out of a messy situation. Hence problem formulation is one of the most critical phases of problem solving. But exercises are *preformulated* problems. They do not require formulation nor do they provide the information that was required to formulate them. It is precisely this information which is generally needed to solve a problem creatively.

The ability to solve an exercise is not equivalent to the ability to solve a problem. Exercises are usually formulated so as to have only one correct answer and one way of reaching it. Problems have neither of these properties.

In a conversation with one of my colleagues, I was asked how I would go about determining the probability that the next ball drawn from an urn would be black if I knew the proportion and number of black balls that had previously been drawn. He told me that the urn contained only black and white balls. I replied that I would first find out how the urn had been filled. "No," he said, "that is not permissible." "Why?" I asked, "Certainly you have such information." "No, I don't," he replied. "Then how do you know the urn contains only black and white balls?" I asked. "I have it on good authority," he answered. "Then let me talk to that authority," I countered. In disgust he told me to forget about the whole thing because I clearly missed the point. I certainly did.

An essential part of problem solving lies in determining what information is relevant and in collecting it. To deprive a student of the experience of rectifying and seeking out such information is to miss most of the point of problem solving. Furthermore, it overlooks the fact that it is harder to ask the right question than it is to find the right answer.

CURRICULA

Today's education is based on three organizing concepts: subjects, courses, and curricula. The amount of choice among them that a student is allowed increases with his age, but even at the "end" his choices are severely limited. The constraints are justified by the assumption that the teacher knows best what the student needs to know. But, as I argued earlier, this is not, and has not been the case. What justification was there for the four years of Latin I was required to take in high school? I cannot recall ever having used trigonometry since then either. We do not know what today's students will require tomorrow. It is for this reason that I argued that it is not nearly as important that a student learns any particular subject as it is that he learns how to learn and how to enjoy doing so.

Subjects, disciplines, and even professions are convenient ways of labeling and filing knowledge. But the world is not organized in the same way as our knowledge of it is. There are no physical, chemical, biological, psychological, sociological, or other unidisciplinary problems. The disciplines and subjects are not different parts of the world; they are different ways of looking at the world. Hence any problem can be looked at from the point of view of any discipline. For example, a doctor may see an elderly woman's lack of good health as a consequence of her weak heart; an architect may see it as deriving from her having to walk up three flights of stairs to her inadequate apartment; an economist may see it as due to her lack of income; and a sociologist as a consequence of her family's indifference.

Progress comes as much from creative reorganization of what we already know as from discovery of new things. Einstein's contribution to physics was organizational. All the facts available to him were available to others. In the last two decades science itself has undergone extensive reorganization with the emergence of many new "interdisciplines" such as cybernetics, operations research, communications sciences, and general systems. A filing system can always be reorganized without changing its content, but doing so may increase our access to, and understanding of, that content. Therefore, we should not imbed our current ways of classifying knowledge in students' minds as fixed categories. They should be encouraged to organize their learning in ways that best serve them, not us.

When we isolate a subject we inhibit exploration of its relationship to other subjects. Disciplines are craft unions preoccupied with preserving their academic perogatives. Academic departments do not organize knowledge; they organize teachers and disorganize knowledge. Disciplinary departments and bounded subjects are antithetical to Systems Age education.

A curriculum is a solution to a problem that does not exist. Even if it did exist its solution would change rapidly with respect to time and place. Curricula as now conceived are a denial of the rapid rate of cultural and technological change.

Because what one learns is not nearly as important as learning how to learn, and because questions are at least as important as answers, students should be free to design their own curricula. (To be sure, faculty members should be available to provide help.) It is at least as revealing of a student's quality to evaluate the curriculum he has designed as it is to evaluate what he has gotten out of it. To design a curriculum is to ask a set of questions. What he gets out of it is a set of answers.

SELECTION OF SCHOOLS
Much of social progress derives from the struggle for survival. This is as true for organizations as it is for species. Public schools have not had to be concerned with their survival; they are subsidized and have captive customers. They do not have to compete to survive, nor do they have to satisfy their customers to do so. As a result, most school-age children and their parents are in a trapped state. They must take what education is provided to them in a particular school at a particular location.

Any supplier of a service who has assured resources and an assured market has little or no incentive to provide a satisfactory service or to improve it. Public schools are no exception. To survive all they need do is comply with regulations. Experimentation and research on learning and teaching are discouraged; standardization and mechanization of education are encouraged.

Christopher Jenks, a Harvard education scholar, has designed a system to overcome these shortcomings. It is called "the voucher" system and is currently being tried in San Jose, California. What follows is my own variation on Jenks' theme.

The parents of each school-age child would be given an educational voucher worth a specified number of dollars payable by the government to a school that receives it. This voucher would cover tuition and transportation (if required) to any public school, and part or all of tuition in private schools. Parents could apply to any school for admission of their child. They would not have to use one to which their child is assigned because of proximity or political jurisdiction. Children could apply to any primary or secondary school just as young adults do to college today, but cost would not be a factor except for private schools.

Schools that have more applicants than they can accommodate would be required to select from among them at *random*. This would assure as much heterogeneity of the student body as the applications permit. It would also make desegregation of schools possible.

Public schools would have no source of income other than what they receive by cashing in the vouchers they receive. Hence if they do not attract and retain applicants, they would go out of business. Private schools could charge whatever they wanted but parents would have to pay the difference. Private schools that accept vouchers could only redeem them if they selected among applicants at random. This would create competition between public and private schools as well as between public schools.

The voucher system would encourage differences between schools. Needed specialization would take place. For example, if there were a large number of retarded or deaf children requiring education, schools would develop that specialize in their education. (Parents of handicapped children might be given an appropriately larger educational allowance for them.)

By introducing the market mechanism into the educational system its consumers would be encouraged to become familiar with the alternative schools available to their children. Each community would provide a clearing house for information about schools including evaluations by both children and parents.

In this system, schools would learn more effectively from their successes and failures and they would be more adaptive. Individual schools would tend to be more responsive to the needs and desires of the neighborhood of which they are part. Their administrators would be more likely to involve parents and students in planning and policy making. Schools would become more participative as well as more progressive.

CONTINUING EDUCATION

Two trends are developing that will eventually converge and change the educational process considerably. We can, and should, accelerate their convergence.

First, because of the rapid development of new knowledge and the rapid obsolescence of the old, those who have left school are increasingly faced with the need for further education, updating. Most white-collar workers above the clerical level already require occasional reimmersion in the formal educational process. This is particularly true of those in the professions. Witness, for example, the profusion of executive and management development programs.

Norman Macrae of *The Economist* tried to put some numbers on this trend:

> A man who is successful enough today to reach a fairly busy job at the age of 30, so busy that he cannot take sabbatical periods of study, is likely by the age of 60 to have only about one-eighth of the scientific (including business scientific) knowledge that he ought to have for proper functioning in his job; and the more learnedly scientific his job sounds, the greater this deficiency will be.
>
> The remedy . . . has got to be some system for much more continuous lifetime re-education for businessmen and bureaucrats at most levels. This will be one of the big problems of 1972–2012. (p. x)

The percent of time spent in learning while at work is bound to increase; hence the distinction between work and learning will become less and less important. Learning will be part of work, and work a part of learning.

Second, increasing numbers of young people are interrupting their formal education for some work experience or exposure to the real world. Many try to combine the two. Furthermore, increasing numbers of graduate students are employed on research and service projects in their universities which deal with real-world problems and provide relevant work experience. Hence just as learning is taking an increasing portion of what used to be years of uninterrupted work, work is entering what used to be years of uninterrupted schooling. Graduation from education to work will be lost in a life pattern in which both go on continuously after an age that is likely to decrease over time.

As these trends develop they will increasingly conflict with incrementally conceived education. The end points of high school and college have always been arbitrary but were convenient in an era in which an educational qualification would last as long as the person who received it. But the life of such qualifications is rapidly shrinking. For example, the medicine practiced at the end of this century will be very different from that of today. Hence a qualification to practice medicine today will not be a relevant qualification then. But most of those who enter medical practice today will still be practicing then. As a result, many professionals and subprofessionals will require repeated requalification (as is already the case for airline pilots and computer programmers). Degrees will become less meaningful and many will become irrelevant. Licenses and certificates requiring periodic renewal are likely to become the rule.

These developments indicate the need for reconceptualizing education as a continuing lifelong process in which the distinctions between formal and informal education and between work, play, and learning become unimportant.

CONCLUSION

There are, of course, many aspects of education that I have not discussed here. I have focused attention on learning that should be the product of the educational process. I have tried to show that we are in the midst of an educational crisis that derives from a conception of education that was suitable for the Machine Age, but not for the Systems Age.

We currently have an industrialized educational system that minimizes the number of choices available to students and that regulates almost every aspect of their behavior. It operates on the assumption that there is only one correct way to do anything, including learning. A teleological system orientation suggests that choice be maximized both in what is learned and how it is learned. It suggests that the emphasis on teaching be reduced and that the purposefulness of students be placed in focus by attempting to motivate them to learn and learn well.

BIBLIOGRAPHY

Henry, J., *Culture against Man,* New York: Random House, 1963.

Ireson, W. G., "Preparation for Business in Engineering Schools," in *The Education of American Businessmen,* F. C. Pierson et al., New York: McGraw-Hill, 1959.

Laing, R. D., *The Politics of Experience,* New York: Ballentine Books, 1967.

Macrae, N., *The Economist,* (January 22, 1972), p. x.

Porter, J. C., M. W. Sasieni, E. S. Marks, and R. L. Ackoff, "The Use of Simulation as a Pedagogical Device," *Management Science, 12* (February 1966), pp. B-170–B-179.

Wolfle, D., "Editorial," *Science, 173* (July 9, 1971), p. 109.

CHAPTER 15

NEVER LET YOUR SCHOOLING INTERFERE WITH YOUR EDUCATION

Every child is an artist. The problem is how to remain an artist when he grows up.

Picasso

TEACHING DISCOURAGES CREATIVITY

In Chapter 12 it was shown that creativity involves providing unexpected answers to questions and solutions to problems and exercises. Here is an example of how teaching almost discouraged creativity by indicating that it was unacceptable.

Adherence to Type

One year, after many of struggling with students' handwriting on term papers, I issued a set of specifications as to how I wanted their papers presented. They were to be typed, double spaced, on 8½-by-11-inch white paper, unlined, with approximately a one-inch margin on all sides.

When I distributed these instructions at the beginning of the semester, I asked if there were any questions. There were several, which I answered. They did not require modification of my specifications.

Among the papers I received at the end of the semester was one that was typed across the long dimension of the paper rather than the short one, as is the usual practice. At the end of this paper the author wrote, "Aha. I gotcha."

My initial reaction was anger, because it was apparent that the student knew perfectly well what I wanted. However, on reflection I realized

---

From *Ackoff's Fables* (Wiley, 1991).

that he took my specifications as a challenge. What he had done was creative, and this was more important than the content of his paper, which was not bad. I gave him an A, but admonished him that the next time he did it it would no longer be creative.

Moral: Teachers kill creativity by inducing students to give them the answers that students think teachers expect. Answers that are expected cannot be creative.

OBSOLESCENCE OF WHAT HAS BEEN LEARNED

Within a short time after graduation many, if not most, graduates practice in a field other than the one in which they were educated. . . . Not one member of the faculty in the department of The Wharton School from which I . . . retired had ever taken a course, let alone a degree, in a business school.

The accelerating rate of change, particularly technological, rapidly obsoletes much of what we know. It reduces the effectiveness of experience as a teacher. The fact that one has driven an automobile for 25 years does not equip one to pilot a jet airplane or a spacecraft. It has been estimated that about 50 percent of what is currently relevant in most professions will not be relevant within five years. Such transience of knowledge is reflected in the story of the ex-student who, a decade after graduation, visited his old professor of economics. When the ex-student entered the professor's office, he was grading examinations. The ex-student picked one up and looked through it. Then he remarked to the professor, "This is the same set of questions you gave us 10 years ago." "Yes," said the professor, "but the answers have changed."

There appear to be a few subjects that we can be relatively sure students will need. Traditionally, we have taken these to be reading, writing, and arithmetic. However, arithmetic is no longer necessary; a hand calculator is faster, more accurate, and can carry out more mathematical operations than most brains. Furthermore, we already have machines that can read print aloud and can convert voice to print. They may eventually replace the need to read and write, at least in part.

My point is not that it will not be advantageous to be able to read, write, and calculate, but that these abilities may well not be needed. In the future, there may not be any subject that must be known for a

useful adulthood other than how to use the machines that know the subjects needed.

FROM DATA TO WISDOM

> An ounce of information is worth a pound of data.
>
> An ounce of knowledge is worth a pound of information.
>
> An ounce of understanding is worth a pound of knowledge.

Despite this, most of the time spent in school is devoted to the transmission of information and ways of obtaining it. Less time is devoted to
the transmission of knowledge and ways of obtaining it *(analytic thinking)*.
Virtually no time is spent in transmitting understanding or ways of obtaining it *(synthetic thinking)*. Furthermore, the distinctions between data,
information, and so on up to wisdom are seldom made in the educational process, leaving students unaware of their ignorance. They not
only don't know, they don't know what they don't know.

The reason so little understanding is transmitted by teachers is that they
have so little to transmit. They are more likely to know *what* is right than
why it is right. Most why questions do not have unique and simple answers, and therefore are difficult to use in examinations or to grade when
they are used. Explanations require discussion if they are to produce understanding. The ability to lead fruitful discussions is not an attribute of
most teachers. Therefore, to break this educational log jam we have to develop ways by which students can gain understanding without having it
taught to them. The fact is that most of the understanding that most of
us acquire we acquire on our own, without it having been taught to us.
Thus, what is required of the educational system is release of this ability
to gain understanding on our own and encouragement to use it. Such a
release may even enable teachers to gain some understanding.

Data are symbols that represent the properties of objects and events. Information consists of processed data, the processing directed at increasing
its usefulness. For example, census takers collect data. The Bureau of the
Census processes that data, converting it into information that is presented
in the numerous tables published in the *Statistical Abstracts*. Like data, information also represents the properties of objects and events, but it does
so more compactly and usefully than data. The difference between data
and information is functional, not structural.

Information is contained in *descriptions,* answers to questions that begin with such words as who, what, when, where, and how many. *Knowledge* is conveyed by instructions, answers to how-to questions. *Understanding* is conveyed by explanations, answers to why questions.

Information, knowledge, and understanding enable us to increase efficiency, not effectiveness. The efficiency of behavior or an act is measured relative to an objective by determining either the amount of resources required to obtain that objective with a specified probability, or the probability of obtaining that objective with a specified amount of resources. The value of the objective(s) pursued is not relevant in determining efficiency, but it is relevant in determining effectiveness. *Effectiveness is evaluated efficiency.* It is efficiency multiplied by value, efficiency for a valued outcome.

Intelligence is the ability to increase efficiency; wisdom is the ability to increase effectiveness.

The difference between efficiency and effectiveness—that which differentiates wisdom from understanding, knowledge, information, and data—is reflected in the difference between development and growth. Growth does not require an increase in value; development does. Therefore, development requires an increase in wisdom as well as understanding, knowledge, and information.

Wisdom deals with values. It involves the exercise of judgment. Evaluations of efficiency are all based on a logic that, in principle, can be programmed into a computer and automated. These evaluative principles are impersonal. We can speak of the efficiency of an act independently of the actor. Not so for effectiveness. A judgment of the value of an act is never independent of the judge, and seldom is the same for two judges.

From all this I infer that although we are able to develop computerized information-, knowledge-, and understanding-generating systems, we will never be able to generate wisdom by such systems. It may well be that wisdom—which is essential for the pursuit of ideals or ultimately valued ends—is the characteristic that differentiates man from machines. For this reason, if no other, the educational process should allocate as much time to the development and exercise of wisdom as it does to the development and exercise of intelligence.

Not only does schooling do little or nothing about the generation of understanding and the development of wisdom, it does little about even the collection of data and the generation of information. There are great subtleties involved in the collection of data and its conversion into information. Most of these subtleties are not revealed in the educational process. Most of us have to learn them the hard way.

On Foaming at the Mouth

When Busch beer was being introduced to the market, I was asked to determine how beer drinkers compared its taste with competitive products. My colleagues and I designed what we thought was a good procedure for conducting the taste tests required. We took Busch and three other beers, removed all identification from their bottles, and then labeled the beers using letters—A, B, C, D, and E. We formed two groups of Busch beer using different letters for each group. We wanted to determine how reliable were the comparisons made by our subjects.

Only regular drinkers of one of the four brands of beer used in the test were subjects. They were invited to beer-tasting evenings at prominent hotels in the centers of the cities in which the tests were conducted. Each subject was given five bottles of beer and asked to rank them by taste. They were free to conduct their trials as they saw fit.

The average ranking of each beer was then determined. Much to our surprise, the difference in the average rankings of the two differently labeled groups of Busch beer was very different. This made no sense and, of course, cast considerable doubt on the reliability of the results.

I lamented over this to August A. Busch III, CEO of Anheuser-Busch companies but then a junior vice president in charge of the Busch brand. He expressed no surprise at the results. He asked me how people actually make their choices between competing brands. Do they line up bottles of the competing brands and sip-test them, as we had them do in our test? Of course not. Then why didn't we have them test the brands as they would normally?

We went back to the drawing board and redesigned the test. This time we placed cases of unmarked bottles of the competing beers in the homes of regular beer drinkers and gave them a month to compare the brands in any way they wanted. At the end of a month we collected their rankings. The results were completely different from those we had obtained in the first test, and they corresponded to the ranking of the market shares of the beers tested. In addition, the rankings of the two cases of differently lettered Busch beer were essentially the same.

Moral: The right information cannot be extracted from the wrong data.

In retrospect, the reason for the failure of the first beer taste test and the success of the second was obvious. As a pipe smoker, for example, I often tried a pipeful of tobacco I had never tried before. I frequently enjoyed that first pipeful enough to buy a package of that tobacco. In most cases I was unable to finish it. Preferences over the long haul can be quite different from those over the short haul. The staying power of a product is at least as important as the initial impression it makes.

Poor teaching of inferential statistics has led to major errors in processing data into information. Students are taught to perform numerous statistical operations without understanding them at all. As a result, they extract misinformation from data and cannot tell the difference between the information and misinformation produced by others. Among the more common types of error frequently committed are the following:

First, statistics provide a way of arriving at inferences from a sample drawn in a prescribed way from a well-specified population to that population. Inferences arrived at from samples drawn in other ways are not valid. Nevertheless, they are commonly made. For example, one research team studied the characteristics of 30 ulcer patients in a particular hospital to which they had access. They drew inferences from their study of this group of patients to ulcer patients in general. Such inferences are completely unjustified. What they had was not a random sample drawn from the large population of interest to them, but a smaller population of interest. Treating it as a random sample is illegitimate, so are inferences drawn from one population to another.

Second, correlation analysis is one of the most frequently used ways of processing data. It provides a measure of the association between variables, the degree to which they tend to change in the same or opposite directions. For example, height and weight of people are correlated positively because they tend to increase/decrease together. Unfortunately, those who find a correlation between variables often erroneously infer that one of them *causes* the changes in the other. This is as wrong as inferring from their correlation that an increase in weight will produce an increase in height. The conclusion drawn from correlation—as was done frequently in studies of the relationship between cigarette smoking and lung cancer—may be right, but the inferential process by which it was obtained is wrong.

Third, in estimating the value of a variable, two types of error can be made: overestimation and underestimation. (Corresponding types of error are involved in the other major activity of inferential statistics: testing hypotheses.) Either of these types of error can be reduced by

changing statistical estimating procedures. However, whenever the probability of one of these types of error is decreased, the probability of the
other is increased. To determine which combination of these types of
error is more desirable requires knowledge of the costs associated with
each. Few of those who use statistics to make estimates know the costs
of error or are even aware of their relevance. They use conventional estimating procedures, almost all of which assume costs of error that are
much more likely to be wrong than right. For example, it is commonly
assumed that the cost of an overestimate of a specified magnitude is equal
to the cost of an underestimate of the same magnitude. Can you imagine estimating the percentage of a chemical in a drug that is poisonous
beyond a certain concentration and assuming that overestimating that
percentage is just as costly as underestimating it by the same amount?
The underestimate can result in death, but the overestimate may only reduce the potency of the drug.

When we speak of the lack of understanding produced by school, we
should include lack of understanding of the methods by which we extract
information, knowledge, and understanding from data.

THE MEDIUM VERSUS THE MESSAGE

Schools seem able to survive the serious trouble they are in with little if
any change. This is not because little is done, but because what is done
has little effect. What is done has little effect because the trouble schools
are in is generally diagnosed incorrectly. Diagnostic efforts focus on what
is taught, the content of teaching, the messages it delivers. However,
much (if not most) of what students learn in the educational process is
not derived from what is taught, but from how it is taught. In education,
perhaps more than in any other domain, *the medium is the message*.

The principal characteristic of the educational process that affects what
is learned and needs to be unlearned is its focus on what appears to be
problem solving.

THE FOCUS ON SO-CALLED PROBLEMS

The focus on problem solving is responsible for a great deal of the learning and unlearning students must engage in after they leave school.
Throughout their formal education, students are evaluated by their ability to solve problems that are *given* to them. Therefore, it is only natural

for them to go out into the world assuming that problems will continue to be given to them. However, nothing could be further from the truth. Outside of school, problems are seldom "given"; they usually have to be taken, extracted from complex situations. Students are not taught how to do this. They are not even made aware of the need to do it.

Problems, Exercises, and Questions.   Most of what most teachers consider to be problems are not problems at all; they are exercises or questions, and most teachers, hence students, are unaware of the very important differences between them.

Look Before You Speak

I was once given the following problem by an eminent statistician: You dip into a bowl containing only black and white balls and pull out m black balls and n white balls. Now, if you dip into the bowl again without replacing the balls you withdrew previously and pull out one ball, what is the probability that it will be white?

I told him I would answer his question after he told me how he knew the bowl contained only white and black balls. "That," he said, "would ruin the problem." He didn't realize that he had already done so. Instead, he reformulated the problem.

This time, he said, the balls are all white on the outside and are contained in a clear bowl into which I could look. Some of the balls have black cores; the cores of the others are white. Now, he continued, if you dip into this bowl and pull out m balls that, when split open, reveal black cores and n balls that reveal white cores, what is the probability that if you dip into the bowl again and withdrew one ball it would have a white core?

"How," I asked, "do you know the balls have only white or black cores?"

He turned away in disgust and abandoned his effort to test me.

Moral: An exercise is a problem from which at least some of the information required to formulate it is denied to the one asked to solve it.

The very popular case method of teaching uses exercises, not problems. Much of the information used to formulate these exercises has been filtered out. To be sure, they contain what the author considers to be all the relevant information. But separation of the relevant information from the irrelevant is a critical part of problem formulation and solving, and what is relevant to one problem solver may not be to another. Nevertheless, some argue that what is learned in dealing with cases is useful in dealing with real problems. This is like arguing that learning how to box with one hand tied behind one's back is a good way to learn how to box with both hands.

A question is an exercise from which the reason for wanting to solve it has been removed. It is an unmotivated exercise, a problem with no context. *Nevertheless, the reasons for wanting to answer a question determines what is the right answer to it.* For example, even the question "How much is two plus two?" has no meaning out of context. The answer is not the same when the two refers to degrees Fahrenheit as it is when it applies to chairs.

To learn how to answer questions or solve exercises is not to learn how to solve problems; and to learn how to solve problems that are *given* is not to learn how to *take* problems from real situations, how to *formulate* them. For example, a recent study received national attention when it cited a growing shortage of university professors. It urged solution of this problem. However, it struck me that professors who are in class for no more than three to nine hours per week and who often give courses they have frequently given before are hardly being overworked, even if they are engaged in research. The formulation of the problem as a shortage of professors not only assumes that the amount of teaching they currently do is just right, it also assumes, among other things, that:

1. The number of courses required of students is just right, and fewer would be bad.
2. The number of contact hours between students and teachers is just right, and fewer would be bad.
3. The number of weeks per session is just right, and more would be bad.
4. The number of sessions per year is just right, and more would be bad.

Not one of these assumptions seems obviously true to me. What does seem obvious is that it would be easier and quicker to get rid of the shortage by manipulating the variables affected by the assumptions I have listed than by trying to produce more professors. Producing more professors might well perpetuate currently inefficient and ineffective practices.

A wrong solution to the right problem is generally better than the right solution to the wrong problem, because one usually gets feedback that enables one to correct wrong solutions, but not wrong problems. Wrong problems are perpetuated by right solutions to them.

Problems and Disciplinarity.   Schools beyond the elementary level are organized into disciplinary departments, and so are the courses and curricula they offer. The disciplines provide a convenient way of labeling and filing knowledge. But the world is not organized the way schools are. There are no physical, chemical, biological, psychological, sociological, or any type of disciplinary problems. Disciplinary adjectives before the word "problem" reveal absolutely nothing about the problem; what they reveal are the points of view of the persons looking at the problem.

Down on the Stairs Up

A while ago some of my professorial colleagues and I were meeting with leaders of the self-development effort in the Philadelphia neighborhood previously referred to, Mantua. A member of the community broke into the meeting with bad news. That morning an 83-year-old woman who lived in the neighborhood and was very active in its development effort had gone to the area's only free health clinic for her monthly checkup. She had been told she was fine and left for home, a fourth-floor walkup. While climbing the third flight of stairs on the way to her rooms, she had a heart attack and died.

The silence that followed this announcement was eventually broken by the professor of community medicine, who said, "I told you we need more doctors at the clinic. If we had them, we'd be able to make house calls and this sort of thing wouldn't happen."

After another silence the professor of economics spoke up. "You know, there are plenty of doctors in Philadelphia who will make house calls. She just couldn't afford one. If her welfare or medical benefits had been adequate, she could have called one and this wouldn't have happened."

The professor of architecture then asked why elevators weren't required in all multiple-dwelling units of more than three floors.

Finally, the professor of social work spoke up. "You all seem to be unaware of the fact that she has a son who is a graduate of our university's law school. He is now a senior partner in a very prestigious law firm located in center city. He, his wife, and two children live in a very

nice bungalow in an affluent suburb. If that woman and her son had not
been alienated, she would have had no stairs to climb and all the money
she needed to call a private practitioner."

Moral: There are as many realities as there are minds contemplating
them.

Learning how to determine what point(s) of view will produce the
best treatment of a problem should be, but seldom is, an essential part of
education.

Knowledge and understanding come as much from creative reorganization of what we already know as from the discovery of new things.
Therefore, students should not be led to believe that current ways of classifying information, knowledge, and understanding involve fixed categories that are inherent in the nature of things. They should be
encouraged to organize their learning in ways that best serve them, not
the educational system. When we isolate and put boundaries around a
subject, we inhibit exploration of its relationship by experts in other subjects. Disciplines are used to organize craft unions that are preoccupied
with preserving their academic prerogatives. Academic departments and
curricula do not organize knowledge; they organize teachers and *disor-*
ganize knowledge.

It is important for students to realize that the best place to deal with
a problem is not necessarily where the problem appears. For example,
we don't try to treat headaches with brain surgery, but by swallowing a
pill.

Problems Are Abstractions. Perhaps the most damaging problem-
related misconception promulgated by the educational process is that
problems are objects of direct experience. Problems are not experienced:
they are abstractions extracted from experience by analysis. They are as
related to what is experienced as atoms are related to tables. Tables are experienced, not atoms. What we experience are dynamic situations that
consist of complex systems of problems, not individual or isolated problems. I call such systems *messes.* . . .

Therefore, when a mess, which is a system of problems, is taken apart,
it loses its essential properties and so does each of its parts. The behavior
of a mess depends more on how the treatments of its parts interact than
on how they act independently of each other. A partial solution to a

whole system of problems is better than whole solutions of each of its parts taken separately. Nevertheless, students are taught to treat problems as separable, self-contained units. They are unaware of the existence or nature of messes and, of course, of ways of dealing with them.

By observing the way the educational system is organized and managed, students come to believe that a system's performance can be improved by improving the performance of each of its parts taken separately. Even in business schools, students do not learn that effective management of organized behavior is management of interactions, not actions. They are not even made aware of the differences between these types of management. What they are taught is that if they improve the performance of each part of a corporation taken separately, the performance of the corporation as a whole will be improved. This is absolutely false. Fortunately, improving the performance of each part taken separately does not necessarily make the whole perform as badly as possible. If it did, few corporations would survive as long as they do.

The quality of education provided by a school is not the sum of the qualities of the education provided by each of its departments, but the product of their interactions. Dealing with messes and organizations as a whole, with interactions rather than actions, requires synthetic, not analytic, thinking. . . .

TEACHING AND LEARNING

Recall a portion of the earlier quotation from Illich: "The pupil is . . . 'schooled' to confuse teaching with learning . . ." The reason is that teachers confuse the two; they assume that teaching is an efficient producer of learning. One would think that this assumption would be seriously questioned by educators. After all, they are aware that we learned our first language well without having it taught to us, but seldom learn nearly as well a second language that is taught to us. We learn a great deal more from our experience than we do from those who are experienced.

Go and Stop Driving

When my son, Alan, completed his first year at the California Institute of the Arts in Valencia, California, he returned to Philadelphia for the summer. He began almost immediately to work on me to buy an automobile for him. He reasoned that it would save him and me money when he went to or came from the West Coast, and he argued that a car was virtually essential for survival in California. I was not convinced, and refused. After a number of his unsuccessful efforts to change my mind, he became sufficiently desperate to look for a job. He found one working for a tree surgeon.

In the first week he fell out of a tree and hurt his leg enough to make it impossible for him to retain the job. Then he really went to work on me. He became a thorough and continuous pest. Finally, in an effort to make my own summer bearable, I told him I would lend him the money required to buy a car. This cheered him considerably. He went off enthusiastically in search of a car. Several days later he announced that he had found one. A friend of his was willing to sell him a 12-year-old Chevy for a very low price. I expressed the opinion that such a car was very unlikely to get him back to the West Coast, and was very likely to lead to his loss of a friend. My son assured me I was wrong on both counts. He told me he had taken the car to a third friend, who was a skilled auto mechanic, and he had checked the car over. It was fine.

Despite my advice to the contrary, my son bought that car and took off for the West Coast. The car broke down a number of times on the way, requiring repairs the cost of which exceeded the cost of the car. Eventually my son reached Los Vegas, where the car broke down and was no longer repairable. He disposed of it as scrap and hitchhiked the rest of the way back to his school. He also lost a friend.

When he returned home the following summer he wanted to know how I knew what would happen to him, the car, and his friendship. Because, I said, I had done essentially the same thing when I was his age. Then he wanted to know why I hadn't told him this. I asked him if he thought it would have made any difference. After a moment's reflection, he said, "No."

Moral: One can learn a great deal from one's own mistakes, but practically nothing from those made by others.

There are many things we insist on learning for ourselves. We resent having them taught to us. Observation of a child for a short time makes this apparent.

There are a variety of ways of learning without being taught. The effectiveness of each varies with time, the place, the subject matter, and the learner. Therefore, students should have maximum freedom to select those ways of learning that best suit them. Before considering ways of learning that are superior to being taught, consider some of the deficiencies of teaching.

WHAT'S WRONG WITH TEACHING?

Four things are wrong with teaching. First, it is more concerned with transmitting than receiving. Second, it assumes ignorance on the part of students. Third, it discourages, if not kills, creativity. Fourth, it normally uses tests and examinations to determine what students have learned, and they do not do so effectively. Consider each of these deficiencies in turn.

Transmitting versus Receiving. We learn more by talking than by listening, but most teachers do all or most of the talking, imposing silence on their students most of the time. Talking gives us an opportunity to discover—become aware of—what we know and don't know. Children who are seen but not heard do not learn very much. It would be much better educationally if they were heard, even if not seen.

A Very Loud Silence

In my last year as a graduate student in philosophy at the University of Pennsylvania, the philosophy department hired as an assistant professor a recent Ph.D. from Columbia University. While there, he had studied under John Dewey, who was America's best known philosopher at that time. Not surprisingly, the new assistant professor considered himself an authority on Dewey.

In his first semester at Penn, this young professor offered a course in contemporary philosophy focusing on Dewey's work. Several of the precocious and arrogant graduate students who signed up for the course, including me, also considered themselves to be experts on Dewey. Therefore, in the first few sessions, the young professor never got more than a few minutes into his prepared presentation before questions began to be asked, throwing him off his course. In none of these initial sessions was he able to complete his prepared presentation, because the questions and their discussion did not let up until the end of the class. The young professor was annoyed and thoroughly frustrated. He was able neither to demonstrate his expertise in the subject matter of the course nor to differentiate himself from the students. Therefore, he opened the fourth session of the seminar by announcing that from then on there would be no questions or discussion until he had completed his prepared presentation.

When the professor finished his presentation that day and indicated that he was ready for questions and discussion, there was spontaneous silence in the room. After repeated but futile requests from the professor for discussion, he dismissed the class. The class had been a bore because it contained little the students did not already know.

The silent treatment, now deliberate, continued in the next two classes. Finally the frustrated young professor announced a return to the earlier format in which questions and discussion were permitted at any time. The class returned to normal. Learning and fun resumed.

Moral: Silence is sometimes more eloquent than words.

Although our talking to others is a good way to find out what *we* think about a subject, it is often a very poor way of learning what *they* think about it.

Back Talk

A corporation's chief executive officer whom I know well initiated communication sessions between himself and all his employees. Once each year he visited each of his company's sites and gave a talk on the state of the company to all the employees located there. After his prepared remarks, he opened the floor for discussion and questions. There was usually plenty of both.

One year, shortly after completion of the executive's tour, a very damaging strike was called against his company by its unionized hourly-paid employees. The executive told me he could not understand their behavior. None of the issues over which the strike was called were raised at any of his communication sessions. "Why?" he asked.

I told him his meetings with the company's employees had been arranged for him to communicate to them, not for them to communicate to him. "Why not?" he asked. "They were free to raise any issues they wanted." I pointed out that in a meeting he calls and in which he makes a formal presentation, people tend to raise questions or issues they think he expects or wants, particularly if they respect him, as they did. Would a parishioner publicly ask embarrassing questions of a minister after he had completed a sermon? One cannot hold an extended discussion of an important issue from a floor occupied by a large audience. I said that if he wanted to hear what his employees wanted to say he would have to ask them to arrange a meeting in which they made a presentation to him and he did the listening and subsequent questioning.

He did just that and it worked.

Moral: It is very difficult to listen while talking.

Assuming Ignorance of Students.   Teachers frequently underestimate the amount their students already know. Such underestimation is not restricted to teachers in school. Many managers assume they know more about their subordinates' jobs than their subordinates do. This has become less and less true with increasing technological content of work and increasing education of workers. Nevertheless, few managers have learned to ask their subordinates for advice.

They Never Asked Me

In the early 1980s I participated in the introduction of a quality-of-work-life program at Alcoa's Tennessee Operations. Managers at all levels were asked to establish boards consisting of themselves, their immediate superiors, and their immediate subordinates. These boards were empowered to do anything they could with the resources available to them that would improve the quality of work life of their members, provided that what they did did not prevent any other units from doing what they wanted. A procedure was set up to handle possible differences between units.

Very shortly after the boards were established, two participating unionized workers who took the rolls of sheet aluminum off the end of the mills that produced them did something that saved the Operations a very significant amount of money. The rolls of aluminum coming off the end of the mill were cylinders about five feet long, hollow in the middle. These were set on end near the end of the mill, where they remained until a forklift moved them to a storage area. The forklift was often delayed because of such things as an obstruction in the access aisle, mechanical failure of the truck, a run-down battery, and so on.

When the truck was delayed for a relatively long time, which happened frequently, the space in which the cylinders were temporarily stored filled up, leaving no room for others coming off the end of the mill. Then the two men unloading the mill would move some of the cylinders back by placing a foot against the bottom of the upright cylinder, pulling the top so as to tip it slightly, and rolling it to a new location farther from the end of the mill. Rolling the cylinder on the concrete floor crimped the edge of the sheet on the outside of the cylinder. This was a defect many purchasers would not accept. They returned many of these rolls. Reworking these rolls was very costly to the Operations.

Shortly after the quality-of-work-life program had been initiated, the two men who unloaded the mill acquired from the shipping room a number of sheets of very heavy quilted paper in which the rolls were wrapped when shipped. They laid several layers of this paper on the floor where the cylinders were normally stored temporarily. When they rolled cylinders over this softer surface, their edges were less damaged than previously. This saved the company a significant amount of money.

When I was told what these men had done, I went down to the shop floor to congratulate them. They were proud of their accomplishment and pleased with the congratulations. While chatting with them I asked how long they had known of the solution they had just implemented. Blushing, one of them mumbled, "About 15 years."

Surprised, I then asked the obvious question: "Why did you wait so long to implement it?" I will never forget their answer: "Because those sons of bitches never asked us before."

Moral: The less we expect from others, the less we are likely to get from them.

What one learns depends not only on what questions one asks of others, but also on what questions they answer. In the Soviet Union I once encountered an outrageous refusal to answer a question.

The Guest of Horror

In the 1970s I was one of the very few foreigners who attended an international conference held in the Azerbaijan Soviet Socialist Republic at Baku. We were herded into a corner and seated around an interpreter who whispered his simultaneous translations of the proceedings to us.

In one of the plenary sessions a senior and distinguished Russian scientist delivered a paper on the use of Game Theory in forecasting. It was not a good paper; his understanding of both Game Theory and forecasting left a lot to be desired.

After the paper had been delivered, the floor was opened for discussion. A young man rose and asked a very astute question that got right at the basic flaw in the presentation. Much to my surprise, the old man who delivered the paper ignored the question and called on another young man who had indicated that he, too, had a question. The second young man, obviously angered by the old man's failure to answer the first question, repeated that question.

The old man was furious, and blurted out, "When you have contributed to this field with such distinction as merits my attention, I will give it to you and your questions. Until then, I have no intention of doing so."

Now I was furious. I indicated that I had a question. As I was one of the guests of honor, the old man called on me immediately. I repeated the question asked by the two young men.

The old man was stunned and very angry. He began to mutter something, stopped, and left the auditorium with no further word. The session was immediately adjourned by its chairman.

Moral: Learning begins with questions we cannot answer; it ends with questions we can. . . .

TESTS AND EXAMINATIONS

The tests used by many educational institutions to determine the suitability of applicants have come under such an intense barrage of criticism that I hardly need dwell on them here. Suffice it to say that whatever it is they measure, it is not the ability to learn. At most, it is what has been learned; at worst, what has been memorized. There is no pressure on the authors of these examinations to make them measure what institutions want, because the institutions have come to want what these tests measure without knowing what this is.

How much students learn depends on more than the ability to learn; it also depends on opportunities to learn. The lack of such opportunities is responsible for the poor performance of many students, even those with a great ability to learn. High scores on tests are evidence of an ability to take tests, not necessarily of an ability to learn. Tests should provide an opportunity for learning, but seldom do. In many cases they don't even measure what has been learned.

On Reassembling a Broken Language

In order to receive my doctorate in philosophy I had to demonstrate proficiency in two languages, one primary and the other secondary. I chose French as my primary language and German as the secondary. Both examinations consisted of a written translation of a passage from an undesignated book, without the use of a dictionary in the primary-language examination, and with a dictionary in the other.

The prospect of the French examination was not worrisome; I had studied French for three years in high school and four years in college. However, because it had been about five years since my last course, I needed to familiarize myself with that language. To this end I withdrew from the philosophy section of the university's library the first book in French I saw. It happened to be a book by Renan, *L'Avenir de Science (The Future of Science)*. I dipped into this book periodically over the summer, using a dictionary to reinforce and expand my French vocabulary.

German was another matter. I had never studied this language. At a friend's suggestion I bought a little book called *Minimum German* and went to work trying to learn the elements of that language. The effort was excruciating. After a few weeks I gave up and placed the little hope I had of passing the German examination on my ability to use a dictionary. Then an unexpected and seemingly very fortunate thing happened: a classmate who has been raised by German-born parents and who was himself fluent in the language offered to tutor me. He had to take the same examination as I, but German was no problem for him.

He began to tutor me, but before long neither of us could stand the pain. I found the memorization required to learn the language abhorrent, and he found my ineptness discouraging. For the sake of our friendship, we gave up.

Fall came and with it the two examinations. The one in French came first. Incredibly, it consisted of a passage from Renan's book, a passage I remembered having translated that summer. I passed this one easily.

The French connection did not reduce my apprehensiveness about the German examination. My friend and ex-tutor was full of confidence.

We went into the examination together. The passage we were asked to translate was taken from Hegel's *Philosophy of Right*. The passage was very difficult. It has been wisely said of Hegel that his work cannot be translated into German, let alone any other language.

I went to work on the assigned passage, furiously using a dictionary. I finished translating the passage about a half hour short of the three hours we had available. When I read what I had written, it made absolutely no sense. I was convinced there was no way my translation could be accepted. In desperation, I got a fresh examination book (in which we wrote our translations) and, using what I knew of Hegel but not of German, I wrote in English what I thought Hegel had said in the passage we were given.

Lo and behold, I passed the examination! However, my friend and ex-tutor, who translated the passage from Hegel literally, didn't. I think he still blames me for this.

Moral: Examinations are not so much a matter of revealing how much one knows as of concealing what one does not know.

An Alternative to Teachers

About a decade ago, Fernando Solana, then secretary of education in Mexico, wanted to bring education to the large number of rural communities in his country. There were not enough qualified teachers to supply these communities. Solana engaged recent graduates from nearby high schools, promising them a college education if they would spend a few years in rural teaching. Subsequent tests given to students taught by these high school graduates and to students taught by professionals in Mexico City's schools revealed no significant difference in their educational attainment.

Conclusion

The deficiencies in the educational system cannot be removed by changing only the content of education. It requires fundamental redesign of the educational system and the processes in which it engages. The messages its structure and processes deliver are more seriously misleading and counterproductive than any messages delivered in courses.

What serves education well at any one time and place may not do so at another, or for different students. Therefore, we must give up the search for one best educational system, one that operates optimally regardless of time, place, and students. What is required is a system that can learn in, and adapt to, the conditions under which it must operate.

Summarizing, the educational system should

1. Preserve individual differences among students, and encourage students to develop their unique combinations of competencies, not mold themselves into standardized, branded products.

2. Focus on learning, not teaching, enabling students to learn how best to learn and motivating them to want to learn continuously.

3. Synthesize what students learn so as to produce understanding if not wisdom (not merely transmit information and knowledge), and emphasize the interrelationships between subjects and disciplines, particularly between science, technology, and the arts and humanities.

4. Enable students to deal with systems as a whole rather than reducing them by analysis to more easily treated parts.

5. Encourage the continuous redesign of educational institutions and processes so they can be debureaucratized, demonopolized, and adapted to changing conditions and students, allowing students, their parents, and other stakeholders to participate in such redesign and in planning its implementation.

CHAPTER 16

CRIME

If you give to a thief, he cannot steal from you and he is no longer a thief.

William Saroyan

An increasing number of people find the effect of increasing crime on the quality of life to be intolerable. As a consequence "law and order" has become a major political issue. The proposed remedies can be classified as reactive, preactive, and interactive. Let us consider each of these in turn.

THE REACTIVIST ON CRIME

The reactive portion of the public responds to increasing crime rates by increasing its demand for stricter laws more effectively enforced; for more, better equipped, and less constrained police; for longer and more punitive imprisonment of those convicted; and for fewer paroles. . . . In short, the reactivist responds to increasing crime with increasing repression. He argues for discipline and deterrence because he attributes rising crime rates to increasing permissiveness in society and in the family.

The reactivist views the criminal as one who is inherently evil, hence incorrigible. The criminal is taken to be exclusively, or at least primarily, responsible for his criminal act. After all, the reactivist argues, look at how many others there are who, though in the same circumstances as the criminal, do not turn to crime.

The reactivist believes treatment of criminals should be directed primarily at protecting society from them. This means secure imprisonment, exile, or execution. Next, those imprisoned should be punished for their transgressions, and, hopefully, through suffering, driven to

---

Adapted from *Redesigning the Future* (Wiley, 1974).

penitence and purged of their criminality. Finally, their treatment should be such as to deter others from crime by instilling fear of punishment within them.

The reactivist resents the use of public funds for support and treatment of criminals, but he grudgingly accepts the need to do so. Not only does he want the system of treatment to be inexpensive, but he also wants it to be unobtrusive—out of sight, out of mind.

When prisoners protest, demonstrate, or riot as they recently did at Attica, the reactivist seeks more repression. He empathizes with the heavily armed guards who must face down the violent prisoners. . . . In brief, the reactivist attempts to deal with crime by dividing people into two classes, the good and the bad. He wants the bad to be apprehended and isolated behind a wall, and he wants this done at minimal cost to the good. He feels that the bad deserve little better than the worst possible treatment. He believes that nothing short of purgatory will produce penitence and that the fear of punishment is the most effective deterrent of crime.

This attitude toward crime has dominated in our country for some time. Not only has it failed to bring crime under control, but it has produced a criminality crisis. Further reactive responses to this crisis will only make it worse.

THE PREACTIVIST ON CRIME

Preactivists and interactivists believe that crime is a joint product of the individual and society. The following passages from Ramsey Clark reflect this belief:

> The anxieties arising from technology cause most of our instability and heighten the desire to manifest contempt for our existing values and to escape to something different. Addicts, alcoholics, and the mentally ill are products of that anxiety and contribute most of the crime in America.
>
> It is the poor, the slum dweller, the disadvantaged who suffer most, and most tragically, the crime of America. It is here that the clear connection between crime and the harvest of poverty—ignorance, disease, slums, discrimination, segregation, despair and injustice—is manifest.
>
> The basic solution for most crime is economic—homes, health, education, employment, beauty. If the law is to be enforced—and rights fulfilled for the poor we must end poverty.

Having recognized that the roots of crime go deeply into society, the preactivist despairs of bringing about the fundamental social changes necessary to uproot it and turns instead to reform of the criminal justice system. He argues that reform of this system, not repression of the criminal, is required: "You cannot discipline this turbulent, independent, young mass society as if it were a child. Repression is the one clear course toward irreconcilable division and revolution in America."

The preactivist advocates less punitive and more humane corrective treatment of convicts, and more public and private assistance to those leaving corrective institutions. And he seeks to supplement these reforms with more community agencies and public programs that can divert and redirect potential criminals.

Ramsey Clark prepared what is probably the most comprehensive preactive critique of, and set of reforms for, the criminal justice system. His main points are based on a breakdown of this system into its basic elements: police, prosecution, courts, and corrections.

His analysis of the current deficiencies within each of these elements reveals several basic needs. More and better personnel and facilities are required to improve the quality of their performance. This, in turn, requires higher salaries to attract more and better qualified personnel, and more investment in better and more facilities. As a result, larger public expenditures are called for. Ramsey Clark lamented, "At a time when our major domestic concern is crime and violence, the nation spends more on household pets than on police."

Clark also called for emphasis on correction rather than punishment of offenders:

> There is no effort within the criminal justice system that holds a fraction of the potential to reduce crime offered by a vigorous, thoughtful corrections program. Not even efforts directed at the underlying causes of crime, such as health services, education, employment and decent housing, offer the same immediate potential at near the cost.

He points out that despite this: "Ninety-five per cent of all expenditure in the entire corrections effort of the nation is for custody—iron bars, stone walls, guards. Five per cent is for hope—health services, education, developing employment skills."

Prison, according to the preactive reformer, should not seek penitence from its inmates because, as Clark says,

Remorse comes from within. No prison will create it. But for those who pose America's crime problem penitence has little meaning. By and large, their lives are so empty, they are so full of frustration and despair, they are so sick in mind and body, and their entire life experience providing them grist for thought is so totally lacking in charity that contemplation is more likely to cause anger at society's sins than remorse for their own.

Preactivists, like Clark, believe that a large proportion of offenders are mentally ill and are therefore in need of medical treatment and therapy: "The opportunity for treatment of the mentally ill in prison is virtually nonexistent. Most prisoners suffered from some mental disturbance at the time they committed crime. More have mental health problems on leaving prison than on entering."

Preactive reform efforts are directed toward change of the criminal justice system so that offenders can be rehabilitated effectively. They attempt to make prisons more like hospitals than dungeons, and to give education a central role in correctional programs. Rewards are advocated as incentives to good behavior rather than punishment as a disincentive to bad.

Preactivists seek to protect at least the minimal rights of offenders. Some proposals call for the matching of each prisoner with a civilian as an effective avenue of complaint. Others have proposed such alternatives as use of ombudsmen, "inspector generals," or unannounced periodic civilian inspections of prisons.

A principal objective of preactive reform is to make sentences better reflect the seriousness of the crime and the likelihood of correction of the offender. As Ramsey Clark observed: "Ten-year sentences in lieu of two-year sentences—because we are angry—will not reduce crime. It is not the length of the sentence but the effectiveness of the correctional program that will make the difference."

Furthermore, preactivists want to match the treatment of an offender with the nature of his offense.

The preactivist advocates programs that will divert the young, particularly those living in slums, from criminality—recreational programs, adult supervision, summer camps, employment, and drug addiction programs. For the preactivist the social worker is a major weapon against criminality and recidivism—the return to crime of those who have been in prison.

In sum, the preactivist appeals to our sense of justice and humanity to pull us through the crisis of crime until we have removed the underlying causes of crime. This, as Ramsey Clark argues, should enable us "to achieve needed reforms, to offer fulfillment, human dignity and reverence for life."

THE INTERACTIVE APPROACH TO CRIME

Preactivists recognize that the roots of crime lie in society, in social conditions such as poverty, discrimination, poor health, lack of education, and substandard and congested housing. But they do not believe that these conditions can be changed quickly enough to affect the crisis in crime. Thus, as preactivists normally do, they accept the environment and seek to reform the criminal justice system within it. The interactivist, on the other hand, does not believe that even the reforms proposed by preactivists are possible without some fundamental changes in society. He does not believe, for example, that the money required to carry out preactive reforms can be extracted out of our society as it currently operates. Therefore, the interactivist does not believe that changes in society and the criminal justice system are separable.

The interactivist assumes a more aggressive posture toward the social environment of crime than the preactivist does. He tries to use the crisis in crime to bring about changes in those aspects of society that breed it. He believes society needs correction even more than the criminal does, and that correcting the criminal without correcting the conditions that breed criminality cannot significantly reduce crime. This orientation leads to an inversion of the problems usually associated with criminal justice. The most fundamental of such transformations is that involving the concept of responsibility for crime.

Recall that the reactivist believes the criminal to be exclusively or primarily responsible for the crime he commits. The preactivist believes that the individual and his environment are jointly responsible for most crimes and, therefore, that criminality is like a disease: the germs must be there in the environment and the individual must be susceptible to them. The interactivist, on the other hand, holds society primarily responsible for crime. He takes the individual's susceptibility to crime to be a product of social influences—an acquired characteristic, not an innate disposition.

Therefore, the interactivist develops a strategy for treating the criminal that is based on the assumption that *his criminal act is the consequence of a crime committed by society against him.* Then, when a person steals to avert starvation, for example, the threat of starvation is taken to be a social crime that requires more attention than the individual theft does. Such crimes can only be significantly reduced by eliminating the possibility of starvation. Race rioting can only be eliminated by removing racial discrimination. This view does *not* imply that the individual criminal requires no treatment but that the treatment he receives is directed to undoing the damage that has been done to him.

The interactivist believes that justice should be more concerned with protecting the individual from society than with protecting society from the criminal. If the criminal is taken to be one whom society has wronged, then the justice system should protect him from further abuse by society. Because the interactivist takes the principal function of the criminal justice system to be the *correction of society,* punishment of either the criminal or society is irrelevant.

Before considering how the criminal might be treated in an interactive criminal justice system some concepts that are central to such a concept should be clarified.

Types of Offender

The performance of a criminal justice system depends primarily on the relationship between the type of offender and the way he is treated. A very large number of ways of classifying offenders—most based on the nature of the crime rather than of the criminal—have been developed. But since the system is supposed to treat the criminal, not the crime, the interactivist bases his classification on three characteristics of the offender.

1. *Those who are dangerous to others or their property* and, therefore, from whom society should be protected. Such a person engages in, or is inclined to, unprovoked aggression on the person of others, or unprovoked destructiveness of property, either for its own sake or for personal gain (where socially acceptable alternatives are available and the need is not desperate).

2. *Those who are dangerous to themselves* and, therefore, should be protected from themselves. A self-destructive person may be either physically or mentally ill and may endanger himself (and/or others) as a result of his illness. He is his own victim, as in drug abuse.

3. *Those who are dangerous to no one but who are in danger.* Such an offender is forced into crime by external conditions that he could not overcome. He may be easily pressured, provoked, or influenced into offensive acts by others, or by a personal need deriving from scarcity of a resource essential for survival but not provided by society or others within it; for example, hunger or the need to belong.

Individuals need not be "pure" types; they may incorporate characteristics of several types, and these characteristics may change over time.

Types of Treatment

The treatment of an offender is a resultant of the type of facility used and the way it is managed. Here too "pure" types can be identified. These, taken in relation to the perspectives of society on the offender, may be said to comprise philosophies of correction.

1. *Deterrent* (controlling). Such treatment is intended to prevent aggression or destruction in or out of a facility, at the time of detention or subsequently. The threat of punishment for doing something and the promise of reward for not doing it are both deterrents, or are intended to be so.

2. *Clinical* (therapeutic). Such treatment is intended to cure, reduce, or stabilize physical or mental illness, or a character defect recognized as pathological and believed to be actually or potentially responsible for self-destructive or antisocial behavior.

3. *Supportive* (protecting). Such treatment is intended to remove its recipient from antisocial influences or forces applied to him that he cannot resist except at great cost or risk; to protect him from threats of harm; and to provide him with physical and emotional care of which he has been deprived and which he needs.

Actual treatments frequently blend these pure types in varying proportions. Some clinical procedures, for example, require a good deal of control as well as support, especially at some stages.

Deterrence, therapy, and support do not in themselves necessarily require the placement of anyone in a closed facility. Security, therefore, ought not to be looked at as an aspect of treatment.

Very different types of offender may sometimes need some security. Few are likely to need a high degree of it all the time. Security measures are required in case other methods of control break down. The first task, therefore, is to ensure that these other methods, which should be an inherent part of a facility's organization and management, are well designed and are in fact working as well as possible. Physical security becomes necessary only insofar as social security breaks down. If a facility's staff is able to maintain it as an open facility, there is no need for a perimeter.

Security measures may be required to safeguard either the boundary of a facility or to protect groups or individuals inside from each other or from themselves. The level of security maintained should depend in either case on the frequency expected in the breakdown of social controls. Physical security should be a reserve system, for emergency use only. Where the emergencies become too frequent the ground rules of the social control system have to be changed.

Now let us be more specific.

Treatment of Those Dangerous to Others

Those who are believed by the interactivist to be dangerous to others would normally be thought of by the reactivist as intrinsically evil. The reactivist would "lock them up." The interactivist recognizes that others have to be protected from them but this does not require punitive incarceration. Rather, treatment of those dangerous to others should be designed to provide them with a full and satisfying life while protecting others from them as long as they remain threatening. Depriving such an offender of completely free access to others does not necessarily require denying them access to him.

The offender believed to be dangerous to others would be placed in a community that differs from others in only several respects. Its members would be watched sufficiently to assure their not harming one another, and they would not have the freedom to leave until they were believed to be cured. Others who desire access to them could have it. For example, the criminal's family could come to visit or live with him in this "coeducational" community. He would have the opportunity to work for a living in that community and support himself and others—like his family—in or out of the community. Furthermore, he would pay rent, taxes, and buy the goods and services he needs for normal living. Society at large would cover the costs of security and surveillance, and of therapeutic and correctional programs provided in the community.

The correctional community should have a sound economic base, producing goods and services required both inside and out. Its business and industry could be based on supplying local, state, and federal government with goods and services they require. Private industries would be encouraged to open branches in such communities. Governments would contract with them to build and operate such facilities. Publicly supported colleges and universities would be required to provide educational programs within the community.

When a convict is no longer dangerous to others he would be free either to leave or remain. "Corrected" in this context means not only that he no longer poses a threat to others but also that he has the skills and resources necessary, and the opportunity, to reenter society in an environment other than the one that produced his criminality.

Those who commit crimes within such a community would be withdrawn to another in which separation, surveillance, and security of inmates would be greater. There would be a hierarchy of such communities, but each would be designed to be as normal as possible. This means that they should also be designed to be essentially self-supporting.

Inmates who show signs of progress would be given furloughs to visit others outside the community. Such leaves would be increased in frequency and duration as the offender improves.

Such communities as are described here might be preferred by many who have not committed crimes to those in which they live. They need not commit crimes to get access to them. Such communities should be open to outsiders. The correctional community should be so designed as to make the inmates reluctant to leave and outsiders anxious to enter. Voluntary movement into these communities would constitute a significant pressure for social change in so-called normal communities.

Personnel who administer and maintain such communities for the state would be required to live within them for at least part of their time. They would, of course, be free to come and go as they wanted.

Those who cannot imagine such a community should reconsider the former West Berlin, which met many of the conditions I have set down. All ingress and egress was controlled, but within it a normal productive life can be lived. Significant differences do not reduce the similarities.

It is not surprising that reflective and responsible prisoners in the current system desire to change it in directions similar to those described here. For example, *The Philadelphia Evening Bulletin* reported (January 18, 1972):

The inmates at Washington State Prison are . . . asking for $1 million to build a prison they designed themselves.

. . . The plan was conceived by the convicts themselves, the architect was a prisoner. . . .

Architect-inmate Don Anthony White . . . said his design is "simple . . . Like it has windows and lots of light so that residents can let the world in. And the windows open to allow fresh air in."

"It is designed to exemplify a normal living situation, so that we, as abnormal people from an abnormal situation, can see what normalcy is and relate," White said.

. . . Correctional staff and families would live right in the complex.

"Residents would study or leave the facility on a work-release basis and those who worked would pay room and board," White continued. "This would eliminate greatly the dependence of the individual as well as the cost of the project.

"Even at maximum outlay, the state would be paying approximately half what it is currently paying to keep us here. . . . And keeping us here is unproductive."

Interactive correctional communities could be experimental in many ways. New types of low-cost housing could be tried without the restrictions of archaic building codes. In particular, prefabricated units that could be assembled by the inmates, or units that could be manufactured by them could be used for their own housing. Innovations in education, transportation, environmental control, and almost every type of social service and facility could be tested in such communities. Such communities could also be operated as experiments in participative democracy. They could incorporate many of the adaptive-learning procedures advocated in this book. They might well become model communities for others to emulate.

Treatment of Those Dangerous to Themselves

Those convicts who are believed to be dangerous to themselves—for example, alcoholics and addicts—would be placed in a community whose principal function is to provide the medical services they require. In other respects this community would be much like one for those dangerous to others. There would, of course, be modifications in the type of security system used. Wherever possible inmates would be used to help take care of each other as has been done so successfully by Alcoholics Anonymous. When a convict no longer constitutes a threat to himself he would be allowed to return to normal society if he so desires.

The community for those dangerous to themselves would be open to anyone who wants treatment within it. There is evidence that it would be used voluntarily by many. For example, consider the following report which appeared in *Parade* (July 23, 1972):

> Instead of jail, Minnesota now sentences drunks to three days in one of 52 new "detoxification centers." There, the alcoholic is given a bath, bed, sleeping pill, and some "morning after" psychological counseling.
>
> The detoxification centers are so successful that 50 per cent of admissions are now voluntary. Moreover, nearly a third of those who come to the centers, sign up for long-term rehabilitation, also offered by the state.

Treatment of Those Dangerous to No One

Even if one assumes that most crimes are due to social conditions it does not follow that every criminal has been damaged by society or is dangerous to himself or others. Some have responded to a unique nonrepetitive set of (1) internal or (2) external conditions. Crimes of passion and need may be of the first type; political crimes may be of the second type.

A person who steals food to avert starvation may not be dangerous to himself or others once the threat of starvation is removed. He needs a job or income more than he needs punishment. Societal revenge should not be the basis for treatment of such an offender; individual welfare should be.

A juvenile who has been forced to commit a crime by others is not helped by detention, but by being removed from the pressures that forced him to crime and by being given proper adult guidance.

Those criminals who are judged not to be dangerous to others or themselves but to have responded to social conditions not under their control, are best treated by removal from those conditions. Punishment in any form is not likely to have any positive effect on them. They should be permitted to function in society in a useful way.

This is particularly true of juveniles and young adults. Instances of their being treated within society by removal of the pressures that produced their crime are increasing. For example, *Parade* reported on an experiment at Yoke Crest near Harrisburg, Pennsylvania:

> . . . in a converted 20-room former mansion that has no cells, locks or bars, 19 convicts are serving sentences for serious crimes ranging from attempted murder to embezzlement.

The residents are free to move in and out of the home, as are their neighbors.

> Eventually the resident looks for a job, then goes to work on the outside, while still living at Yoke Crest. When he has saved enough money, found a place to live and proven himself able to function in the normal world, he "graduates." Even after leaving Yoke Crest, however, he is asked to come back for a group session every two weeks or so. . . .

It costs about half as much to keep a man at Yoke Crest as it does to keep him in prison and his stay is usually shorter.

Classification of Convicts

It is clear that in the concept of correction presented here classification plays a major role. Two kinds of classification are involved: classification of individuals and of treatments.

How an offender is classified depends not only on the classification system used but also on the amount of information about him that is available to the classifier. It also depends on the orientation of the classifier, who inevitably brings his own and his community's biases to bear, and the number and variety of facilities available for handling the offender. Thus classification varies with time and place. Therefore, it should be reviewed periodically or whenever new information about the offender or a new type of facility becomes available. No disposition of a convict should ever be final.

The best predictor of what an offender's behavior will be after he is released can be his behavior before release *if* the pre- and postrelease environments are similar. Because of this the interactivist seeks to create communities of convicts that are as normal as possible, and to provide them with as much interaction with normal communities as security considerations permit.

Errors in classification are always possible. In the current criminal justice system a convict is seldom given the benefit of any doubt; he is usually given the harshest treatment that is justified by the available information about him. This is a consequence of placing a higher cost on turning someone loose prematurely than on retaining someone longer and more restrictively than is necessary. Concern with security currently dominates concern with rehabilitation. The interactivist seeks to reverse this priority.

Now let us consider interactive views of some other aspects of the criminal justice system.

The Courts

It is clear that legislative bodies have the decision-making function in democratic societies, and that the executive branch of government has responsibility for supplying the legislative branch with the information it needs and for implementing the decisions made. What is not clear is who has the control and problem-identification functions. These functions are not currently systematized nor does any part of government have designated responsibility for them. The interactivist believes these functions should be performed, at least in part, by the courts.

According to the interactivist the courts should not only have the function of enforcing the law but also for evaluating it. This means that the courts should serve as a memory and comparator in an adaptive-learning system of government such as is described in Chapter 2 and the Appendix. It should also have at least partial responsibility for the diagnostic function. In order to perform these functions, the courts would require submission by legislative bodies of explicit statements of the expected effects of laws they have enacted and the bases on which these expectations rest. The courts would then compare actual performance with what was expected and if the differences are found to be significant, they would signal a "deviant." Diagnosis would then be required. The courts and/or legislative bodies should be provided with researchers who are capable of carrying out the required diagnosis. If the diagnoses are performed by groups serving the legislature, then the courts should review the results. Whoever performs the diagnostic work, the courts should maintain a record of it and the corrective actions taken. They should prepare summary reports of the control process periodically and release them to the public. This would enable public pressure to develop when legislation fails to do what it was intended to do.

Courts, aided by government attorneys, should also serve as symptom and presymptom identifiers. By analyzing the types of cases brought before them, and how the mix changes over time, the courts and government attorneys can identify significant changes in social behavior and conditions. Attention to these changes would indicate whether governmental action is required. Hence the courts should also provide legislative bodies with formulations of problems to which their attention should be given.

As I have already indicated, society should be tried in court along with each alleged criminal. It should be the court's responsibility to determine what social conditions, if any, are responsible for the crime—such as inadequate parental care, poor education, lack of satisfying work, and so on. Information of this type should be accumulated and analyzed. The results should be disseminated to both the public and legislators.

In brief, the courts should provide much needed feedback to legislative and administrative branches of government and to the public on society's actual performance. This would facilitate more effective response to, and anticipation of, social threats and opportunities.

Law

It is much easier to pass a new law than it is to modify or eliminate an old one. The body of law is large, hence exhibits a great deal of inertia.

To the interactivist crimes that are committed provide an implicit critique of society, hence of its laws. Analysis of crimes can make the critique explicit and indicate what changes are needed. Laws that the general public does not respect do more harm than good because they invite widespread violation and thus undermine respect for the law in general. This was the case, for example, when alcoholic beverages were prohibited in the United States, or when, in some cities, activities on Sundays were severely restricted by "blue laws." There are many obsolete laws on the books, laws that are disregarded; for example, laws that prohibit sexual intercourse on Sundays in some places. When a law is generally disregarded, analysis of the reasons for it offers an opportunity for social improvement.

The military draft is a case in point. The morality of a draft law and an undeclared war are brought into question by conscientious objectors and draft dodgers. Many argue that there is no practical alternative to such a law, particularly when a nation is involved in war, declared or not. There obviously is, as Professor Ronald A. Howard of Stanford University has observed:

> A fairly obvious use of the pricing system is in the manning of the armed forces. We should simply pay high enough wages and fringe incentives to volunteers to attract whatever number and variety were required by our military commitments; there would be no draft. Those members of society who had what were to them more desirable life opportunities than serving in the armed

forces would be free to follow them. Since there would be no compulsion, every serviceman would have willingly accepted his lot and, consequently, could be expected to perform his duties with greater enthusiasm and efficiency. Of course, the expense of such a military establishment would exceed present cost under the draft system. This cost would be passed on to all of society by increased taxes, thus sharing the burden of military service indirectly among all taxpayers. If the nation were to engage in an unpopular war, it is probable that the pay of the servicemen would have to be increased to attract the necessary number. The increasingly high expenses would serve as a very proper feedback on the true cost of the whole adventure. Conversely, a war that had the support of the populace would find many dedicated citizens who would serve for nominal pay.

Consider another example of how lawbreaking can be used to indicate where the law should be changed and how. I visited Iran a few years ago as a scientific consultant provided by the United Nations. In a conversation with one of Iran's cabinet ministers he put the following problem to me. As best I can remember his words, he said:

We have a national monopoly, a state-owned tobacco industry which is the second largest source of income for the government; the first being the oil industry. We have factories which produce a number of different brands of cigarettes that are sold through government licensed stores for from 15¢ to 35¢ per pack in American money. We also import American cigarettes and sell them for 55¢ and make a good profit from these sales. But this profit has been decreasing because of increasing smuggling. Smugglers bring American cigarettes in from Kuwait on small fishing boats at night. They are brought up to the major cities, like Teheran, where they are sold by unlicensed street vendors for about 50¢ per pack. This illegal business has been growing rapidly, thus reducing government sales and profits.

The reward we offer for information leading to apprehension of smugglers does not lead to many arrests, so we are considering increasing the reward. Clearly, if we make it too high it would be self-defeating. Is it possible to determine the amount of reward that would maximize government's net profit?

In the conversation that followed I probed to determine how profitable the government's importation and sale of American cigarettes was. Once this was established we determined how much profit was being made by the smuggling operation. It turned out that the smugglers were making a larger profit per pack than was the government even though they sold a pack for less. Therefore, I recommended that the government either go into the "smuggling business" itself or legalize and tax it enough to yield the desired level of profit. Unfortunately, I do not know if anything ever came of this suggestion.

The same kind of thinking involved in my suggestion to Iran has led some states and local governments to legalize gambling, or some forms of it, and to derive an income from it by taxation. Governmentally operated lotteries are becoming commonplace. Recall that one of the major sources of revenue for federal and state governments is taxes on alcoholic beverages. Some states, like Pennsylvania, even control its distribution and sale. England handles narcotics in much the same way. Doing so not only enables her to reduce illegal traffic in drugs considerably, but also to identify and treat a large number of addicts.

Laws that are frequently broken should be reexamined and reevaluated periodically. This does not imply that all frequent offenses should be legalized; but it does mean that possibilities for innovative improvement of law and society would be increased.

Police

Preactivists have suggested many possible reforms that would increase the effectiveness of the police. Most of these are directed at raising the rate of apprehension of offenders, not at crime prevention. Crime prevention has never been a central function of the police. The interactivist believes it should be, hence advocates creation of a new preventive police force. The preventive police officer (man or woman) would have no power of law enforcement or arrest. He would not be armed in any way. But he would be conspicuously uniformed so that he could be easily identified.

The preventive policeman's principal function would require his getting to know the neighborhood to which he is assigned and the people in it. To facilitate this process, he would be required to live in that neighborhood. The neighborhood should be small enough so that he can cover all of it on foot or bicycle. He would be there to help people or to help them get help whenever they needed it. He would be expected to know and understand the conditions in his neighborhood that breed crime and thus direct the activities of appropriate public and private agencies to their correction. His activity in the community would be completely positive—oriented to making it a better place in which to live.

When he sees criminality developing he would take corrective action, but if apprehension or forceful intervention is required, he would call on others to perform it.

This preventive policeman should be able to be contacted by anyone in his area at any time, day or night. When someone in his area is arrested he would be responsible for being sure the one apprehended knows his rights and receives whatever assistance he requires; for example, that proper legal aid is available. He would similarly help any ex-convicts who return to his area.

He would work with schools, clubs, and other organizations in the community to help make it as self-policing an area as possible. Put another way, his principal function would be to protect people from society and other who might abuse or misuse them. The preventive officer would testify in court on the crime-producing conditions operating on anyone from his area who is being tried for a crime. He would serve as a witness against the state, not as a witness for it.

The preventive policeman would require all the skills and training of a social worker and more, but his orientation would not be toward the alleviation of suffering so much as toward the removal of its causes.

Victims of Crime

Those victims of crime who can least afford to sustain the losses imposed by it often cannot afford insurance of person and property against crime. Property is not insurable in many low-income neighborhoods because of their high crime rate. The interactivist believes that where insurance against crime is not otherwise available, government should either provide it or subsidize private companies that do so. The amount paid out by government to victims of crime would provide valuable feedback on the effectiveness of anticrime programs. It would also provide a more reasonable basis for determining how much should be spent on efforts to reduce crime. If the cost to the public of such a government-backed insurance program increased too rapidly it would indicate the need to invest more, or to invest more effectively, in efforts to prevent crime.

Even if a criminal is not primarily responsible for his crime, he should be made more aware of the cost of crime to its victims. Therefore, wherever possible, the criminal should repay the government or the appropriate insurance company for its payment to the victim(s) of his crime for the loss or damage incurred. He could do so only if he could earn money, but he could do so in the communities I have described above.

SUMMARY

In this chapter I have described how reactivists, preactivists, and interactivists respond to the crisis of crime. The reactivist believes that the criminal alone is responsible for crime. Therefore, the reactive community treats increased crime with increased repression—more law and law enforcement, if not more order. This means more police, arrests, and convictions; and longer sentences, fewer paroles, and more secure and punitive treatment of those convicted. Treatment of the individual convict is directed at protecting society from him and at punishing him. The intention behind punishment is to produce penitence and to deter others from committing crimes.

The reactive attitude toward crime currently dominates most American communities. In the background, however, there is a growing demand for liberalizing reforms of the criminal justice system.

The liberal reformer normally has a preactive attitude toward crime. He conceptualizes it as a type of illness that possesses the criminal, the source of which is his environment. The environment, however, is usually taken to be too hard to control or to require too much time to bring under control. Therefore, preactive reforms are largely restricted to the elements of the criminal justice system. They are directed at producing more enlightened and humane police, prosecution, and courts. Proposed treatment of convicts is based on the belief that most of them can be corrected or cured through appropriate medical, psychiatric, and educational services, and by a type of detention that does not deprive them of their dignity and self-respect. Preactivists prefer to treat the convict in the normal community, when possible, reserving prison for those who are a serious threat to others.

The interactivist places primary responsibility for crime on society or social conditions. Therefore, each element of the criminal justice system is reconceived so as to lead to social changes that reduce society's crime-producing capabilities. Criminals are classified as dangerous to others, themselves, or no one. The interactivist advocates secure but otherwise normal and supportive communities for those who are believed to be dangerous to others or themselves; communities in which they can lead a full and satisfying life, into which they can bring their families, and to which their friends can come freely. Treatment would be readily available. Such communities would provide considerable opportunities for participative government and experimentation with new social facilities and functions.

The convict who is dangerous to no one would not be incarcerated in any way, but would be relocated in a normal community so that the pressures that produced his crime are not present. He would be given a chance at a normal life in an improved environment.

Commitment of convicts would terminate when, and as soon as, they are no longer dangerous to themselves or others. Sentences would not be of predetermined duration.

Interactive courts would play a central role in society's management system. They would have primary responsibility for society's control function: evaluating consequences of legislation and diagnosing failures. They would also have the function of identifying current and coming problems. Society would be constantly on trial before them.

Laws would be continuously reviewed and occasionally revised in the interactive community. Laws that cannot be enforced or do not have popular support undermine respect for the law in general. Their revision or withdrawal would be undertaken systematically.

The interactivist believes that police should take on an additional function: protecting individuals from their environment. A new arm of the police is advocated, one which has no power of arrest or law enforcement but which is involved in preventing crime, in assisting individuals who are misused or mistreated by others or by society in general. Preventive police would have responsibility for seeing to it that society's obligations to its members are being fulfilled. The objective of this function is to minimize social crimes of which individuals are victims.

Finally, the interactivist believes government should see to it that victims of crimes are compensated for losses or damage due to crime. Criminals should repay the government or its agents for such payment. Such an obligation by the criminal only has meaning if he can earn money while "incarcerated." He could do so in the communities the interactivist advocates for offenders.

If crime is to be reduced, victims of it must understand the criminal at least as well as he understands them. If, as the interactivist believes, most criminal acts are the product of social crimes against the criminal, then, in a sense, all actual and potential victims of crime share responsibility for society's criminality. Criminals will not be corrected until society is.

BIBLIOGRAPHY

Clark, R., *Crime in America,* New York: Pocket Books, 1971.

Howard, R. A., "Free for All," *Management Science, 13* (1967), B–681–B–685.

CHAPTER 17

THE EFFECT OF ADVERTISING ON SALES: A STUDY OF RELATIONS

In this case study, the relationship between the amount spent on advertising, its timing, media usage, and sales of a consumer product, beer, is explored experimentally in some depth. The case reveals how research can be used to illuminate such relationships and how complex and counterintuitive they may be. The simple relational assumptions that go into many advertising decisions can be very costly and reduce their effectiveness significantly.

Just before mid-1961, Mr. August A. Busch, Jr., then President and Chairman of the Board of Anheuser-Busch, Inc., asked my colleagues and me if we could evaluate an advertising decision he was about to make. In that year Budweiser, the largest selling beer in the United States, was budgeted to receive about $15 million worth of advertising. Mr. Busch had been approached by the vice president of marketing with a request for an additional $1,200,000 to be spent on advertising in twelve marketing areas. The vice president had defended his proposal on the basis of a projected increase in sales that he believed it would produce. Mr. Busch explained that he was confronted with such a proposal every year and that he always accepted it. He intended to do the same again, but, he asked, "Is there some way I can find out at the end of the year whether I got what I paid for?" We said we would think about it and come back with some suggestions.

The proposal we presented to Mr. Busch shortly thereafter consisted of allowing the marketing department to select any six of the twelve areas it wanted and giving it $600,000 for additional advertising. The remaining six areas would not be touched and would be used as "controls." This biased selection procedure was intended to overcome some

This case is adapted from Ackoff and Emshoff. Advertising Research at Anheuser-Busch, Inc. (1963–68), *Sloan Management Review,* Winter 1975, pp. 1–15.

of the opposition that the marketing department had to any effort to evaluate its proposal.

Earlier we had developed an equation for forecasting monthly sales in each marketing area. Our plan was to measure the deviation of actual monthly sales from the forecast for each marketing area in the test. Using the statistical characteristics of the forecasts, we estimated that we had a ninety-five percent chance of detecting a four percent increase in sales in the areas with additional advertising. Since the increase predicted by the marketing department was in excess of this amount, Mr. Busch authorized the test, and it was initiated.

The test was conducted over the last six months of 1961 yielding seventy-two (12×6) observations. *The analysis of these data failed to* reveal any *significant difference* between the test and *control* areas. Nevertheless the control areas did better on average than was forecast. Therefore, we assumed that all the sales above those forecast were attributable to the increased advertising and evaluated the results accordingly. Even under this assumption the increased amount of advertising was *not* justified by the deliberately overestimated increase in sales attributed to it.

Encouraged by these results, Mr. Busch asked us to design research directed at determining what amount *should* be spent on advertising. However, he wanted to proceed with caution, because he believed that much of Budweiser's success, which was leading the beer market with a share of 8.14 percent in 1962, was due to its quality and the effectiveness with which this was communicated through its advertising. When we suggested research involving experimentation with marketing areas, he authorized use of fifteen such areas provided they did not include any of the company's major markets.

Constrained in this way, we sought an experimental design that would maximize learning about advertising expenditures. Our design effort was guided by two methodological principles. First, we knew that the company advertised for only one reason: *to* increase *sales*. Therefore, we were determined to measure the effect of advertising on sales and not, as is usually done, on one or more easily measured intervening variables such as recall of messages or attitudes toward the product. For this reason, we decided to continue to use deviations of actual from forecast sales as the variable to be observed. This allowed us to cancel out much of the effect on sales of factors other than advertising. Therefore, efforts to improve forecasting of monthly marketing-area sales were continuous.

Second, we were committed to an attempt to explain the causal effect of advertising on consumer purchases, not merely to find statistical correlations between them. Our search of the marketing literature for such an explanation was futile; all it uncovered were correlations and regressions (associations) between advertising and sales. These usually showed that increases (or decreases) in the former were associated with increases (or decreases) in the latter. From such associations it was almost universally inferred, incorrectly, that increases in advertising *produce* increases in sales almost without limit. We believed that these analyses really showed that most companies forecast next year's sales quite accurately and that they set their advertising budgets as a fixed percentage of predicted sales. Put another way: forecasts of increased sales produce increased advertising.

Our commitment to experimentation derived from a determination to find a causal connection between advertising and sales, not merely an association between them: to develop an ability to manipulate advertising to produce the desired effects on sales that could be observed.

Since we had no tested theory to go on, we fabricated our own. Our hunch was that advertising could be considered to be a stimulus and sales a *response* to it. A great deal is known about the general nature of stimulus-response functions. They usually take the form shown; Figure 17.1. Therefore, we formulated the following hypothesis:

A small amount of advertising has virtually no effect on sales, but as the amount is increased it pushes the response through a threshold after which it produces an increasing effect. This effect decreases and flattens out once the respondents are *saturated;* that is, they either turn off further exposure to the stimulus or are consuming up to their capabilities or capacities. A response to further increases in advertising remains relatively unchanged until the respondents reach *supersaturation,* a "fed-up" point beyond which they respond negatively.

In an earlier study we had done for the Lamp Division of the General Electric Company (Waid, Clark, and Ackoff, 1956) we found such a relationship between the frequency of sales calls (stimuli) and purchases (responses). In the sales-call context, the idea of supersaturation is not as shocking as it is in advertising. Clearly there is an amount of a salesman's presence that is intolerable to a buyer. Beyond this, one would expect the buyer to try to get rid of the salesman by discontinuing his purchases. Similarly, we felt reasonably sure that if, for example, *all* television advertising were for one product, the public would react negatively.

Figure 17.1
A Typical Stimulus-Response Function

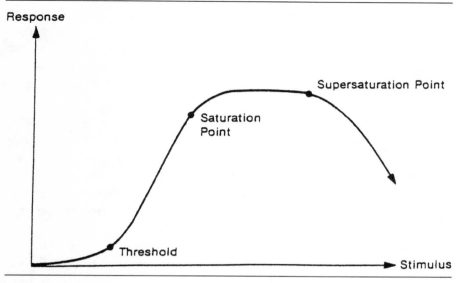

A minimal experiment would have involved applying the same percentage change in advertising expenditures to each of the fifteen marketing areas allotted to us and comparing the results obtained from them with those obtained from an equal number of control (unchanged) areas. However, we needed only nine areas to obtain the level of accuracy set as our target: to be able to detect a two percent difference in sales ninety-five percent of the time. To introduce two different treatments—one involving an increase and the other a decrease in advertising expenditures—required eighteen test areas, three more than were available. However, even an experiment with two different treatments would yield only three points: the average effect of each treatment and that of the control group. The difficulty this presented derived from the fact that every configuration of three points except one, V-shaped, could be fitted to the relationship we wanted to test. Therefore, there was a very low probability that a three-level experiment would disconfirm our hypothetical relationship; thus it was a very poor test of the validity of this relationship.

For these reasons we decided to ask for three different treatments and a control group, even though this would require twenty-seven marketing areas plus nine under control. Four experimental points could disconfirm our theory as easily as it could confirm it and hence would have provided a reasonable test of it.

We had nothing to go on but our intuition in selecting the experimental treatment levels: a fifty percent reduction and a fifty and 100 percent increase in budgeted levels of advertising. We wanted to make changes large enough to produce observable effects on sales, assuming such changes had any effect; thus, if there were no observable effects, this fact could not be dismissed because the changes were believed to be too small. Two increases rather than decreases were selected to make the experiment more palatable to the marketing department.

When this four-level design was presented, it was rejected because it involved the use of too many marketing areas. Mr. Busch agreed, however, to our use of eighteen (rather than fifteen) areas *provided* that we changed the reduction in advertising from fifty to twenty-five percent. He felt that a fifty percent reduction might irreparably damage the areas so treated. This left us with a three-level experiment: minus twenty-five, zero, and fifty percent changes from budget.

We were not completely happy with this outcome, because it did not provide an adequate test of our theory, but we were pleased that we had the opportunity to conduct even a limited experiment. We were reasonably sure that if it produced "interesting" results, restrictions on future experiments would be lifted.

A $3 \times 3 \times 3$ factorially designed experiment was prepared in which two other important marketing variables were explicitly controlled: the amount *spent on sales effort* (on salesmen) and the amount *spent on point-of-sales materials (displays,* signs, etc.) (see Figure 17.2). We would also have liked to control *pricing,* but this was precluded.

Marketing areas were selected randomly from the "permissible list" and randomly assigned to the twenty-seven treatments. The use of this list could obviously bias our results, but again our hope was that the results would justify further experiments and that they would not be so restricted.

The experiment was carried out over twelve months, yielding twelve observations of each marketing area. We were able to reach a conclusion at the end of six months, but the experiment was continued to build up confidence in the results. This did not work, however, because the results were too much at variance with expectations within the company and its advertising agency. The three points shown in Figure 17.3 fell into the only configuration, V-shaped, that was inconsistent with our hypothesis because the relationship being tested had no V in it. In addition, we found no significant interaction between advertising, sales effort, and

Figure 17.2
The 3 × 3 × 3 Experiment

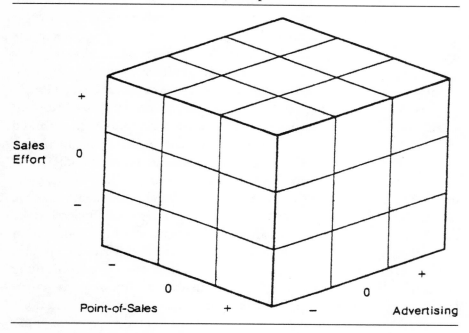

Figure 17.3
Results of First Experiment (1962)

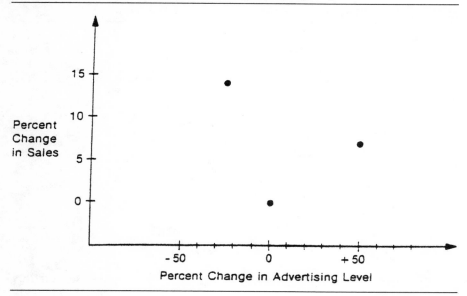

point-of-sales expenditures—a surprising but not unacceptable result—and that current levels of sales effort and point-of sales expenditures were close to optimal. The last result was readily accepted.

No one found much difficulty in believing that a fifty percent increase in advertising produced a seven percent increase in sales, but only Mr. Busch and Mr. Vogel, the new vice president of marketing, were willing to consider seriously the possibility that a twenty-five percent reduction of advertising could produce a fourteen percent increase in sales. Even they were not ready to act on this finding, but they wanted to take a "closer look." They asked us to design another experiment that would check these results and would be more convincing to others.

We had to set our theory straight before designing the next experiment. The preceding experiment appeared to reject the theory, but we had grown fond of it, perhaps because so many who were supposed to be in "the know" thought it was ridiculous. Thus we sought a modification of the theory that would make it consistent with the experimental results.

It occurred to us that there might be two or more distinct consuming populations in each marketing area and that each had a response curve like the one we had assumed but that these were separated along a horizontal scale (as shown in Figure 17.4). Then the aggregated response

Figure 17.4
Response Function of Segmented Population

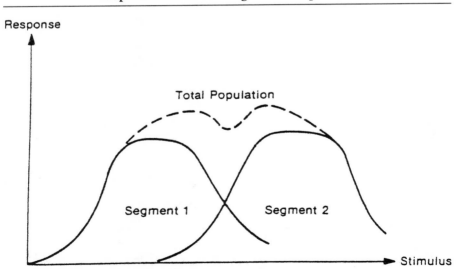

curve would have a V in it. When this possibility was presented to Mr. Vogel, he thought it quite reasonable and suggested that the markets might be segmented into three parts: heavy, moderate, and light beer drinkers. This made sense to us. One would expect the heavy users of a product to be more sensitive to its advertising than moderate users, and the moderate users, to be more sensitive than light users. We looked for some way of testing this assumption and found one.

It would have been very time consuming and costly to determine how many beer drinkers of each type there were in each marketing area. We had neither the time nor the money required to do so. However, we did know from previous studies that beer consumption correlated positively with discretionary income within the range of income in which most beer drinkers fall. Thus we determined the average discretionary income in each marketing area that had been used in the previous experiment and compared it with the average deviations from forecast sales in each area. There was a positive correlation between these deviations and average discretionary income, leading some credence to the user-level segmentation assumption.

We revised our theory to incorporate three response functions for each marketing area. This meant that the aggregated response functions for markets as a whole could differ significantly because of different proportions of heavy, moderate, and light beer drinkers.

Armed with this revised theory, we decided that we would like seven different advertising treatments so that we could adequately test it. We wanted to replicate the earlier experiment and add treatments further out on both sides of the scale. Seven treatments were selected: minus one hundred percent (no advertising), minus fifty, minus twenty five, zero, fifty, one hundred, and two hundred percent. Because of improvements in our forecasting methods, only six areas were required for each treatment. This design was accepted with only slight modification: the number of test areas in the two extreme treatments was reduced.

This experiment was also conducted over a twelve-month period. Fortunately, the results obtained from the treatments that had been used in the first experiment were the same as in the earlier experiment. When plotted, the seven points fell on a curve such as the one shown in Figure 17.5. There were two deviations from our expectations. First, only two, not three, "humps" appeared. We did not take this seriously, because the points act on the right were so far apart that there could well be a third hump concealed by the interpolation between the points. It was harder

Figure 17.5
Results of Second Advertising-Level Experiment (1963)

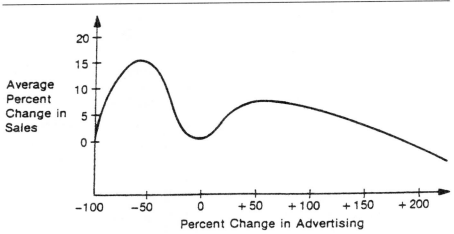

to explain the finding that the areas in which all advertising had been eliminated survived the year with no significant difference in performance from the control areas. Hardly anyone believed this result. The believers attributed it to the long history, strength, and exposure of Budweiser in the market place. We suggested further tests of the effect of complete elimination of advertising.

There was no such problem with the areas that had received a two hundred percent increase in advertising. The distributors in these areas complained constantly during the experiment about the overexposure and the unfavorable feedback they were getting from the "trade" and consumers.

Mr. Vogel and we agreed that the generally negative, if not hostile, reception of the research by the company's advertising agencies derived from the fact that their income was threatened by the results. They were paid in the conventional way: a fixed percentage of the amount spent by the company on advertising. This struck us as irrational, because it discouraged the agency from acting in the company's best interests. A change was made in the way of compensating the agencies. A scheme was developed by which agency fees were increased if sales increased with no increase in advertising or advertising decreased with no decrease in sales. This provided an incentive that encouraged the agency to collaborate in the research effort and to initiate its own research. The income of the Budweiser agency benefited from this change. It has since initiated such a compensation scheme with some of its other clients.

Although a willingness to act on our findings had not yet developed, there was growing agreement on the desirability of continuing the research. The second experiment was continued with particular attention to the areas from which all advertising had been removed. The objective was to determine how long it would take before any deterioration of sales could be detected and at what rate it would take place. We also wanted to determine how much effort would be required to recapture lost sales.

At the same time research was initiated into the relative effectiveness of different media. While this research was going on, the first opportunity to apply results from the earlier work presented itself.

Mr. Busch wanted to make more cash available to meet some commitments he had made. He asked Mr. Vogel and us if this could be done. We jointly proposed that advertising be reduced by fifteen percent in twenty-five of the smallest markets. The markets were chosen to minimize any possible long-run harmful effects. The proposed changes were capable of yielding more than the amount Mr. Busch needed. We also pointed out that we could maintain very close watch over the areas affected and report immediately on any reduction of sales that might occur in them. We predicted, however, that the proposed decrease in advertising would produce about a five percent increase in sales. Despite his skepticism about the increase, Mr. Busch decided to go ahead.

The predicted results were obtained within six months. As a consequence, the number of "reduction areas" was increased to fifty and the amount of the reductions was increased to twenty-five percent. From then on, more and more areas were similarly treated, and the reductions were gradually increased until the advertising expenditure per barrel was $0.80 in contrast to $1.89 when the research was initiated. During this period (1962–1968), sales of Budweiser increased from approximately 7.5 million to 14.5 million barrels, and its market share increased from 8.14 to 12.94 percent.

Returning to the experiment that involved complete deprivation of advertising, the areas thus deprived showed no response until *more than a year and a half* after the experiment was initiated. From then on a small decline was noted each month. This was allowed to continue only long enough to provide good estimates of the deterioration rate. Moves to correct these markets were then made. The markets were restored to their normal growth rate in about six months with only their normal amount of advertising.

These results led to a new line of speculation. Would it not be possible to *pulse* advertising, using an off-and-on pattern, and obtain the same effectiveness as that obtained by continuous advertising? We came to think of advertising as a motion picture which, of course, is really a sequence of motionless pictures. If sixteen still photographs are taken and projected per second, the appearance of motion is created because images are retained in the retina between exposures. We felt the same should be true for advertising.

Two types of pulsing were considered. In one, advertising expenditures in all media are off or on together. In the other, only one medium is used at any time, but the media are alternated. We designed an experiment to test the first of these types of pulse. It involved four treatments: one control (I) and three pulsing patterns (II, III, and IV), as shown in Table 17.1. In addition, the level of expenditure in each was varied, as shown in Table 17.2. The marketing areas used in this experiment were classified by median income and growth rates.

One of the pulsing patterns was found to be significantly better than the others and slightly better than normal advertising when accompanied by a high level of expenditure. Another pattern was found to be best when accompanied by a low level of expenditure.

The pulsing patterns were found to interact significantly with median income level and the growth rate of the market area. Subsequent experimentation revealed no significant difference between time pulsing and media pulsing, but media pulsing was easier to administer.

These results were cautiously incorporated into small reductions of advertising expenditures that were made in series. It was only after one change was demonstrated to have the predicted effect that the next change was made. Regular monthly checks on the performance of each marketing area were initiated and continue to this day.

Table 17.1
Pulsing Patterns

	I	II	III	IV
Spring	x	x	o	x
Summer	x	o	x	x
Fall	x	x	o	o
Winter	x	o	x	o

Table 17.2
Percentage of Local Budget Spent by
Pulsing Pattern and Advertising Level

Advertising Level	Pulsing Pattern (%)			
	I	*II*	*III*	*IV*
High	150	100	100	100
Low	100	50	50	50

In the early experiments on advertising expenditures, the budgets for experimental areas were set by the research team, but the way additional moneys were allocated to media or reductions made was left entirely to the advertising agency. Five media were involved: billboards, magazines, newspapers, radio, and television. We analyzed the relationship between the actual changes in media allocations made by the agency and changes in sales in each marketing area. This preliminary analysis indicated no significant differences between magazines, newspapers, and radio, but it suggested that television was slightly superior and that billboards were substantially inferior.

An experiment was designed to test these tentative findings (see Table 17.3). Magazines were not included in this experiment because they could not be controlled within small areas. (They were investigated separately at a later date.) A distinction was made between local and national television. In each of twenty areas only one medium was used; in another twenty each medium was combined with national television.

The results showed that national television was slightly superior to any local medium. Local television (with or without national television) and radio were more effective than newspapers or billboards. Billboards were the least effective. This required explanation.

First, a number of observations were made to determine how much information could be conveyed by a billboard. We found that little more than the product name and a slogan could be conveyed. This meant that

Table 17.3
Media Experiment: Number and Treatments of Marketing Areas

	Newspaper	Local TV	Billboard	Radio
No national TV	5	5	5	5
National TV	5	5	5	5

billboards could do little more than remind one of the existence of an already familiar product; they cannot convey much new information. Our second set of observations showed that the typical urban dweller in the United States saw (but did not necessarily notice) the word Budweiser on signs, displays, or beer containers almost ten times per day. He hardly needed additional reminding of its existence. On the basis of these findings virtually all billboard advertising was discontinued. The company had been spending about twenty percent of its advertising budget on this medium.

It would be foolish, of course, to claim that the improvement in company performance was due entirely to changes in advertising. Other types of changes, some based on research and some not, were also made during this period. One thing is clear: the changes induced by the research described here did not hurt Anheuser–Busch.

A little bit of understanding can go a long way, but one may have to go a long way to get a little bit of understanding.

CHAPTER 18

ON PAIRS AND TRIOS: THE SMALLEST SOCIAL SYSTEMS

Those of us whose work focuses on social systems tend to be concerned with ones that are large and complex, for example, corporations, institutions, governments, nations, coalitions of nations, and the world. There is nothing wrong with this tendency, but because of it we miss an opportunity to do some useful work and to have fun by focusing on the smallest social systems: pairs and trios. The effort to do so described here was carried out as a labor of love rather than as professionally motivated research. Therefore, it does not obey the rigorous demands of acceptable science. For this reason I tell it as a story rather than present it as a research report.

BACKGROUND

In 1946 C. West Churchman and I were strongly attracted by C. G. Jung's personality categories, *introversion* and *extroversion*. We inquired as to whether any tests had been developed to determine into which of these types particular individuals fell. We learned there were several such tests, and obtained copies of each. Then we gave each of the tests to each of a sample of graduate students. To our surprise, different tests for determining what were allegedly the same properties when applied to the same person yielded significantly different results. We discussed this with several clinical psychologists whom we knew and who were familiar with Jung's work. They expressed no surprise at our findings and explained that they did not consider paper-and-pencil tests a suitable substitute for clinical interviews. Following their advice, we arranged for several of them independently to determine the type into which each of a set of graduate students fell. Once again we obtained inconsistent results.

From "On Pairs and Trios: The Smallest Social Systems," *Systems Research,* Dec. 1996, pp. 435–446.

Churchman and I thought of two possible explanations of such in-consistency. First, perhaps Jung's types were nonsense. We found this hard to believe and, furthermore, if we accepted it, it would leave us at a dead end. Second, perhaps Jung's concepts involved two or more di-mensions, and different tests and different clinicians were using one di-mension to the exclusion of the other(s). This turned out to be the case.

To understand this type of explanation suppose all males could be clas-sified as either (American) *football players* or *not football players*. Suppose further that to be a football player one had to be both *big* (over a speci-fied height) and *heavy* (over a specified weight). Then we could prepare a little table (Figure 18.1) showing the four possible types of males. Four is the minimal number of types because each variable cannot be divided into less than two categories.

Now imagine a person who falls in the *big-light* category. An observer who employed only the size category would see this person as a football player, but one who used only the weight category would not. Their judgments would be reversed for a person who was small but heavy. Churchman and I suspected that something like this was going on with

Figure 18.1
Example of a Two-Dimensional Type

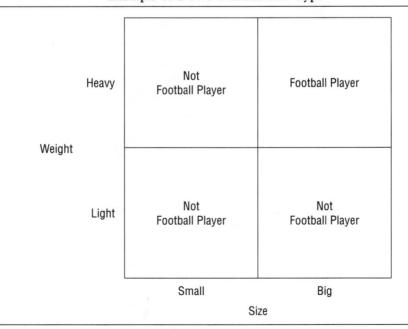

respect to introversion–extroversion. Therefore, we directed our efforts to determining what the underlying dimensions of introversion and extroversion might be.

Returning to Jung's writing we extracted every one of his descriptions of the types and found that they fell into two categories: those that dealt with (1) how the environment affects an individual, and (2) how an individual affects the environment. Furthermore, it was apparent that Jung took *self* and the *environment* to be exclusive and exhaustive categories. Therefore, the complement of the effect of the environment on an individual is the effect of the self on the individual, and similarly, the complement of the effect of the individual on the environment is the effect of the individual on self.

We then developed ratio measures of each of these effects. We took the function formed by the probability of an individual's response to environmental stimuli of different intensity (Figure 18.2). This was a measure of an individual's sensitivity to his/her environment. Those who are more sensitive to their environments than their selves we labelled *objectiverts,* and those more sensitive to self, *subjectiverts.* We took the function

Figure 18.2
Effect of Environment on Individual

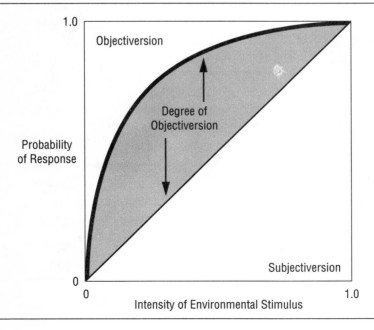

formed by a plot of the cumulative probability of behavior against the intensity of its effect on the environment to provide a measure of *externalization* and *internalization* (Figure 18.3).

By combining the two scales and the two categories associated with each, we obtain the four (basic) personality types shown in Figure 18.4.

1. *Subjective-Internalizers* (SIs): characteristically respond to internal rather than external stimuli, and do so by changing themselves.
2. *Subjective-Externalizers* (SEs): characteristically respond to internal rather than external stimuli, and do so by changing their environments.
3. *Objective-Internalizers* (OIs): characteristically respond to external rather than internal stimuli, and do so by changing themselves.
4. *Objective-Externalizers* (OEs): characteristically respond to external rather than internal stimuli, and do so by changing their environments.

Churchman and I equated the subjective-internalizer with Jung's introvert, and the objective-externalizer with Jung's extrovert. We called

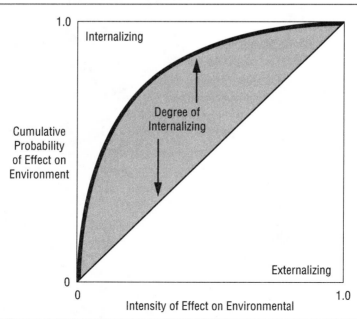

Figure 18.3
Effect of Individual on Environment

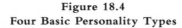

Figure 18.4
Four Basic Personality Types

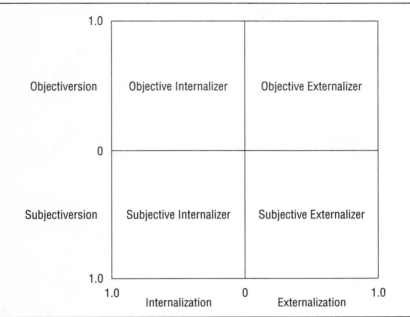

these categories *pure* types and the other two, subjective-externalizer and objective-internalizer, *mixed* types. The pure types are oriented to self or environment in both directions (that is, as input and output), but the mixed types are oriented to self in one direction and environment in the other.

At this point in the development of our thinking we went back to the students used in our earlier tests to determine where they fell in the 'personality space' we had constructed. We found that about three-quarters of them fell into the mixed types. Furthermore, when we re-examined the tests for introversion-extroversion and the recorded clinical interviews that had been used earlier to classify the students, we found that each test and interview had a clearly discernible bias toward one of the two dimensions we had identified. This explained the inconsistency of both the test results and the clinical judgments. For example, a test that focused exclusively on the effect of an individual on his/her environment/self would judge an externalizer to be an extrovert. But if that individual were also a subjectivert, a test that focuses on the effects of environment/self on the individual, would judge that same individual to be an introvert.

Churchman and I subsequently made finer distinctions in the personality space. First, we introduced a fifth type, the *centravert,* shown in Figure 18.5. The centravert falls in the middle section of both scales. Then we divided the personality space into the nine types shown in Figure 18.6. However, the four or five basic types turned out to be all we needed for most subsequent applications.

SOME PROTOTYPES

The nature of the types we came up with is illuminated by the use of prototypes.

Objective–Externalizer

The roles played by actor John Wayne in his motion pictures, if not John Wayne himself, was a model of extroversion, objective externalizing. In virtually all of his parts he was swept up in a cause not of his own making, but one presented to or imposed on him by his environment. In each case he undertook doing something about an undesirable external

Figure 18.5
Five Basic Personality Types

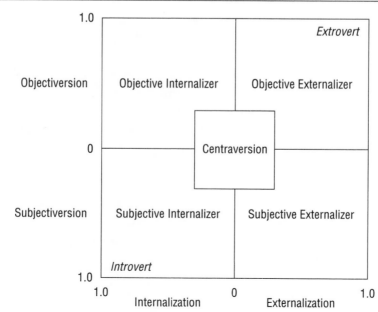

Figure 18.6
Nine Basic Personality Types

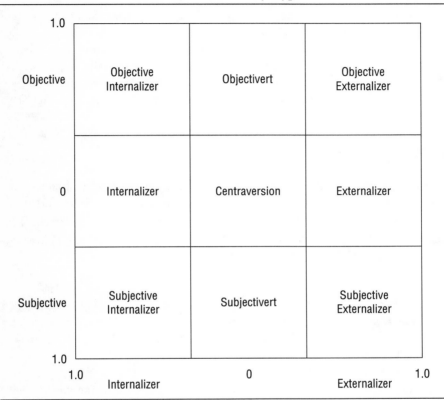

situation, usually manipulating or otherwise affecting others significantly. The causes he supported were not intellectual, not based on ideas but on environmental conditions. The characters he played were seldom seen in acts of reflection or introspection. They lacked depth, subtlety, and self-consciousness but they had big hearts and cared about the welfare of others.

Subjective-Externalizer

Joan of Arc was a model of the subjective-externalizer. She was as dedicated to changing her environment as any of John Wayne's characters, but unlike them she was driven from within, reacting to an inner voice or vision rather than an external state of affairs. This is reflected in a description of her provided by the *Encyclopaedia Britannica* (11th edition):

. . . her vivacity . . . was the direct outcome of an abnormally sensitive nervous temperament . . .

As she grew to womanhood she became inclined to silence, and spent much of her time in silence and prayer.

. . . while active in the performance of her duties . . . inwardly she was engrossed with thought reaching far beyond the circle of her daily concerns.

. . . she had become imbued with a sense of having a mission to free France from the English. She heard the voices of St. Michael, St. Catherine and St. Margaret urging her on. (v. 15, p. 420)

Objective-Internalizer

Another heroine, Florence Nightingale, was a model of the objective internalizer. She was extremely sensitive to the needs of others and dedicated herself to satisfying them even at a considerable cost to herself. This accommodating, self-sacrificing approach to external needs is also reflected in the *Encyclopaedia's* description of her:

From her earliest years . . . her great delight was to nurse and bandage her dolls. Her first living patient was a shepherd's dog. From tending animals she passed to human beings, and wherever there was sorrow or suffering she was sure to be found. Her most ardent desire was to use her talents for the benefit of humanity . . . (v. 19, p. 684)

The story of Miss Nightingale's labours at Scutari is one of the brightest pages in English annals. She gave herself body and soul, to the work. She would stand for twenty hours at a stretch to see the wounded accommodated. She regularly took her place in the operation-room, to hearten the sufferers by her presence and sympathy, and at night she would make her solitary round of the wards, lamp in hand, stopping here and there to speak a kindly word to some patient . . . For a time Miss Nightingale was herself prostrated with fever, but she refused to leave her post, and remained at Scutari till Turkey was evacuated by the British in July 1856. (v. 19, p. 685)

Subjective-Internalizer

Most hermits and recluses are introverts, subjective-internalizers. However, withdrawal from the environment and involvement with oneself does not have to be as extreme as it is in the case of hermits. Nevertheless, for Vincent Van Gogh it was fairly extreme. Although his paintings were frequently of nature, they were not efforts to depict what he saw, but what he felt about what he saw. They were pictures of what went on inside himself. He tried to satisfy his own needs, not those of others, or he would have painted more conventionally and saleably, which he was very capable of doing. His few efforts to form partnerships, as with Gaugin and Toulouse Lautrec, were very short-lived. He could not live or work with others. He was unable to tolerate the discipline imposed by the many schools he attended and, therefore, left all of them before completion of his programs. In April, 1889, he asked to be temporarily shut up in the asylum at Saint-Remy-de-Provence. He spent much of the following year in solitary confinement.

His biography in the *Encyclopaedia Britannica* contains such descriptive passages and phrases as the following:

> . . . he wrestled with temperamental difficulties and sought his true means of self expression . . .
> . . . his love was rejected by a London girl in 1874. His burning desire for human affection thwarted, he became and remained increasingly solitary.
> [In 1880] he sank into despair, cut himself off from everyone.
> . . . he strove to respect natural appearances and yet to convey by emphatic contours and heightened effects of colour the reality of his own feelings about the subject. (15th edition, 1974, v. 8, pp. 231–233)

PAIRS

Once we had developed a satisfactory way to type individuals, it was natural to ask how well individuals of the same type or different types interact. What are the characteristics of the system created by their interactions? Our thinking on this question began with two contradictory bits of so-called common sense: (1) likes attract each other, and (2) unlikes attract each other.

We leaned towards the belief that unlikes attract each other and likes repel each other because we thought likes probably compete for carrying out the same functions, while unlikes probably cooperate in this regard. For example, it seemed to us that an internalizer might be perfectly willing to let an externalizer manipulate the environment when such manipulation is necessary, as in repairing a defective faucet at home. Two externalizers, however, might conflict over who should make the repair. Similarly, a subjectivert is more likely to allow an objectivert to describe what happened in the environment than is another objectivert. On the other hand, an objectivert is much more likely to allow a subjectivert to plan their joint activity than to allow another objectivert to do so.

To test these hypotheses it was necessary to develop a measure of the similarity/dissimilarity of two types, that is, positions in the personality space such as A and B in Figure 18.7. Two measures suggested themselves. The first had to do with the distances of these points from the point of centraversion *(C)*. We used the absolute difference of their distances from this point: $|AC - BC|$. Obviously, if A and B are at the same point, then the difference between their distances from C is zero. We said that such a pair was perfectly *balanced*. Therefore, the absolute difference $|AC - BC|$ was taken as a measure of *imbalance*. Note that the imbalance is at a maximum when one individual is at the point of centraversion *(C)* and the other is at one of the corners of the space.

Second, the angle between lines AC and BC also seemed relevant. If A and B lie on the same straight line drawn through C, but on different sides of it, then the angle between them was taken to be 180°. (Figure 18.7 shows a balanced pair with a 180° angle between them.) Where A and B are not on the same straight line through C, we took the smaller of the two angles they form as the relevant one. This meant that 180° was the maximum angle and 0°, the minimum. This minimum occurred for two points on the same line through C on different sides of C. We used

Figure 18.7
A Symmetrical Balanced Pair

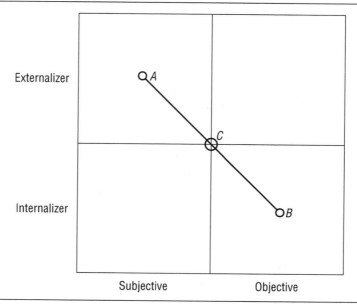

Subjective   Objective

the side of this angle as a measure of the pair's *symmetry or complementarity*. A pair whose angle was 180° was taken to be the most symmetrical or complementary; a pair whose angle was 0° was taken to be the least symmetrical or complementary.

We initially hypothesized that *the greater the imbalance of a pair and the less symmetrical they were, the more difficulty its members had in getting along together.*

Since one of the relevant measures was in terms of distance and the other in terms of angular degrees, initially we had difficulty in seeing how to combine them into a single measure, but a single measure was clearly desirable. A way was suggested to us by one of our colleagues—a physical test. He suggested we think of the personality space as on a solid plane balanced on a point under it at the point of centraversion; and of the individuals located in that space as weights of equal magnitude. Then the measure of the rotational force they would create would be *a measure of their incompatibility*. This force is proportional to the distance from C of a point half-way between the positions of the two individuals. We called this midpoint the *pair-point*. The greater the angle between the individual points (the more symmetrical they are) and the less the absolute difference of the distance between them, the closer their pair-point is to C. Therefore, the distance of their pair-point from the point of centraversion can be used as a measure of their *incompatibility,* that is, their inability to get along together. This measure permitted a reformulation of the pairing hypothesis:

> The ability of a pair to get along together is inversely proportional to the distance of their pair-point from the point of centraversion.

Three characteristics of this measure are important. First, the pair-point of two people who are at the same location in the personality space is the same as that of the individual points; second, a pair-point falls on a boundary only if the position of the pair-points of both members of the pair fall on the same boundary; and, third, the pair-point of two people who are perfectly balanced and perfectly symmetrical will fall at the point of centraversion, hence their distance from that point is zero.

This last condition means that a pair whose positions are equidistant from the point of centraversion, and are on different sides of the same straight line through that point, is the most compatible pair. This condition is satisfied, for example, when both individual personalities lie on the point of centraversion.

The pairing hypothesis seemed plausible to us because we reasoned as follows. Consider a relatively compatible pair, the subjective-externalizer *(A)* and objective-internalizer *(B)* shown in Figure 18.7. If an external problem involving the pair arises, the objective type, *B,* is more likely than *A* to be aware of it. If so, *B* will try to solve the problem by adjusting him/herself. In this case *B* would 'see' and 'solve' the problem without involving *A;* there would be no conflict between them. If, on the other hand, the externalizer *A* perceives this problem he/she is more likely to try to solve the problem by manipulating *B* than him/herself. *B* is likely to respond cooperatively to *A*'s effort to change him/her because he/she is an internalizer. Conflict does not arise here either.

Consider a pair consisting of an introvert, *A,* and an extrovert *B.* Because *B* is sensitive to *A*'s reluctance to be changed by others, *B* will try to solve the problem by manipulating things in their environment, not *A.* In this way *B* acts as a moat around *A* protecting him/her from the environment. On the other hand, if *A* perceives the problem, he/she will try to solve it by changing him/herself. Should *A* try to change *B, B* will respond favorably because he/she is objective. In such a pair *A* serves as a *substitute self* for *B,* a self for *B* to be aware of.

I ran across a case very much like this during a clinical interview of a married couple in their fifties. The husband was a postman and extremely introverted. His wife was a housekeeper and extremely extroverted. When they entered the interview room she took the most comfortable chair and instructed him to sit at her side in a less comfortable chair than was available, which he did. The interview began with her. She answered questions easily and quickly but tended to talk too much. The interviewer frequently had to cut her short in order to move on. Eventually, her interview was completed and the interviewer told the husband that it was now his turn. Up to that point he had not said a word, and he had not looked directly at the interviewer. He continued to avoid looking at the interviewer even when he was being questioned. When the first question was addressed to him, his wife immediately answered it. The interviewer asked her to refrain from answering for her husband. She apologized and said she would. When the second question was directed to him, he did not answer immediately. His wife watched him impatiently and finally could no longer tolerate the delay; once again she answered for him. Although the interviewer cautioned her again, the same thing happened on the next question. The interviewer then asked the wife if she would mind leaving the room and waiting outside until the interview of her husband was completed. Before she could reply her husband spoke up for the first time. He said that he would not stay if his wife left. Their division of labor was close to perfect.

Consider a less well-matched pair, the objective-externalizer *(A)* and objective-internalizer shown *(B)* in Figure 18.8. Both are sensitive to the environment and will compete with respect to interpreting what is going on out there. The externalizer *(A)* will keep trying to correct the internalizer's (*B*'s) interpretation of what is going on. This can become a bone of contention between them. *B* may not react overtly to *A*'s criticism but, because *B* is sensitive to criticism, he/she will resent it. Such resentment may be internalized and accumulate over time. When it does come out it is likely to do so with an intensity that has increased over time, and therefore may appear to *A* to be an over-reaction.

Testing the Pairing Hypothesis

Our first effort to test the pairing hypothesis consisted of identifying pairs of faculty members in our university who had jointly authored one or more published articles. Then we interviewed those involved and estimated their types subjectively. Using these estimates, we determined

Figure 18.8
An Asymmetrical Unbalanced Pair

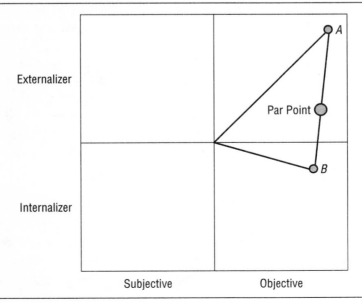

their pair-points and the distances of these points from the point of cen-traversion.

We divided the collaborating pairs into two groups: (1) those who had collaborated only once; and (2) those who had collaborated more than once. Then for each group we determined the average distance of its pair-points from the point of centraversion. This distance was signifi-cantly larger for those who had collaborated only once than for those who had continued to collaborate after their first experience of it. This result, of course, was consistent with our hypothesis.

Next we had clinical psychologists interview and determine the per-sonality type of each member of a number of married couples and a number of divorced couples. The interviewers had no knowledge of the hypothesis being tested. Once again, the location of the pair points and the average distance of those in each group of subjects were estimated. The average distance of the pair-points of the divorced couples from the point of centraversion was significantly greater than that of the still-married couples. The results were consistent with our hypothesis, but they suggested a much stronger test of it.

We used married couples again, but this time we used only those that had been married for 10 years or more. Clinical interviewers, who were not informed of the hypothesis being tested, typed each member of each couple. Then we used two marriage counselors to interview each cou-ple together. The interviewers knew nothing of our hypothesis but were asked to make the following judgment: *Would the couple remarry if they were to learn at this moment that their marriage was not valid and there were no external pressure on them to remarry?* The interviewers had to answer this question independently of each other. Then we used only those couples on which the interviewers had agreed. (This included most of them by far.) Then once again we compared the average distances of the pair-points from the point of centraversion and obtained a significantly larger average distance for those couples that the interviewers judged would not remarry voluntarily.

THREE AND MORE

It occurred to us that if we could characterize the compatibility of pairs, we might be able to do so for larger groups, so we turned to trios. First, we had to define a trio-point. We did this by finding a point to charac-terize the relationship between a pair (*A* and *B*) and a single individual

(D) (see Figure 18.9). Let *P(AB)* represent the pair-point of *A* and *B*. Then we could find the pair point between *P(AB)* and *D* but this would not reflect the fact that *P(AB)* involves two people and *D* only one. Therefore, instead of taking a point midway between *P(AB)* and *D*, we took a point one-third the way from *P(AB)* along the straight line connecting *P(AB)* and *D*.

Such trio-points always fall within the personality space. They can only fall on a boundary of the space when all three points fall on the same boundary. Finally, the trio-point of three people all of whom have the same position in the personality space is at that position. This is the same as it is for two people with the same position.

The principle used in defining the trio-point was used to define points characterizing larger groups. For a quartet, two exclusive pairs are defined—it does not matter which pairs are selected—and their pair-points are determined (Figure 18.10). Then the pair-point of these pair-points is the quartet-point. For a quintet, first a quartet-point is determined for any four of the five. Then the quintet-point is one-fifth the way from the quartet point on a straight line from it to the position of the remaining person in the group.

Figure 18.9
Pair-Point P(AB) and Trio-Point P(AB-D)

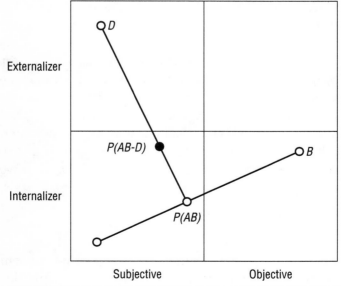

Figure 18.10
A Quartet-Point

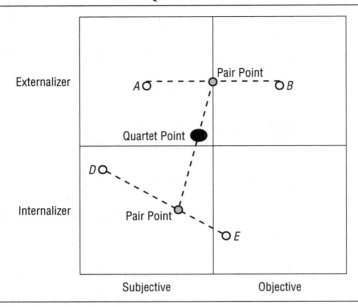

Using this measure, we generalized the pairing-hypothesis as follows:

The ability of the members of a group of *n* directly interacting members to get along together is inversely proportional to the distance of their *n*-point from the point of centraversion.

We have had no opportunity to test this hypothesis either formally or informally, but the personnel department of one large company did. It was interested in using this hypothesis in forming small task forces and teams. We trained some of the members of this department in the use of our clinical interviews and our self-administered test. They later reported to us that they had formed groups using our hypothesis and were convinced that they had obtained more effective teams than they would have obtained otherwise.

THE FAMILY

Families are, in a sense, small teams. Like some but not all teams, families grow and contract, but unlike most other teams their additions are usually infants whose personalities have not yet taken shape. Therefore, we began to focus on the effects on a family of the addition of a child, and the effect of a family on the formation of the child's personality.

Adding a member to a team is an opportunity that may either increase or decrease its compatibility. It seemed to us that in a family situation the formation of the personality of the child is influenced significantly by how the family treats the child. Therefore, we suspected that families tend to shape the personalities of their children so as to increase the compatibility of the family, making it easier for its members to get along together. We also suspected that the influence of a family on the formation of a child's personality was unconscious. Speculation along these lines led to the following *psychogenetic hypothesis:*

> The personality of a child added to a family tends to be formed so as to increase the stability of the family.

If, for example, the personalities of the married couple, A and B, are as shown in Figure 18.11, then the personality of the first-born will tend to be in the vicinity of D which would place the trio-point, $P(AB)$, at the point of centraversion, C. If the couple is well balanced, as they are in Figure 18.7, the first child's personality will tend to form at or near the point of centraversion. To the extent that the first-born's personality is conditioned in this way, that child can convert even a very poorly matched pair into a better matched trio. It is in this sense that a child can stablize an otherwise unstable marriage.

However, there are couples so badly matched that the addition of a third person cannot bring their trio-point to the point of centraversion, although it can bring the trio-point significantly closer to the point of centraversion. The most extreme case possible is shown in Figure 18.12. In this trio, the addition, D, is located as well as possible, but still cannot bring the trio to the point of centraversion, C. But note that the addition of another child, E, located where D is, would bring the family-point to the point of centraversion. Unfortunately, this would occur at a cost to the children D and E: they are too much alike to get along well together.

In a family with good but not perfectly matched husband and wife, the personality of the first child tends to be closer to the point of centraversion than either of the parents. Where this is the case, the personality of the second child is likely to be even closer to the point of centraversion than that of the first child. In general, then, for reasonably well-matched couples—ones whose pair-points, say, are no more than halfway to a

Figure 18.11
An Increase in a Couple's (A and B) Stability by the Addition of a Child (D)

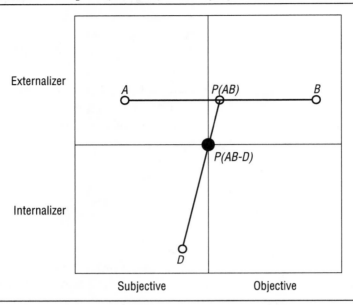

Figure 18.12
The Largest Possible Improvement to the Worst Possible Couple

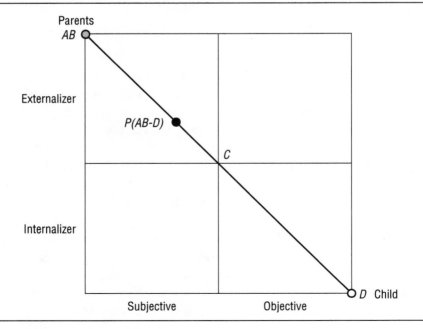

boundary of the personality space—each successive child will have a personality closer to the point of centraversion than those who preceded him/her. This may help explain why large families tend to be more stable than small ones, and why divorce rates are higher among childless couples than among ones with children. Note also that as family size increases, the probability of the family containing a well-matched subgroup increases.

We never tested the personality formation hypothesis rigorously. But we did test it informally on families we knew well. The results certainly seemed to support our hypothesis.

It should be emphasized that the effects of a family on personality formation are almost always the result of pressure applied *unconsciously*. For example, a child born of two introverted parents learns rapidly that he/she can win approval most easily by handling a large part of the family's interactions with its environment. In this way he/she alleviates the parents' problem with the environment. If he/she were to become introverted, he/she would exacerbate their problem and create one for him/herself. Sensing what types of orientation make the family members more compatible, the child's personality tends to move in that direction.

As the members of a married pair grow older their personalities tend to change. They may become either a better or worse pair. Therefore, when children grow up and leave home, the parents may find themselves either on a second honeymoon or in need of separation. At this time in the life of a married pair, either divorce or renewal is quite common.

CULTURES

Given the apparent applicability of our typology to groups of increasing size, it was natural to extend our thinking to societies and their cultures. In another place, Emery and I wrote that culture is to society what personality is to the individual. This suggests that the personality types may also serve as cultural types.

I was able to explore this idea while working on a project for the Arms Control and Disarmament Agency in Washington, DC. With the help of our project officer, Dr Thomas Saaty, a group of experts on foreign countries were brought together. They were exposed to a detailed exposition and discussion of our personality types. Then each expert was given a list of 25 countries and asked to identify the type of any they felt they knew well.

We obtained complete agreement on about 75% of the countries on the list. There was essential agreement on about half of the remainder. Of significance was the fact that the countries on which there was little or no agreement were ones with which the USA had interacted little in recent years.

We then identified a number of international negotiated agreements, such as treaties, involving only countries on which our experts had reached agreement. For each negotiation we then estimated the group-point and its distance from the point of centraversion. Simultaneously, we arranged for a group of political scientists to determine whether each agreement on our list had been successful or not. We then calculated the average distances from centraversion of the successful and the unsuccessful groups. The average distance of the unsuccessful groups was significantly larger than that of the successful groups.

Some Examples (Figure 18.13)

There was complete agreement among our experts that the USA was a subjective-externalizing (SE) nation. It was seen as driven by its own opinions,

Figure 18.13
The "Personality" of Some Nations

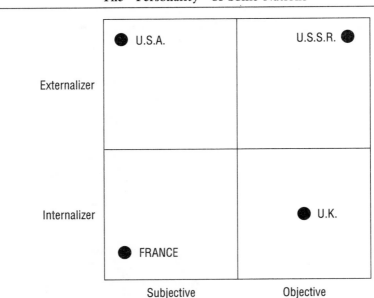

perceptions, needs, and desires rather than those of others (subjective), but it is manipulative of others and its environment (externalizing).

For example, in India in 1957 I found that the USA was characterized as a nation that was willing to give India anything that it wanted to get rid of, whether or not the Indians needed or wanted it. At that time the Indians had asked the USA to sell it liberty ships that had been built for use in World War II and were then being decommissioned. India wanted these ships for intercoastal shipping. However, the USA, fearing that this would enable India to compete with US international shipping, turned down the Indian request and instead offered to sell India its surplus of butter at a bargain price. It made this offer despite the fact that India did not use much butter because of lack of refrigeration equipment. The Indians contrasted this attitude with that of the USSR which, they said, was very sensitive to Indian needs and desires. They also said that although Soviet aid was only a fraction of that given by the USA, it was much more effective because it was sensitive to Indian needs and desires. Whether or not these opinions and attitudes were justified was not as important as their existence.

Experts in the Arms Control and Disarmament Agency classified the USSR as extroverted, OE. If correct, this explained in part the difficulty the USA and the USSR had in getting along together. They were both manipulative of their environments and therefore competed for control of it. The Soviets, however, were primarily driven by external events to which they were much more sensitive than Americans, who were primarily driven by internal conditions.

On the other hand, the UK was uniformly judged to be objective-internalizing (OI), although it was also judged to have been subjective-externalizing during its 'empire days.' This would explain the current friendship of the USA and the UK (SE and OI), and the earlier enmity between them when they were of the same type. This also indicates that the UK had problems with the USSR, but that these were different from those that the USA had. To the UK the USSR appeared to be excessively manipulative, and to the USSR the UK appeared to be excessively passive, reactive as opposed to proactive.

France was typed by our experts as introverted (SI). This would explain why it got along with the USSR better than either the USA or the UK. It also explains why no three of these four countries formed a very stable trio, but that the four formed a relatively stable quartet. France's introversion also explains a frequent complaint about the French by

American tourists: they are inhospitable and resent the American presence. To the French, on the other hand, Americans seem loud and brash, too conspicuous and intrusive.

Canada was seen to be like the UK: objective-internalizing. This is consistent with the traditional friendship between the USA and Canada. It also helps explain the internal strife in Canada between the British derivatives (OI), and the French derivatives (SI). The desire of French Canada to secede from the rest is consistent with its introversion.

West Germany was seen as similar to the USA: subjective-externalizing (SE) but not as extremely so. This explains why the West Germans have had less difficulty in getting along with the British than with the French or Americans.

One of the most persistent conflicts in the world today is that between the Israelis and the surrounding Arabs. Both were seen by our experts as subjective-externalizers (SEs), each trying to manipulate the other to its own ends. There is very little ground for cooperation between them. When the USA enters their conflict in an attempt to facilitate negotiation, it is not likely to succeed because it is another SE. In this situation the UK would be a much more effective negotiator or arbitrator than the USA.

Conclusion

The personality types that have been described here have been used to explain consumption of a variety of products—beer, headache pills, tranquilizers, candy, and pet food—and also to explain the selection of pets and alcohol and narcotic addiction. We suspect the concepts can provide useful insights to the use of any products, things, or services that affect the way a person feels about him/herself.

Clearly, there is a large opportunity for expanded and rigorous work on the effect of personality on small and large groups, and on cultures.

Bibliography

Ackoff, R. L., and Emery, F. E. (1972). *On Purposeful Systems,* Chicago: Aldine Atherton.

Jung, C. G. (1924). *Psychological Types.* New York: Harcourt Brace.

CHAPTER 19

WHY PEOPLE DRINK: TOWARD UNDERSTANDING OBJECTIVES

Understanding human behavior, particularly consuming behavior, is obviously of value to those who provide the products consumed. Few of us understand why we behave as we do, but we are convinced that we have such understanding. Our explanations of our own behavior are often excuses and rationalizations of it. This would be bad enough but, in addition, we tend to infer from our self-misunderstanding to misunderstanding of others. Correct explanations of human behavior, even partial explanations, are often very difficult to come by, even when the behavior involved is commonplace.

In the study described here an explanation was sought for the consumption of alcoholic beverages, a very commonplace event the explanation of which is far from commonplace. This study followed on the heels of the one reported in the last chapter and was also done for Anheuser-Busch, Inc.

Early in 1968 Mr. E. H. Vogel, Jr., then Vice President of Marketing, with whom the work reported in Chapter 11 has been done, asked that we turn our attention to the content of advertising: the quality of messages. We began by surveying organizations that offered message-evaluation services. A great deal of information was collected about each. Using this we selected for closer examination about a half dozen of these organizations, those which most impressed us on paper. We then visited each one and went over their procedures in detail. Finally, we selected the agency that seemed to us to have the soundest procedures, and we made this proposition to it: We would carry out an experimental evaluation of its message evaluations with the understanding that, if the results were favorable, it could use them as it saw fit; if they were not, we would not release information about the study that would identify the organization. The agency agreed.

From *The Art of Problem Solving* (Wiley, 1978).

A-B's principal advertising agency was asked to select fifty of its television commercials equally divided into those it considered to be among its best and its worst. The advertising agency was not restricted to selecting commercials that had actually been used.

The message-evaluation agency was then asked to conduct tests of these commercials in three cities selected by us. It was to identify six commercials that were evaluated as superior and six that were evaluated as inferior in all three cities.

The agency obtained consistent evaluations in two of the three cities, but the third yielded results that were inconsistent with the other two. The city causing the trouble was one in which A-B had a large brewery. We began to suspect that the message evaluations obtained in this city were greatly influenced by the company's presence. Through discussion with others who had conducted similar message evaluations, we learned that they had had similar experiences in cities in which a company was a major economic force. This suggested that most of the public in such cities already had strong opinions, one way or the other, of the company and its products; hence they were not subject to significant influence by advertising.

This led to two actions. First, another city was selected to replace the "brewery city" in the message-evaluation effort. Second, a sequence of carefully monitored reductions in advertising was introduced in the brewery city. Reductions of about $250,000 in annual expenditures were made over a relatively short time, with no effect on sales.

The message-evaluation agency, using the new "third" city, was able to identify the required number of consistently "superior" and "inferior" commercials. These were then used in a designed experiment in which a number of marketing areas were exposed to nothing but the superior commercials, and an equal number were exposed to nothing but the inferior commercials. The amounts spent on advertising in these areas were carefully controlled. The deviation of actual from forecast sales was used as the measure of performance.

We found no significant differences between the performances of the two sets of markets. We concluded that the message evaluations were not related to the effectiveness of the messages, to their ability to affect sales. The only positive value of this conclusion was that it led A-B to discontinue its use of such message-evaluation services. This yielded a modest saving, but the problem originally put to us remained unsolved.

Before continuing with this account, it is worth pausing for a few observations. First, it should be noted how frequently we accept without question the ability of those who render a service to deliver what they promise. We tend to take such an ability for granted. If we require any evidence to support such a belief, we usually take the survival, success, or reputation of the server as sufficient. Such casual acceptance of expensive services can be a costly habit. The more obvious the value of a service appears to be, the more intensively it should be tested, if for no other reason than that its cost tends to be proportional to its "obviousness."

Second, note that an unexpected result (e.g., the behavior of the brewery city) usually represents an opportunity for improvement of performance if we can find an explanation of it. Many significant advances in science, for example, have been the result of looking into anomalies, misfitting observations. Now let us continue with the story.

LOOKING FOR AN EXPLANATION

Our experience with the message-evaluation agency convinced us that we would not be able to evaluate advertising messages adequately without knowing *why* people drink beer and, more generally, alcoholic beverages. When we mentioned this to a marketing manager in another company, he said it was perfectly clear why people drink beer: they like it. When we asked him how he knew this, he replied, "They wouldn't drink it if they didn't." We wanted a less circular and more illuminating "explanation" of drinking behavior.

We initiated an extensive literature search for theories purporting to explain alcohol consumption. All those we found dealt with the abuse rather than normal use of such beverages. Furthermore, not one of the theories had been adequately tested; most were based on a small number of clinical observations. To design and conduct adequate tests of these theories would have required more time, money, and patience than we had. Fortunately we found that someone else had already conducted such tests.

Dr. Fred E. Emery and his colleagues at the Human Resources Centre of The Tavistock Institute in London, with whom we had collaborated over a number of years, had tested most of the available theories with negative results. Emery and his co-workers then devoted their efforts to producing a detailed description of drinking behavior and to extracting from it underlying patterns that might provide a basis for theoretical speculation. They studied about 3000 regular drinkers in England, Ireland, and Norway. Their analysis disclosed three drinking types which Emery named and described somewhat as follows.

Reparative

These are generally middle aged and of either sex. They have not achieved as much as they had hoped to by that stage of their lives, although they are usually far from being failures. They believed they were capable of achieving what they wanted, but also believed that doing so would require sacrifice from others for whom they cared a great deal. For example, achievement might require a move that would displease wife and children. Therefore, they sacrificed their own aspirations in the interests of others but were well adjusted to this state.

Most reparative drinking occurs at the end of the work day rather than on weekends, vacations, or holidays. It usually takes place with a few close friends or members of the family. The reparative is a controlled drinker who seldom gets high or drunk and very rarely becomes an alcoholic. His or her drinking is associated with the transition from the work to the nonwork environment and is seen as a type of self-reward for sacrifices made for others.

Social

These are of either sex but are generally younger than reparative drinkers. They have not yet attained the levels of aspiration, but believe they will and that doing so requires approval and support of others. They are driven by ambition, the desire to get ahead.

Social drinking is heaviest on weekends, holidays, and vacations. It usually takes place in large groups consisting of acquaintances in social settings. The social is a controlled drinker but less so than the reparative. His or her drinking is associated with friendliness and acceptance of and by others. Alcoholic beverages are seen as lubricants of social situations.

Indulgent

These are of any age and either sex. They have not attained the levels of aspiration and never expect to. They consider themselves to be irretrievable failures. They view life as tragic.

The indulgent drinks most heavily when subjected to pressure to achieve. He or she drinks to escape such pressure. The indulgent is the least controlled drinker and is the most likely to get high or drunk and become an alcoholic.

THE MISSING TYPE

We at Wharton found these categories to be exciting and suggestive, but we were disturbed by the fact that there were *three* of them. The only explanation for this could be that there was a single underlying scale on which the three categories represented low, medium, and high ranges. Emery and we agreed, however, that there must be more than one underlying scale. Even if there were only two, and each was minimally divided into two ranges (low and high), their combination would yield *four* types (low-low, low-high, high-low, and high-high).

We suspected that there were two underlying scales because two of Emery's drinking types appeared to be subtypes of two of four personality types that C. West Churchman and I had identified in the late 1940s. In our analysis of C. G. Jung's personality types, *introvert* and *extrovert,* Churchman and I had uncovered two underlying scales, hence four personality types of which introversion and extroversion were only two.

THE MATCHING HYPOTHESIS

Now the initial hunch relating Emery's drinking types to our personality types was as follows.

1. Emery's *reparative* drinkers were *objective internalizers* because they were sensitive and responsive to the needs of others and adapted to them by sacrificing their unfulfilled aspirations. (Not all objective externalizers, of course, are drinkers, let alone reparative drinkers.)
2. Emery's *social* drinkers were *subjective externalizers* because they were primarily driven by their own ambitions and attempted to manipulate others to get what they wanted.

It also occurred to us that Emery's *indulgent* drinkers were divisible into two groups, corresponding to the two "pure" types, introvert and extrovert. If this were so, we hypothesized, introverted drinkers blamed their failures on the environment from which they were trying to escape by drinking; the extroverted drinkers blamed their failures on their own shortcomings and were trying to escape from consciousness of them. At our suggestion Emery re-examined his data on the indulgent and found that, indeed, the two drinking types we had inferred from our theory did exist. He retained the term *indulgent* for the introverted drinker and called the extroverted drinker an *oceanic*. This finding considerably reinforced our conviction that we were on the right track.

Emery had found that most regular drinkers were in the social and reparative groups, which were subclasses of our mixed types. Recall that Churchman and I had found that more people fell into the mixed types than into the pure types. This was also reinforcing.

In addition, Emery had found that most alcoholics were indulgents or oceanics (although most indulgents and oceanics were not alcoholics). Using our typology, we hypothesized two types of alcoholics. First, the introverted (indulgent) alcoholic who would tend to drink himself into a catatonic stupor with little or no consciousness of and interaction with his environment. He would tend to drink alone or with someone who would help protect his privacy. Second, the extroverted (oceanic) alcoholic who would tend to drink himself into un*self*-consciousness and hyperactivity, a manic or orgiastic state. We thought of the role played by Ray Milland in the motion picture, *The Lost Weekend,* as prototypical of the introverted alcoholic, and the type of orgiastic drinking shown in *La Dolce Vita* as prototypical of the extroverted alcoholic. Consistent with our theory was the fact that many orgies—for example, those associated with the Mardi Gras—involved masks and costumes, which provide anonymity and facilitate escape from self. Subsequently, this hypothesis and others led us into studies of alcoholism that, however, are not an integral part of this story.

Our "matching hypothesis" (Figure 19.1)—that Emery's drinking types were subgroups of our personality types—required rigorous testing. This was done in a laboratory into which regular drinkers were brought for observation and interview. Since independent classification of drinkers into the personality and drinking types were to be based in part on judgments made by clinical psychologists, it was first necessary to instruct them in the use of both classification schemes. Instruction and practice was continued until there was a high degree of consistency of judgments made independently by different clinicians, and these agreed with those made by the researchers responsible for the types and theory. Even after the interviewers were "calibrated," several independent judgments were made on each subject.

Figure 19.1
The Matching Hypothesis

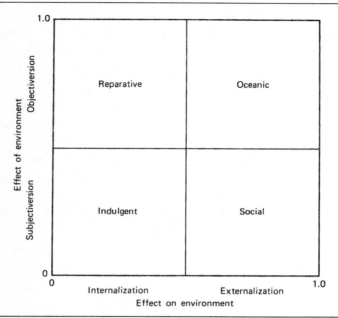

The results of one of the tests of the matching hypothesis, one that used 125 subjects, are shown in Table 19.1. Seventy-six percent of the observations fitted the hypothesis. This is relatively strong confirmation. Most of the mismatches, we believed, were due to lack of perfect precision in the classification procedures.

Having established this link between the drinking types and the personality types, we began a more intensive research program to establish the causal links between our theory and the purposes served by the

Table 19.1
Results of a Test of the Matching Hypothesis (125 Subjects)

Drinking Types	Objective Internalizer (%)	Subjective Externalizer (%)	Objective Externalizer (%)	Subjective Internalizer (%)
Reparative	30	5	7	1
Social	4	31	1	3
Oceanic	0	1	10	0
Indulgent	1	0	1	5

consumption of alcohol among the types. Before we could seek such an explanation, however, we had to develop and validate instruments for measuring the dimensions of our personality types. Although the clinical interviewing procedures had been demonstrated to have sufficient reliability, their cost was too great to employ them on larger samples drawn from multiple locations. Each of the 125 interviews cost approximately $300, and these were conducted in 1968. Even if we were to cut these costs in half, they would have been too large to enable us to deal with large samples in different locations. Consequently, we turned our research to the development of less expensive typing procedures. One direction we took involves the use of a behavioral laboratory in which we hoped to be able to reduce or eliminate clinical interviewing costs by collecting data on an individual's personality by observing his behavior in specially designed situations. The other direction we took involved the design of self-administered paper-and-pencil tests that a subject could take without supervision.

The behavioral situation we developed worked well; it provided rich and reliable readings on both personality scales, but the cost and the time required were too great, particularly when we had to operate in different cities. Nevertheless we found that the information obtained from this laboratory situation enabled us to design a substantially more efficient and shortened interviewing procedure to be used by the clinicians. Eventually we were able to obtain an accurate and reliable clinical typing of a subject for about $35.

The development of an acceptable self-administered paper-and-pencil test took more than two years. Two criteria of acceptability were imposed on this effort. First, there had to be at least a seventy-five percent agreement between the results of the test and clinical evaluations. Second, there was to be no bias in the classification of those subjects about whom there was disagreement between test and clinic. This would assure us of acceptable "collective" accuracy when we went into the field and used large numbers of subjects. Fortunately, A-B's management understood the methodological issues and did not press us into going into the field prematurely.

THE MATURATION HYPOTHESIS

Once an acceptable test was developed, research could be directed to testing the hypotheses formulated to explain drinking behavior. The hypothesis formulated to do so was suggested by the earlier hypothesis about the two types of alcoholics and by the fact that most alcoholics came from the pure rather than the mixed types. In addition, it made use of the following intermediate "maturation hypothesis":

> As those in the pure types (introversion and extroversion) grow older they tend to become more introverted and extroverted, to move away from the point of centraversion. As those in the mixed types mature they tend to move toward centraversion.

By interviewing the spouse of middle- and older-aged couples in the clinic and extracting from each descriptions of the change in personality that had occurred in the other over the years, data were obtained that supported this hypothesis. This led to our "drinking hypothesis."

THE DRINKING HYPOTHESIS

> Alcoholic beverages are used to produce short-run transformations in personality of the same type produced by maturation in the long run.

This hypothesis implies that introverts and extroverts drink to become more introverted and extroverted, respectively; however, the mixed types drink to become more centraverted.

We did not feel we could test this hypothesis by interviewing techniques, because we doubted that most drinkers were aware of their reasons for drinking (not to be confused with their rationalizations of it), and, if they were, they might be unwilling to reveal their reasons in an interview. Therefore, my colleague James Emshoff designed a rather complex but very effective behavioral test of this hypothesis.

Through a field survey, 250 regular drinkers were identified and invited to participate in an effort by Anheuser-Busch to select one of four newly developed beers to bring out on the market. They were invited to a meeting place at which, when they arrived, they were first given the paper-and-pencil personality-typing test previously referred to. They were then told they would be given an opportunity to taste and test the four new beers, but before doing so they would be shown the television commercials that had been prepared for each brand.

The television commercials had been prepared by the advertising agency in story-board form. Each commercial consisted of three scenes.

In the first a person who was clearly of one of the four personality types was shown in a situation that was characteristic of that type. In the second scene the same person was shown drinking one of the four new brands of beer while its virtues were extolled by an announcer. Each brand had been given a three-letter name selected from a list of names that had been demonstrated to have no value connotations. The names used were Bix, Zim, Waz, and Biv. In the third scene the same person was shown with his personality significantly transformed in the direction predicted by the "drinking hypothesis."

After being shown these commercials, the subjects were allowed to taste the beers as much as they wanted, how they wanted, and to discuss them with each other. Each brand was contained in the same type of bottle with identical labels except for the name printed on them. Furthermore, and most important, was the fact unknown to the subjects: all four of the beers were exactly the same, from the same brew of the same brewery.

The subjects were not only asked to express their preferences, which they did with no difficulty, they were also asked to select one of the brands, a case of which would be given to them to take home. The percentage that chose the brand corresponding to their personality type was much larger than one would expect by chance. Furthermore, all the subjects believed the brands were different and that they could tell the difference between them. Most felt that at least one of the four brands was not fit for human consumption.*

These results not only confirmed the drinking hypothesis but also suggested an important direction for further research. A survey was designed and carried out in which beer drinkers were asked to characterize those whom they believed typically drank each major brand of beer marketed in their areas. This survey was carried out in six cities; 1200 subjects were interviewed. The results clearly revealed that each beer was perceived as having an appeal to particular personality clusters. Further research showed that those who drank each brand of beer did in fact fall into these perceived clusters. The personalities associated with each brand not surprisingly corresponded to those of the people usually shown in

---

* These results showed that *in the short run only* drinkers could be induced to perceive differences that were not there. The experiment did not show that drinkers could be induced *not* to perceive differences that were there. Both Emery and we found distinctive taste preferences in each personality type. This meant that if a beer were to appeal to a particular type it had to have certain physical characteristics and not have others.

their commercials. The personality segments found to be associated with four major brands of beer are shown in Figure 19.2.

MATCHING TYPES AND BEERS

Using this knowledge, it was possible to determine by further surveys what personality types drank each of the three brands A–B produces: Michelob, Budweiser, and Busch. Although these were found to have some overlap, in the main they were found to appeal to different personality segments of the market. This enabled us to determine which segments each brand was and was not reaching. From these surveys we were also able to estimate what portion of the beer consumed was consumed by each type. These portions varied significantly. Using this informaton, we were then able to specify target market segments to be reached either by existing brands or by new ones, *and now we knew what kind of advertising messages would be most effective in doing so.*

For example, although it was found that Michelob had most of its market in one part of the personality space, a small portion of its consumers were drawn from a different part of this space, a part in which the largest percentage of beer drinkers fell. This led to an advertising campaign

Figure 19.2
Personality Segments Associated with Different Brands of Beer

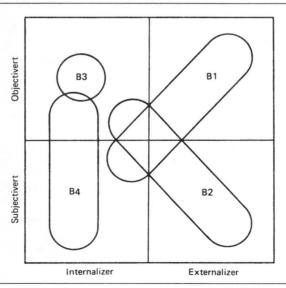

directed at the second segment. The campaign succeeded in significantly increasing this brand's share of the target market.

The implications of these results to the preparation of advertising messages and the design of products is clear, but the typology and the theory based on it could be used in another less apparent way. We hypothesized different usage of different media by different personality types. For example, we predicted that reparative drinkers (objective internalizers) would watch more television than social drinkers (subjective externalizers), because reparatives are more likely to observe others and socials are more likely to be doing things, participating. The chances that a reparative will watch at least six hours of television on a nonwork day, for example, are more than two and a half times greater than for a social. This ratio is even higher for indulgents, as one would expect. It is also possible to predict which magazine appeals to each type. For example, *Playboy* is almost twice as likely to be read by an oceanic as by an indulgent; the reverse is true for *Readers Digest*. Objective types (oceanics and reparatives) read newspapers more regularly and thoroughly than subjectives.

By combining information on the segmentation of the market with the information gained about the use of media, it became possible to combine messages and media in such a way as to direct advertising messages at particular market segments in a more effective way.

Our typology and personality theory has enabled A-B to gain insights into marketing phenomena that do not involve advertising. For example, research was undertaken for the company to determine what happens in a market when a new competitor enters it. In particular, the company was interested in identifying the personality characteristics of those who are most likely to try a new brand when it is introduced, those who switch to it as their regular brand, and the way others subsequently learn about the brand. Research was conducted in a number of markets that had experienced new brand entries in the relatively recent past. This work revealed that different personality types have significantly different likelihoods of trying new products. One of the types purchases new products thirty percent faster than the overall average. A second type does so slightly more than average, a third type slightly less, and the fourth type forty percent less than average. Furthermore, we found that those who are identified as early triers are influenced by advertising differently from those who switch to the product after it becomes established. The understanding thus gained enabled Anheuser-Busch to develop more effective advertising and other marketing strategies at appropriate times before, during, and after the introduction of new products.

Knowledge is power, and understanding is control; they are double-edged swords. To obtain knowledge and understanding of human behavior is to gain the ability to control the behavior of others more effectively either in one's own or their interests. Like any instrument, knowledge and understanding can be used for either good or evil—for example, an axe can be used to free a person from a burning building or to murder him. The use of every instrument necessarily involves ethical and moral judgments which cannot be avoided by the manager who uses the knowledge and understanding produced by research or by the researcher who produces them.

The understanding of drinking behavior developed in the research described here can be used to either intensify or ameliorate the "drinking problem." Fortunately, Anheuser-Busch believes it is in the long-run interests of the producers of alcoholic beverages as well as of their consumers to ameliorate it. One of the principal ways the company is using this understanding is in the development of more effective ways of preventing and treating alcoholism.

CHAPTER 20

CORPORATE PERESTROIKA: THE INTERNAL MARKET ECONOMY

*P*erestroika, the Russian word for "restructuring," is applied to the recent efforts in the old Soviet Union to convert from a centrally planned and controlled economy to a market economy. Not one centrally planned and controlled national economy has ever attained as high a level of economic development as has been reached by national market economies. Of course, not every national market economy has flourished, but every economy that has, has been a market economy. Recognizing that their country has developed economically as much as it can with a centrally planned and controlled economy, Gorbachev and now Yeltsin have tried to convert the old Soviet Union to a national market economy.

Curiously, in our country, which, of course, has a market economy, most organizations, institutions, and government agencies operate with centrally planned and controlled economies. Their internal economies are more like the national economy that the old Soviet Union is trying to get rid of than the national economy that we have. Unfortunately, many, if not most, of our corporate and institutional economies are currently in decline, in part because, like the Soviet Union, they contain and are constrained by many units that are bureaucratic monopolies.

In search of economies of scale, centrally planned and controlled economies in nations and corporations tend to create monopolistic providers of goods and services. For example, in corporations, accounting, personnel, and R&D departments are usually deliberately organized as subsidized monopolies. They are subsidized in the sense that the users of their products or services do not pay for them directly; the supplying units are supported financially by funds that are allocated to

From "Corporate Perestroika: The Internal Market Economy," in *Internal Markets,* William E. Halal, Ali Geranmayeh, and John Pourdehnad (Eds.), pp. 15–26 (Wiley, 1993).

them from above. The pool from which these funds are drawn is filled by a "tax" allocated from above to the units served. Monopolistic units that are subsidized are generally insensitive and unresponsive to the users of their services, but they are sensitive and responsive to the desires of the higher-level units that subsidize them. These higher level units are even more removed from the units served than the serving units. As a result, they are often unaware of, or unresponsive to, the needs and desires of the internal users of monopolistically provided goods and services.

However, this is only the beginning of the problems that centrally planned and controlled economies create within nations, institutions, and public and private organizations. Other problems include oversizing, excessive layers of management, and spans of control that are too small. Bureaucracies try to ensure their survival by becoming as large as possible because they operate on the (not unreasonable) assumption that the larger they are, the more difficult they are to eliminate. As a result, oversizing has become a congenital problem in many American organizations. Centralized economic planning and control allows subordinate organizational units to become bloated largely because those in control are rarely aware of the overpopulation in each of the units they control. Companies operate using the so-called information supplied by the managers of these bureaucratic units, but this information is usually generated by managers to justify whatever their units are doing, however inefficient they may be. The current rash of down- and right-sizing activities in American corporations reflects the growing awareness of the complete lack of population control that centralized management has.

Bloating is especially prevalent in corporate headquarters. For example, when Clark Equipment Company got into serious financial difficulty and converted from a centrally planned economy to an internal market, its headquarters was reduced from about 450 people to about 70, and its performance improved.

In addition, because salaries are usually attached to ranks in American organizations, people are often promoted to managerial ranks, not because a manager is needed, but because this is the only way to obtain additional compensation for them. To justify the promotion, one or two people are assigned to them. This makes for very small spans of control, which, in turn, leads to excessive layering. On average, the United States has approximately two and a half times as many managers and layers of management as the Japanese have.

Centrally planned and controlled economies also stimulate the growing costs of internally provided products and services because the supplying units do not need to compare their costs and prices with those of external suppliers of the same products and services. As a result, they seldom know what their internal costs actually are. Therefore, they have no systematic way of "benchmarking" their costs. In contrast, units operating in a competitive economy cannot survive without knowing and meeting the prices at which their competitors are providing comparable goods and services.

Transfer pricing, which is the surrogate for market pricing in a centrally planned and controlled economy, produces intense internal conflict and competition. Peter Drucker once observed that competition within corporations is much more intense than competition between them and, moreover, is a lot less ethical. Corporate units usually have much more cooperative relationships with their external suppliers than with their internal sources of goods and services.

It is almost impossible to determine the economic value of a subsidized internal monopolistic provider of a service or product—for example, a corporate computing or telecommunication center, a centralized R&D unit, or a human resources or organizational development department. In a market economy, users, not subsidizers, evaluate suppliers and express their evaluation in a way that counts, by their purchases.

The managers of most so-called business units within corporations do not know what their total costs are. In particular, they seldom know how much capital they employ and what the cost of that capital is. Their cost of capital is usually hidden in costs allocated to them from above. Allocated costs are sometimes as high as 40% of the total unit costs. How can managers reasonably be held responsible for the financial performance of their units when they neither know nor can control a large portion of their costs, their costs of capital in particular?

MACRO- VERSUS MICROECONOMIES

The macroeconomy of the United States involves relatively autonomous competitive suppliers of goods and services. Some regulation of these units is required because, among other things, they do not have perfect information about the market. Further, they do not always behave ethically or in the best interests of their stakeholders, their environments, or the systems that contain them. What centralized control there is is supposed to provide only enough regulation to enable the market to operate effectively.

Why do we have one type of economy at the national level and another at the organizational level? Some argue that the economic problems of a nation are of a different magnitude and complexity than those of companies. However, this is not so; for example, IBM and AT&T are among the largest economies in the world. Very few nations have larger economies. Even fewer are as complex.

Such considerations lead to the question, What effects would organizing corporations and public institutions around internal market economies have? Would their performance be better or worse?

INTERNAL MARKET ECONOMIES

With a few minor exceptions, corporations operating within an internal market economy operate as profit centers. Units within corporations are managed either as profit or as cost centers. In an internal market economy virtually all units, including executive offices, operate as profit centers. The only exceptions to this requirement are units whose output cannot or should not be provided to any external user, and which have only one internal user. The corporate secretary, for example, serves the chief executive officer and no one else. Therefore, this secretary should operate as a cost center attached to the executive office, which in turn should operate as a profit center. A unit that produces a product whose composition is secret for competitive reasons would also not be expected to operate as a profit center and, therefore, would be expected to operate as a cost center that is a part of a profit center.

Not all profit centers are expected to be profitable, but their profitability is taken into account in evaluating their performance. For example, a company may retain an unprofitable unit because of the prestige it brings the parent (e.g., Steuben Glass at Corning) or because its product is used as a loss leader. It may also be used to produce a product or provide a service that is required to complete or round out a product or service line.

Subject to the minimal constraints discussed below, profit centers should have the freedom (1) to buy any service or product they want from whatever source they want and (2) to sell their outputs to whomever they want at whatever price they want or are willing to accept. Because some corporate units may lack relevant information about other corporate units, and, more importantly, about the complex interactions among units, they might not act in the best interests of the corporation as a whole. Therefore, higher-level units must be able to intervene when lower-level units fail to act in the best interests of the whole of which they are part. The only justification for a corporation that consists of units operating as business units is the value that the corporation adds to them. One way it can do so is to require internal purchasers of goods or services that are provided by another internal unit to give the internal supplying unit the opportunity to meet externally quoted prices. However, even if the internal supplier meets or goes under an externally quoted price, the internal buyer can elect to use the external supplier for other than cost reasons, for example, because of the quality of products or services provided.

A corporation with an internal market economy can add value to its units only if it has the ability to intervene effectively in their buying and selling decisions, but it should intervene only when doing so clearly benefits the corporation as a whole. This can be accomplished through interventions of the following type.

Executive Overrides

At times a corporate executive may believe that a purchase made by a subordinate unit from an external source, even at a lower price than an internal supplier would charge, would be harmful to the corporation. In such a case, the executive can require that the purchase be made from the internal supplier, but that executive must pay for the difference between the internal and the external price. This means that the buying unit will *not* have to pay more than it would have had to pay if it had been free to buy from the external source. In addition, since an executive who overrides a subordinate unit will also be a profit center or part of one, he or she will have to consider explicitly the benefits as well as the costs of such interventions.

In one case, an executive vice president consistently required one internal unit to buy a major component of its product line from another internal unit. In many cases the component could have been obtained externally for less money. As a result, at the end of the year the vice president had been charged several million dollars for his overrides. He then reevaluated his policy and decided to free the units to do as they wanted the following year. Not only did each improve its financial performance, but these previously antagonistic units became friendly and cooperative, and the executive stopped feeling like a referee of a prize fight.

When a corporate executive believes that a sale to an external customer that an internal unit wants to make is not in the corporation's best interests, he or she can override that sale, but only by providing the internal unit with the amount of profit it would have made from that sale. This means that a selling unit will never have to sell its output at a price lower than it wants to.

When a manager believes that an external purchase or sale should never be made, he or she can act like a government relative to his or her subordinate units by establishing appropriate restrictive rules or regulations. The federal government of the United States prevents the sale of certain (e.g., military) products to certain foreign countries because it considers such sales to be against our national interests. Corporate managers may act similarly. For example, they may preclude use of an external processor to make a food product sold by the company because the product's formula is considered to be of competitive value. Coca Cola is not about to allow an external supplier to make Coke syrup for it.

The Executive Unit

As noted earlier, the executive unit operates as a profit center. It incurs costs when it overrides purchasing or selling decisions of subordinate internal units. It also incurs other types of cost, for example, for externally provided consulting or staff services, for interest on money it has borrowed, and for taxes and dividends it has to pay.

The executive unit also has two major sources of income. First, it charges for the operating and investment capital it supplies to subordinate units. These units then know what capital they are using and pay for that capital at a cost related to their riskiness and what it costs the corporation to acquire it. (Where a subordinate unit is set up as a wholly owned but separate corporation, it may be given the option of obtaining capital wherever it wants.) The second source of income to the executive unit is a tax it imposes on the profitability of each unit. This tax should cover the operating cost of the executive unit. The tax rate should be established in advance of the period in which it is to be applied and, with the participation of the taxed units. That is, there should be no taxation without representation. (The circular organization facilitates such representation.)

Operating an executive unit as a profit center helps assure that it is efficient and that the tax it levies is kept low.

Profit Accumulation

Each profit center should be permitted to accumulate profit up to a level set for that unit. (This level may vary by unit.) Profit up to the limit should be available to the unit for any use it desires as long as that use does not have an adverse effect on any other part of the corporation or the corporation as a whole. Accumulations of capital in excess of the specified amount should be passed up to the next higher level of the organization for its use or for transmission to a still higher level. A unit that provides its excess profit to a higher-level unit should be paid interest on it by that higher-level unit at a rate that is no less than what the leading unit can obtain outside the corporation.

PUBLIC-SECTOR APPLICATIONS

The use of internal market economies is by no means restricted to private for-profit organizations. It can and has been used effectively in the public sector. For example, a voucher system for supporting public schools was developed by Christopher Jenks of Harvard University and publicized by Milton Friedman.

[The discussion of a voucher system is deleted because a variation of this system was discussed in Chapter 15.]

In another example, a centralized licensing bureau in Mexico City had a terrible record of inefficiency and poor service. It was broken up into small offices in each section of the city. The income of each office was derived exclusively from a fee paid to it by the city government for each license it issued. (The amount varied by type of license.) Those wanting a license could obtain it from any office. Unlike the former centralized bureaucratic monopoly, the new offices could only survive by attracting and satisfying customers. Service time decreased, service quality increased, and overall costs and corruption within the offices decreased.

An internal market economy can be employed by many government service agencies, and to the extent that it is, the public's pressure to privatize these services might significantly decrease.

POSSIBLE OBJECTIONS

Proposals for the introduction of a market economy in an organization usually give rise to four types of concerns.

First, skeptics argue that the additional amount of accounting required by such a system would be horrendous. Not true. The amount of accounting required is actually reduced. Most of the accounting and reporting currently done by organizational units is to facilitate their control by higher level units. In an internal market economy, only profit-and-loss statements and balance sheets need to be provided to higher level units. Any additional information requested by higher level units should be paid for by those units. This requirement has a strong tendency to reduce the amount of unnecessary accounting information flowing within organizations, particularly up.

Second, some argue that an internal market economy will increase conflict and competition between internal units. Again, not true. Most organizational units have much better relations with their external suppliers than they do with internal units (1) whose services or products they are forced to use, or (2) with which they also compete for scarce resources. Internal suppliers who must compete with external suppliers for internal customers' business are much more responsive to these customers than monopolistic internal suppliers.

The corporate computing center of one very large corporation provided services to all units of the corporation without charge. Its costs were covered by corporate headquarters. These funds were extracted from overhead payments made by every corporate unit. The units using the center complained continuously about the poor service it provided and wanted to engage more responsive external services. Units making little or no use of the center resented the overhead assessment that did not take their lack of usage into account. On the other hand, the computing center head complained about the unreasonable requests and expectations of users of his center. These dissatisfactions led to the CEO's request for an evaluation of the center's output to determine whether it was worth its high cost.

Despite heroic efforts to determine that unit's worth, it could not be done. The schedules of production operations, which constituted the major output of the center, were significantly modified by plant managers before they were applied, and no record was kept of these modifications.

Following the suggestion made to him, the CEO converted the computing center into a profit center whose services had to be paid for by using units at a price set by the serving unit. However, users were allowed to use external services, and the center was permitted to sell its services to external customers.

Within a few months, the number of computers in the center was reduced by half. Nevertheless, the center was doing almost all the work required by internal units. Now that they had to pay for it, however, these units significantly reduced the amount of computing they requested. Moreover, they were much more satisfied with the services they received. In addition, the center acquired a number of external customers whom it served very profitably. It obtained a return on the investment higher than that obtained by any other unit in the corporation.

In another case, a diversified food manufacturer had a large market research unit with a monopoly on corporate work. Most of the units that had to use it regarded it poorly because they felt the research unit was unresponsive to their needs and offered inferior service. It too was converted into a profit center with the requirement that it become profitable within two years or else be eliminated. However, it was given freedom to sell its services to whomever it wanted. On the other hand, its internal users were given freedom to obtain their market research wherever they wanted. Every one of them initially moved to external suppliers. As a result, the internal unit was forced to look for external work. It eventually succeeded, but only after significantly improving the quality of its services. In time, it became a thriving business. Internal units became curious about its success and began to try it again. This time they found it responsive to their needs. Internal demand became so great that the unit had to reduce, but not eliminate, its external work. It did not have to sacrifice profitability to do so.

A third argument for rejecting the adoption of an internal market economy is that it cannot be installed in a part of an organization, only in the whole. This, it is asserted, may be very difficult, if not impossible, to arrange. Difficult, yes, but impossible, no. In 1988, the Kodak Apparatus Division—Kodak's manufacturing arm that produces copiers, X-ray equipment, medical devices, cameras (i.e., everything but film)—converted to an internal market economy. Its first problem was that the corporation of which it was a part did not want to convert to an internal market economy. As a result, KAD had to operate as a market-oriented economy within a centrally planned and controlled economy.

Kodak continued to charge KAD for services, and KAD could not break the charges down into those for services it used and those it didn't. Therefore, KAD had to develop surrogate costs. It treated the estimated cost of corporately provided services that it did not use as a tax. Furthermore, it had to continue reporting to the corporation as it had before converting to an internal market economy. Therefore, it had to maintain one set of books for the corporation and another for itself.

One year after its conversion, KAD's effectiveness had increased so much that the corporation began to pay attention to it. The corporation as a whole did not convert to an internal market economy, but KAD's experience led to changes in the corporate bookkeeping system that allowed it to operate more easily with an internal market economy. Other Kodak units have since followed suit.

Like KAD in Kodak, the research and development unit of Esso Petroleum Canada also converted to an internal market economy within a centrally controlled corporate economy, but in this case the containing unit tried to facilitate the conversion. It did so because it considered the conversion to be a trial which, if successful, would lead it to support similar conversions of other of its units, and eventually of the whole.

A fourth reason often given for not taking the idea of an internal market economy seriously is that certain internal service functions cannot "reasonably" be expected to obtain external customers. Accounting and legal departments are often cited as examples. Nevertheless, one corporation headquartered in a small city in the Midwest converted both its accounting and legal departments into profitable business units. Many local small and medium-sized companies lacked access to high quality professional accountants and attorneys and wanted their services badly. This enabled the accounting and legal departments to sell services externally at a very good price. As a consequence, the quality of their services improved significantly to retain external customers. The external contacts also led to the formation of several significant strategic alliances.

Another company that occupied a number of buildings in a suburb of a major metropolitan area converted its facilities-and-services department (buildings, grounds, and utilities) into a profit center that operated within a corporate internal market economy. All of its internal users shifted to outside agencies from which they obtained better services at a lower cost than had been provided by the internal unit. As a result, the service department gradually shrank and was eventually eliminated at a considerable saving to the company.

ADVANTAGES OF AN INTERNAL MARKET ECONOMY

A number of the benefits of an internal market economy have already been identified: in particular, increased responsiveness of internal suppliers, better quality and lower cost of internally supplied services and products, continuous rightsizing, elimination of fluff, debureaucratization, demonopolization, and so on. A few other advantages are worth mentioning.

First, because virtually every corporate unit operating within an internal market economy becomes a profit center, similar measures of performance can be applied to all of them. This makes it possible to compare performances of units that were previously not comparable, for example, manufacturing and accounting.

Second, the manager of a profit center within an internal market economy is necessarily a general manager of a semiautonomous business unit, which provides all unit managers with opportunities to improve and display their general management skills. Therefore, executives are better able to evaluate the general management ability of their subordinates.

Third, when units are converted to profit centers and acquire autonomy, their managers are in a much better position to obtain all the information they require to manage well. They become more concerned with finding the information they need than with providing requested information to their superiors.

CONCLUSIONS

Because conversion to an internal market economy raises a number of problems of adaptation, it is not a task that attracts the fainthearted; it requires considerable courage. Moreover, conversion to an internal market economy is risky for those managers whose units either are unable to compete effectively in the open market or are no longer needed within the corporation. Such units are very likely to be eliminated in an internal market economy. That they should be eliminated offers little solace to those who are affected. The possibility of creating activities that will use excess personnel productively is seldom considered in such circumstances. Nevertheless, the managers who are responsible for the excess are generally retained and moved to another unproductive activity.

A major obstruction to the conversion to an internal market economy is the reluctance of many higher level managers to share with their subordinates information to which they alone have had access. To be sure, information is power, and many managers are not willing to share their power. Unfortunately, they fail to recognize that there are two kinds of power: power-over and power-to. Power-over is authority to command, whereas power-to is the ability to implement. The relationship between these two types of power becomes increasingly negative as the educational level of those managed and the technical content of their jobs increase. Internal market economies may decrease managers' power-over, but they more than make up for this loss by increasing their power-to. This truth is no consolation to those who value power-over for its own sake. Those who want authority for its own sake and ignore its consequences do not fit into a democratic organization.

Installing internal market economies in American corporations can allow them to increase their effectiveness by an order of magnitude. Such restructuring is as important to our country on the microeconomics level as it was to the Soviet Union on the macroeconomics level. Without it, we are destined to experience continued economic stagnation.

CHAPTER 21

DESIGN OF
MANAGEMENT SYSTEMS

A man who excels in drive and leadership but is not skilled in the three intellectual functions of management [policy-making, decision-taking, and control] may be compared to a man on a unicycle—the unicyclist gives a virtuoso display over the short term, but a delivery boy on a tricycle will make steadier progress and carry a more useful load.

Stafford Beer

The product of an idealized design should be an ideal-seeking system. Such a system must be capable of pursuing its ideals with increasing effectiveness under both constant and changing conditions; it must be capable of *learning* and *adapting*.

To adapt is to respond to an internal or external change in such a way as to maintain or improve performance. The change to which adaptation is a response may present either a threat or an opportunity. For example, the appearance of a new competitor may present a threat; the disappearance of an old one, an opportunity. Both require an ability to detect changes that can or do affect performance and to respond to them with corrective or exploitative action. Such action may consist of a change in either the system itself or its environment. For example, if it suddenly turns cold, one can either put on additional clothing (change oneself) or turn up the heat (change the environment). Furthermore, the change to which adaptation is a response may occur either by choice or without it. The demise of a competitor, for example, may occur independently or because of what a corporation does.

From *Creating the Corporate Future* (Wiley, 1981).

The concept of adaptation used here is much richer than the one used in association with the theory of evolution. In that theory, adaptation refers to only involuntary responses to external changes, and the responses consist of internal changes. This restricted connotation of the concept derives from the fact that the theory of evolution is preoccupied with nonpurposeful systems, and when it deals with purposeful systems it is not concerned with their purposefulness. Here we are preoccupied entirely with purposeful systems and their purposefulness.

To learn is to improve performance under unchanging conditions. We learn from our own experience and that of others. Such experience can be controlled, as in experimentation, or uncontrolled, as in trial and error. For example, if we improve our rifle shooting at a target with repeated tries, we learn. If, after we have done so, a wind comes up that makes us miss the target, adaptation is called for. We can adapt either by adjusting the sight on the rifle or by aiming into the wind.

Because learning and adaptation, as I deal with them, are purposeful activities (i.e., matters of choice) they can themselves be learned. Learning how to learn and adapt is sometimes called double-loop learning. If we did not have such a capability, this chapter would have been written in vain because it is intended to facilitate just such learning.

A system cannot learn and adapt unless its management can. Therefore, an ideal-seeking system must have a management system that can learn how to learn and adapt.

ADAPTIVE-LEARNING MANAGEMENT SYSTEMS

Management is the control of a purposeful system by a part of that system. It involves three functions: (1) identification of actual and potential problems—that is, threats and opportunities, (2) decision making—deciding what to do and doing it or having it done, and (3) maintenance and improvement of performance under changing and unchanging conditions. A continual supply of information is required to carry out these functions. Therefore, a management system should consist of three interacting subsystems, one for each function, and a management information (sub)system.

The first design presented here is that of a free-standing management system, one that does not interact with any other such system. (The numbers and letters used in describing this system correspond to those used in the schematic diagram provided in Figure 21.1.) Subsequently, adjustments

Figure 21.1
Diagrammatic Representation of a Management System

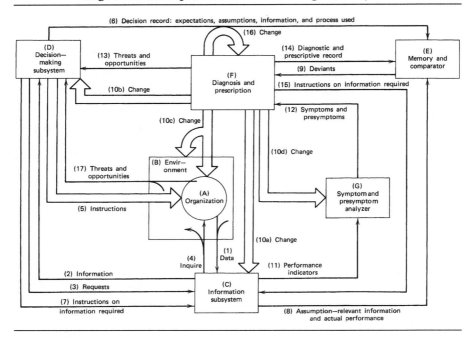

are made to this design to incorporate interactions with other management systems.

The Free-Standing Management System

Management of an organization obviously requires observation of the *organization* managed (A) and its *environment* (B). To observe is to generate *data* (1). Data are symbols that represent properties of objects and events. They are raw material, hence require (data) processing to convert them into *information* (2). Until they are processed they have little or no use in decision making. Information also consists of symbols that represent the properties of objects and events, but these are useful in decision making. Therefore, data processing is a necessary part of the *information subsystem* (C). For example, a great deal of data must be processed to produce the information contained in an annual report.

When those responsible for *decision making* (D) receive information they may find it incomprehensible or unreadable, doubt its validity, or question its completeness. On the other hand, they may accept it but want more. For these or other reasons the receipt of information often leads decision makers to make *requests* (3) for either additional information or reworking of the information already received.

Requests made by decision makers require two additional capabilities of the information subsystem. It should be able to generate new data; hence *inquire* (4) into the organization and its environment so that the necessary data are obtained. It should also be able to reuse data previously obtained. This requires it to store data in a way that makes it possible to retrieve them when desired. A data-storage facility is, of course, a file whether it is in a drawer or a computer. If in a computer, it is called a *data bank*.

Once the old or new data have been processed to produce the information required to fill the requests that initiated the process, it is transmitted to the decision makers. This information–request cycle may be repeated any number of times. Eventually it is stopped because either the decision makers are satisfied or time has run out. Then a decision is made. The output is an *instruction* (5), a message intended to affect the behavior of the managed organization or part of it.

Now consider what is required to monitor and control a decision. Every decision is intended either to make something happen that otherwise would not, or to prevent something from happening that otherwise would. In either case there is an expected outcome and a time by which it is expected. Therefore, control of a decision requires that the expected outcomes and their timing be made explicit. The assumptions on which these expectations are based and the information and decision-making process used in reaching them should also be made explicit. Together these make up the *decision record* (6) which should be stored in an inactive *memory* (E). Human memories are generally much too active for this purpose. They have a way of revising recollections of earlier expectations in light of subsequent experience, as the following case shows.

An industrial equipment manufacturing company initiated a project to determine the level at which its parts inventories should be maintained. In a meeting of the senior managers of the company and the consultant who was to direct the research, the consultant suggested that a little spice be added to the project. What he suggested was that each manager make a guess as to what the effect of the study on the size of the relevant inventories would be, write it on an index card together with his name, place it in an envelope, and seal it. This was done. The envelopes were given to the corporate secretary for storage until the project was over.

After a year, during which the managers played an active role in the study, it was completed. A meeting was called to review the results. After they were presented and discussed, the secretary was called and asked to bring the envelopes down for the "unveiling." He did not appear promptly. Finally, after a few unsuccessful efforts to reach him by phone, he appeared in an apparent state of great distress. He said he could not find the envelopes.

The managers were angry and disappointed, but the consultant said that all was not lost. He suggested that they get a new set of cards and write their original estimates on them. They did so.

The consultant collected the cards and then withdrew the original envelopes from his briefcase. To the embarrassment of the managers he compared the original and the remembered estimates. Their averages differed by a factor of six and, of course, the remembered estimates were much closer to the result obtained.

Without awareness of error, learning is very difficult, if not impossible.

The decision record should be used to *instruct* (7) the information subsystem to provide the information needed to monitor the decision. The *assumptions* on which a decision is based and the *actual performance* of that decision (8) should be checked periodically. The actual and the assumed conditions and the actual and expected outcomes should be compared (E).

When assumed and actual conditions or expected and actual performance agree, nothing need be done. However, *deviations* (9) of actual from assumed conditions and actual from expected performance should be noted and reported. Such deviations indicate that something has either gone wrong or is exceptionally right. To determine what has happened and what should be done about it requires *diagnosis* (F).

The purpose of diagnosis is to find what produced the deviations and to *prescribe* (F) corrective or exploitative action. Although the producers of deviations can be difficult to identify, they are only of four types.

1. *The information used in making the decision was in error.* If this is the case, a *change* in the information subsystem (10a) or the symptom and presymptom analyzer (10d) should be prescribed to prevent repetition of the error. For example, if the data collected on competitive pricing are found to be inaccurate for the purpose for which they are used, a decision may be made to acquire such data in the future from a commercially available service.

2. *The decision-making process may have been faulty.* In such a case, a *change* (10b) in the decision-making subsystem should be made. For example, if a finished-goods inventory is found to exceed expectations but sales are as expected, the decision rules used to set production quantities may require modification.

3. *The decision may not have been implemented as intended.* If this is the case, *changes* (10c) are required. Either the communications from the decision makers to the organization should be improved, or the organization should be changed so that it is more likely to carry out instructions as intended. For example, if it takes much longer than expected to carry out a decision, the implementation procedures or the personnel involved may need to be changed.

4. *The environment may change in a way that was not anticipated.* In such cases a way of better anticipating such changes, decreasing sensitivity to them, or reducing their likelihood of occurrence must be found. Doing so may require any one or a combination of the types of change already mentioned, or a change in the environment itself. For example, if the cost of production exceeds expectations because of an unexpected increase in energy costs, the production process might be redesigned to reduce the amount of energy required or the price at which the product is sold might be increased.

The process initiated by the preparation of a decision record (6) and terminated by a change of the system or its environment (10), is what makes it possible for management to learn and adapt rapidly and effectively.

Now let us consider how threats and opportunities can be identified. First we must identify symptoms and then synthesize them into a diagnosis. We normally use the term symptom to denote an indicator of a threat to the health of an organism or organization. However, it may also refer to an indicator of an opportunity. A symptom is one of a range of values of a variable that usually occurs when something is either exceptionally right or wrong, but seldom occurs when things are normal. An unusually high unit cost of production suggests that something is seriously wrong. An unusually low cost suggests that something is exceptionally right. On the other hand, either a low or a high body temperature suggests that something is wrong. A fever is seldom associated with good health.

The techniques of statistical quality control provide effective ways of defining *normal* and *abnormal* behavior.

Variables used as symptoms are properties of the behavior or performance of organisms and organizations. Such variables can also be used dynamically as *presymptoms* or *omens:* indicators of future threats or opportunities. For example, the range of normal body temperature is about one degree Fahrenheit. Suppose that in five consecutive readings of a person's temperature taken a half hour apart, a normal but rising temperature is observed. This would indicate that unless an intervention occurs the person observed will have a fever in the near future. The same would be true if we observed small but repeated increases in the number of defects coming off a production line.

A presymptom is *nonrandom normal behavior.* Nonrandomness can manifest itself in many different ways, the most familiar being trends or cycles. Such nonrandomness is usually easy to detect by statistical tests or even the naked eye.

A complete management system regularly obtains information on a number of *performance indicators* (11) some of whose values are symptoms. In many organizations that is a function of the controller; in a hospital it is the function of the nurses. Controllers and nurses usually obtain and examine a large number of performance indicators in search of symptoms and presymptoms. Therefore, the information subsystem should be responsible for obtaining and providing such observations. These should be supplied to the *symptom and presymptom analyzer* (G). When *symptoms and presymptoms* (12) are found, they should be sent to the diagnostic function. Once a diagnosis is obtained, the *threats* or *opportunities* detected (13) should be reported to the decision-making subsystem.

A *diagnostic and prescriptive record* (14), much like the decision record, should be issued by the diagnostic and prescriptive subsystem. It should be sent to the memory where its elements can subsequently be compared with the facts that are supplied by the information subsystem in response to *instructions on information required* (15). Deviations should subsequently be reported to the diagnostic and prescriptive subsystem where corrective action should be taken. Such corrective action may involve making any of the changes previously referred to (10a–10d) or changes in its own decision-making process (16). Such changes assure double-loop learning and adaptation—learning how to learn and adapt.

Finally, information on *threats and opportunities* (17) may be sent to the decision-making subsystem from a source within the organization or its environment. For example, such information may come from a superior, a subordinate, a customer, or a supplier.

Note that there are three levels of control in this management system. First, the system as a whole controls the organization of which it is a part. Second, the diagnostic and prescriptive subsystem controls the management system. Third, this subsystem controls itself.

The Computer and Management Systems

Each of the functions that is a part of a management system is subject to computerization, in varying degrees. Much of a management information subsystem can be computerized, but inquiry into other than purely mechanical behavior cannot be carried out by a computer at the present time.

Decision making, for which models and explicit procedures for extracting solutions from them are available, can be computerized. Decisions for which models but no solution-procedures are available can be partially computerized; but decisions for which there are no models cannot be computerized. . . .

The problems for which both models and algorithms are available, or can easily be produced, tend to be ones that are repetitive, routine, and operations-oriented. They are usually ones in which human behavior is not important, and means rather than ends are to be selected. Strategic problems are more difficult to model and solve than tactical or operational. However, the use of models and algorithms on simpler problems frees decision makers so they can spend more time on more important, more complex, and longer-range problems that normally are put aside under the pressure of daily short-run crises.

Models are simplifications of reality; they seldom contain *all* the relevant variables and interactions between them. Therefore, the solutions they yield—however they are obtained—usually require adjustment by decision makers so as to take into account what is missing from the model. For example, in locating a factory or a warehouse there are many relevant variables that do not lend themselves to quantification, such as, the quality and attitudes of the work force available in the area the quality of life the location offers to those moving into it, and accessibility from other locations.

Therefore, even when there are algorithms associated with models, the so-called optimal solutions they yield can seldom be implemented automatically. They usually require review by managers who understand the models and know what important considerations they do not include.

Automation of decision making does not diminish the manager's job; on the contrary, it enlarges it and makes it more difficult. The number of problems confronting him is not reduced because the solutions to most problems create several new and more important ones. If a management system is to learn how to be more effective, then the managers within it must also learn how to cope effectively with problems of increasing complexity.

Now let us return to the other parts of a management system and the extent to which they can be automated.

The memory and comparator and the symptom and presymptom analyzer can be completely computerized, but the diagnostic and prescriptive subsystem can be to only a very limited extent. However, recent developments of diagnostic routines applicable to machines and, to a lesser extent, organisms indicate that development of computerized diagnosis of organizations is not impossible.

There is nothing about a management system that requires any part of it to be computerized. Furthermore, the entire system can reside within one mind, a manager's. At the other end of the spectrum, each function can be performed by different groups or individuals. Where more than one person is involved in such a system (and this is the case in all but very small organizations) they should be managed by the manager whose system it is.

An Example of a Management System

The system described here was developed for a marketing department of a company that produces a high-volume, low-unit cost consumer good. When the system was installed the company had the largest share of its market, about 9 percent. It marketed approximately forty product-package combinations in all of the United States which it divided into 200 market areas. The decision-making component of the management system contained models of each market area. These enabled marketing management, through dialogue with the computer, to set values for variables of five types:

1. Prices.
2. Advertising (levels, media mix, timing, and message).
3. Amount of sales effort.
4. Number and type of sales promotions.

5. Amount and type of point-of-sales materials to be distributed to retailers.

Values of these variables were set monthly by management with the intention of maximizing market share in each area. Its expectations were determined with the help of the computerized models and were fed into the memory and comparator which already had relevant aspects of the decision-making procedure stored in it.

In its first month of operation this system generated forty-two deviants which were sent to the diagnostic and prescriptive team. This team consisted of operations and marketing researchers who had participated in the design of the system. The average error of the expectations was large.

The deviants required varying amounts of time to diagnose. Some took several months. Where appropriate, corrective action was taken. The number of deviants decreased from month to month. By the twelfth month there were only six deviants and the average error had been decreased to one-quarter of what it had been in the first month. By the eighteenth month the system stabilized at an average of two deviants per month and an average error of less than one-sixteenth of what it had been in the first month.

Armed with this system, marketing management more than doubled the company's market share within a decade.

Shortly after this marketing-management system was installed a similar system was requested by production management. One was developed and it eventually reduced operating costs by about $35 million per year. Yet the system had cost only about $300,000 to design and install.

Now consider how a number of such systems can be designed to interact in a corporate environment.

The Embedded Management System

Every corporation has a hierarchical network of management units. If some or all of these units have the type of system I have described, these systems require coordination and integration in order to serve the corporation effectively as a whole. Such coordination and integration can be obtained by use of decision-allocation boards. . . . If the chief planner in each unit is also made responsible for diagnosis and prescription, one board can serve both purposes.

Each unit except those at the lowest level has a decision-allocation board. These boards consist of (1) the person or persons responsible for diagnosis and prescription in that unit, (2) the corresponding person(s) from the level immediately above, and (3) those with the same functions from the units immediately below. Therefore each board except the one at the top has three levels represented on it. The one at the top has only two.

Referring again to Figure 21.1, members of each board receive copies of those reports of threats and opportunities (13) from the management system at the next level below. These derive from changes that have occurred or are anticipated outside the system in which the reports are prepared. The members also receive the reports of deviants (9) and symptoms and presymptoms (12) on which identification of these threats and opportunities is based. This means that copies of these reports are received by those responsible for decision making and diagnosis in each unit at the same level of the unit in which the report was prepared, and by the corresponding persons at the next two higher levels.

Each board has responsibility for determining where and how problems thus identified should be handled. They may be assigned to a higher-level unit, to a combination of lower-level units, or to one of them, including the originating unit. Such a procedure reduces the likelihood of trying to solve problems only where their symptoms appear.

Solutions to problems afflicting units at levels other than the one at which the problem appears can be discussed in these boards. Doing so assures awareness in the solving unit of the effects its solutions have on units at levels immediately above and below it, and it alerts these levels to the impending decision and its possible effects. This makes anticipatory adaptation possible.

One other aspect of creating a system of management systems merits attention. Economies of scale can often be obtained; one individual or group can often perform the same function for a number of different management systems. Each of the functions shown in Figure 21.1, except that of decision making, is subject to partial or complete consolidation across units.

The management system described here was designed to provide management with an ability to learn how to learn and adapt. The design is schematic and general; hence it permits many variations. Some such design should be incorporated into the idealized design of every system. No organization can effectively pursue the future it desires if its management is not capable of continually improving its performance in turbulent as well as stable environments.

THE INFORMATION SUBSYSTEM

The preoccupation of managers and information scientists with management information systems (MISs) is apparent. In fact, more than a few consider such systems to be a panacea for every type of management problem. Enthusiasm for such systems is understandable. They involve managers and information-system designers in a romantic relationship with the most glamorous instrument of our time, the computer. Although such enthusiasm is understandable, some of the excesses to which it has led are not.

Contrary to the impression produced by a large volume of propaganda about MISs, relatively few have met the expectations of the managers who authorized or use them. Many of the near and far misses could have been avoided if some commonly made, false, and usually implicit assumptions underlying their design had been avoided. There seem to be five such assumptions.

Managers Critically Need More Relevant Information

Most MISs are designed on the assumption that one of the most critical handicaps under which managers operate is the *lack of relevant information*. It is obvious that managers lack relevant information. It is not so obvious that if they had it they would perform better or that they need it critically. My experience suggests that many would not perform better because they suffer from an *overabundance of irrelevant information*. This requires explanation.

First note that the consequences of changing the emphasis of management information systems from increasing relevant information to decreasing irrelevant information are considerable. If one is preoccupied with supplying relevant information, as is usually the case, attention is given almost exclusively to the generation, storage, retrieval, and processing of data. The ideal that has emerged from this orientation is that of an infinite pool of data into which a manager may dip and pull out whatever information he wants. The fact is that he is more likely to drown in such a pool than be saved by it.

If, on the other hand, one sees a manager's information problem primarily, but not exclusively, as one arising out of an overabundance of irrelevant information, then the two most important functions of an MIS become *filtration* and *condensation* of information. The MIS literature seldom refers to these functions, or how to carry them out.

Most managers receive more data and information than they can possibly absorb even if they spend all their time trying to do so. They already suffer from an information overload. This makes it necessary for them to separate the relevant from the irrelevant and to search for the kernels in the relevant documents. I receive an average of more than sixty hours of reading material each week, and most managers I know receive at least as much. Of this amount more than half is unsolicited. Despite this very few MISs make any provision for the treatment of such documents.

I have seen a daily stock-status report of approximately 600 pages of computer printout circulated daily to a number of managers. I have also seen book-size requests for major capital expenditures accumulate on managers' desks. Most managers additionally receive at least one journal and two newspapers per day.

Most of us who have suffered from an information overload are aware of the fact that when the amount of information exceeds a certain amount, a supersaturation point, both the amount and percentage of it that we try to absorb decreases. We give up hope of being able to keep up and abandon our efforts to do so. The more we get beyond this point the less we use. Richard L. Meier has shown that social institutions behave in the same way.

Unless the information overload to which managers are subjected is reduced, any additional information made available by an MIS cannot be expected to be used effectively. The need for filtration should be obvious, but it is almost universally ignored in MIS design. Nevertheless, there are profile-based computerized filtration procedures available and in use. For a detailed description of each system see Ackoff, Cowan, et al.

Even relevant documents are usually too long. Most of them can be considerably reduced without loss of content. This is illustrated by a small experiment that a few of my colleagues and I conducted on the operations research literature a number of years ago. By using a panel of well-known experts we identified four recently published articles that every member of the panel independently evaluated as above average, and four articles that every member took to be below average. The authors of the eight articles thus selected were asked (without being informed at the evaluation of their work) to prepare objective examinations of thirty minutes' duration and to provide answers to their questions. The authors were told that graduate students would be given their papers to read and we wanted to test their ability to understand what the authors intended. The examinations were prepared. Then several professional science writers were asked to reduce each article to two-thirds and then one-third of its original length only by eliminating parts of it. They also prepared a brief abstract of each article. These writers were not shown the examinations prepared by the authors.

A group of graduate students who had not previously read the articles were then selected. Each one was given a random selection of four articles, one in its original length, one reduced by one-third, one reduced by two-thirds, and one in abstract form. Each version of the article was read by two students. All were given the same examinations. The average scores on the examinations were then compared.

For the above-average articles there was no significant difference between average test scores for the 100, 67, and 33 percent versions, but there was a significant decrease in the average test scores of those who had read only the abstract. This result suggests that even well-written material can be reduced by at least two-thirds without significant loss of content.

For the below-average articles there was also no significant difference between average test scores among those who had read the 100, 67, and 33 percent versions, but there was a significant *increase* in the average test scores of those who had read only the abstract. This suggested that the optimal length of inferior material is zero.

It seems clear, then, that filtration to select relevant information and condensation of what is selected should be an essential part of an MIS, and that such a system should be capable of handling unsolicited as well as solicited information.

Managers Need the Information They Want

Most designers of MISs determine what information managers need by asking them what they want. Doing so is based on the assumption that managers know what information they need.

For managers to know what information they need (1) they must be aware of each type of decision they should make and (2) they must have an adequate model of each. The second condition, if not the first, is seldom satisfied. The genius of a good manager lies in his ability to manage effectively a system that he does not understand completely. A system that is completely understood does not require the skills of a manager, those of a scientist who understands it or of a clerk who has been programmed by the scientist are sufficient.

It has long been known in science that the less we understand something, the more variables we require to explain it. Therefore, the manager who is asked what information he needs to control something he does not fully understand usually plays it safe and says he wants as much information as he can get. The MIS designer, who understands the system involved even less than the manager does, adds another safety factor and tries to provide everything. The result is an overload of information, most of which is irrelevant. The greater this overload, the less likely a manager is to extract and use whatever relevant information it contains.

The moral is simple: one cannot specify what information is needed for decision making until a valid explanatory model of the decision process and the behavior of the system involved has been constructed. Information systems are subsystems of management systems and, therefore, cannot be adequately designed without understanding the nature of the system managed and the management of it. Such understanding is not likely to be found in those who normally design MISs.

If Managers Are Given the Information They Need, Their Decision Making Will Improve

Even if we grant that managers may not know what information they need surely they would do better if they had the information than they would without it. The following example shows that this assumption is not necessarily true. It involves about as simple a production problem as one can imagine. There are ten products to be made, each requiring time on two machines. M_1 and M_2. Each product must first go to M_1 and then to M_2. The problem consists of finding the order in which to produce the ten items so that the least possible time is required to complete them. Simple enough. All the information required to solve this problem is given in Table 21.1.

Despite the facts that this problem is much simpler than most real production-management problems and all the data needed to solve it are provided, very few managers can solve it. They cannot do it by trying the alternatives because there are more than 3.5 million of them. Yet the problem can be solved in less than a minute *if one knows how.*

Table 21.1
A Production-Sequencing Problem

Product Number	Time Required on Machine M_1	Time Required on Machine M_2
1	7	18
2	3	13
3	12	9
4	14	5
5	20	8
6	4	16
7	2	20
8	9	15
9	19	1
10	6	13

Take the product with the lowest entry in Table 21.1, number 9. Since the entry, 1, appears in the right-hand column, place product 9 last in the sequence and cross out line 9 in the table. Take the product with the lowest remaining entry, number 7, and entry 2. Since 2 appears in the left-hand column, place this product first in the sequence and cross out line 7. Take the product with the lowest remaining entry, number 2, with entry 3. Since this entry appears in the left-hand column, place this product second in the sequence and cross out line 2. Continue to come in from the left for left-hand column entries and from the right for right-hand column entries until all the products have been placed in order. In case of a tie, either may be selected.

The point of this example is that if we know how to use the information needed to solve a problem, we can either program a computer or instruct a clerk how to solve it. We need not waste a manager's time. If we do not know how to solve a problem there is no assurance that having the information required to solve it will help.

In most management problems there are too many possible solutions to expect judgment or intuition to select the best one even if provided with perfect information. Furthermore, when probabilities are involved, as they usually are, the unguided mind has difficulty in aggregating them in a valid way. There are many simple problems involving probabilities in which untutored intuition usually does very badly; for example, what are the correct odds that at least two out of twenty-five people selected at random will have their birthdays on the same day of the year? They are better than even.

The moral: if managers do not know how to use the information they need, then giving it to them will only increase their information overload. If they know how to use it they can instruct someone else to use it for them. This does not mean that managers who do not know how to use the information needed to solve a problem do not need any information. What information managers need to deal with problems is whatever information enables them to do better with it than without it. To identify such information, experimentation may be required. Therefore, in order to obtain an information system that is capable of improvement it must be embedded in a management system that can enable a manager to *learn* what he needs. Without such learning he is bound to ask for and receive more information than he needs.

More Communication Means Better Performance

One characteristic of most MISs is that they provide managers with more information about what other managers and their units are doing. Better flow of information between parts of an organization is generally thought to be desirable because, it is argued, it enables managers to coordinate their activities better and thus improve overall performance. Not only is this not necessarily so, but it seldom is. One hardly expects two competing companies to become more cooperative if each is provided with more and better information about the other. This analogy is not as far-fetched as one might suppose. Competition between parts of a corporation is often more intense than between corporations and, as has been observed, less ethical. A possible consequence of providing corporate parts with more information about each other is revealed by the following example, which is a simplification of a real case, involving a department store and its two principal functions, buying and selling. Buying and selling are handled by the purchasing and merchandising departments respectively. The purchasing department controls the quantity of each item purchased but little else, because competitive conditions largely control selection of brands. It usually buys in quantities that yield maximum quantity discounts, hence has little control over purchase price. This department was given the objective of minimizing the average value of inventory while meeting expected demand.

The merchandising department's main controllable variable was the selling price. This price, of course, affected the amount sold. The department's objective was to maximize gross profit. The manager of this department was assisted by a statistical staff that recorded previous prices and associated amounts sold. From this data the staff put together a price-demand curve for each class of products. The staff provided estimates of the expected (average) demand supplemented by optimistic and pessimistic estimates (Figure 21.2).

In planning ahead the merchandising manager had to select a price at which to sell a product. Call this P_1. He then used the price-demand curve to estimate how much of the product he would need. Naturally, he used the optimistic estimate (Q_1) because he wanted to guard against running out. If he were short his performance would suffer.

Once the merchandising manager had determined this quantity he notified the purchasing manager. The purchasing manager, who had previously worked in the merchandising department, also had access to the price-demand curves. Knowing the merchandising manager's practices, he read over from the quantity Q_1 (in Figure 21.2) and down to the *average* demand curve. His measure of performance required that he stock no more than the quantity Q_2. He so informed the merchandising

Figure 21.2
Price-Demand Curve

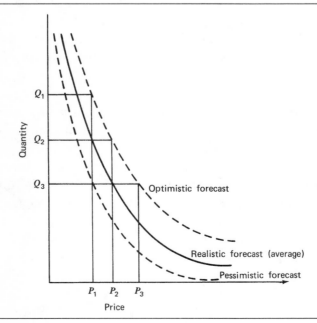

manager who promptly adjusted his price so as to maximize gross sales, given that only Q_2 would be available. He reset the price at P_2. The purchasing manager got word of this and adjusted the order quantity to Q_3. As can easily be seen, if this process were to have continued nothing would have been bought, hence nothing sold. Such a state was not reached because the executive office intervened and prohibited communication between the two managers. This did not remove the cause of the problem, faulty measures of performance, but it did alleviate the consequences.

When organizational units have inappropriate measures of performance that put them in conflict with each other (and this is commonplace), communication between them may hurt overall performance, not help it.

The moral: organizational structure and performance measures should be put right before opening the flood gates and permitting free flow of information between parts of an organization.

A Manager Does Not Have to Know How an Information System Works, Only How to Use It

Most designers of MISs try to make their systems innocuous and unobstructive to managers to avoid frightening them. The designers try to provide managers with easy access to the system and to assure them they need know nothing more about the system than how to use it. The designers usually succeed in keeping managers from knowing any more about the system than this. This leaves managers incapable of evaluating the system as a whole. It often makes them afraid of trying to do so because they do not want to display ignorance. In failing to evaluate their MISs managers delegate much of their control of the organization to the system's designers who, whatever else they are, are seldom competent managers. Let me cite a case in point.

The chief executive of an equipment manufacturing company asked for help with the following problem. One of his larger divisions had installed a computerized production-inventory control system about a year earlier. About $2 million worth of computing equipment had been purchased for the system. The executive had just received a request from the division for permission to replace the original equipment with new equipment that was considerably more costly (and advanced). The division had provided an extensive justification for the request. The executive wanted to know whether the request was really justified. He said that he did not know enough about the system and the relevant equipment to make such an evaluation himself.

A meeting was arranged at the division's headquarters during which I was given an extended and detailed briefing. The system was large but relatively simple. At the heart of it was a computer program for determining a reorder point for each item and its maximum allowable stock level. The computer kept track of stock, ordered items when required, and generated numerous reports on the status of the inventory.

When the briefing was over I was asked if I had any questions. I did. I asked whether, when the system had been installed, there had been many parts whose stock level exceeded the maximum allowable under the new system. I was told there had been many. I asked for a list of about thirty of them and for some graph paper. With the help of the system coordinator and many old reports I began to plot the stock level of the first item on the list over time. When this item came down to the maximum allowable stock level for the first time, much to the surprise of those in attendance, it had been reordered. Continued plotting showed that the item had been reordered every time it approached this maximum level. Clearly, the computer program was confusing the maximum allowable stock level and the reorder point. This turned out to be the case for more than half the items on the list.

Next I asked if they had many paired parts, ones that were used only with each other but were separately numbered; for example, matched nuts and bolts. They had many. A list was produced and I began to check the withdrawals from stock reported for the previous day. For many of the pairs the differences in the numbers recorded were very large. No explanation could be provided.

The system was clearly out of control. To determine this I had asked only simple and obvious questions, ones managers would have asked of a hand-operated system. However, they were ashamed to ask the same questions of a computerized system.

The moral: no MIS should ever be installed unless the managers it serves understand it well enough to evaluate its performance. Managers should control this MISs, not be controlled by them.

ON THE APPROPRIATE DESIGN OF AN MIS

Most of the deficiencies in MISs that I have cited can be avoided if such systems are designed as integral parts of management systems. Unfortunately, this is seldom done. The difference between how MISs are commonly designed and how they should be is illustrated in Table 21.2.

MISs are usually designed as independent systems that are intended to serve all managers (the bottom row of Table 21.2). It is better to design a complete management system for a part of management (the first column). Such a system can be extended relatively easily by adding similar systems for other parts of management. Because of overlapping requirements among such systems, each successive system (column) tends to be easier to design and can share parts of the earlier ones. Furthermore, the ultimate outcome is a comprehensive and completely integrated management system.

When an MIS is designed as an independent system much of its content is irrelevant to the needs of the other subsystems, which are seldom analyzed for their informational requirements. Once an independently designed MIS is installed it often generates so many problems requiring attention from its designers that they never get a chance to get to the other subsystems of management. Most MIS specialists are disinclined under even the best of conditions to deal with other subsystems. They need little excuse to ignore the need for them.

Table 21.2
Alternative Approaches to the Design of Management Systems

Subsystems of a Management System	Organizational Units			
	O_1	O_2	$\cdots$	O_n
1. Problem formulation and identification				
2. Decision making		Way it should be done		
3. Control				
4. Management information system		Way it is usually done		

If and when MIS designers do turn to other subsystems their designs of them are forced to accommodate to the completed MIS. It should be the other way around, the MIS's function should be to serve them. Therefore, if subsystems (rows in Table 21.2) are to be designed in sequence—and it is preferable that they not be—the MIS should come last, not first. In my experience the simplest, most rewarding, and subsequently least restrictive subsystem to develop first is the control subsystem.

Independently designed MISs are seldom endowed with a capability of learning and adapting. They tend to be devoid of either internal or external controls; hence they are not responsive to either their own experience or that of management. Over time they are more likely to deteriorate than improve. This can be avoided by designing an MIS as an integral part of a management system.

BIBLIOGRAPHY

Ackoff, R. L., T. A. Cowan, Peter Davis, et al., *The SCATT Report: Designing a National Scientific and Technological Communication System,* Philadelphia: University of Pennsylvania Press, 1976.

PART IV

SCIENCE

The four selections in this part are intended to provide management and students of management with some of what they should know and understand about science: what it can and can't do; and the difference between scientific methodology and scientific "*myth*ology." The last selection in this section describes how Operations Research, an effort to put science directly to useful and important work, once the recipient of great expectations, devolved in a disappointing way.

It is particularly important for managers to understand that correlation and regression analyses *cannot* establish causal relationships—only experiments can do that.

The invasion of management by pseudoscientific studies using correlation or regression analyses creates a continuous source of misdirection. When someone groups companies into successful and unsuccessful categories, and then finds characteristics that distinguish between them, they cannot, but do, claim to have established a causal connection between the characteristics and success. Even if their claims for such a connection are correct, their method of establishing it is most certainly not.

Ever since Tom Peters published *In Search of Excellence,* a flood of studies has appeared that claim to reveal the secrets to corporate success and longevity. Hopefully these four selections will lead those who read it to take these pompous proclamations with a grain of salt.

CHAPTER 22

THE NATURE OF SCIENCE AND METHODOLOGY

THE MEANING OF "SCIENCE"

Since this is a book about science, we should begin by seeking some common agreement as to what science is. The extensive literature addressed to the definition or characterization of science is filled with inconsistent points of view and demonstrates that an adequate definition is not easy to attain. Part of the difficulty arises from the fact that the meaning of science is not fixed, but is dynamic. As science has evolved, so has its meaning. It takes on new meaning and significance with successive ages. This evolution is not to be stopped by the act of defining. Although we cannot expect to attain an ultimate definition of science, it is desirable to reach some common understanding of the concept in order to proceed. For our purposes it is only necessary to agree on a few of its essential characteristics.

First, we shall consider science as a process of inquiry; that is, as a procedure for (a) answering questions, (b) solving problems, and (c) developing more effective procedures for answering questions and solving problems. We will consider the distinction between questions and problems later.

Science is also frequently taken to be a body of knowledge. We shall concentrate, however, on the process which generates this knowledge rather than on the knowledge itself.

Not all inquiry is scientific. There is a large class of nonscientific inquiry, including what we call "common-sense" inquiry. The difference between these types of inquiry is important. This difference must lie either in subject matter or in method, or both. It has been proposed in the past that common-sense (and other kinds of nonscientific) inquiry is

From *Scientific Method: Optimizing Applied Research Decisions,* in collaboration with J. S. Minas and S. K. Gupta (Wiley, 1962).

concerned with more immediate and practical problems than is science. It has become increasingly clear, however, that science, particularly "applied science," does deal with immediate and pressing problems. On the other hand, philosophic inquiry, for example, is frequently directed toward problems which are neither immediate nor pressing.

Some have argued that common-sense inquiry is qualitatively oriented, whereas scientific inquiry is quantitatively oriented. For example, John Dewey (1938, p. 65) observed:

> The problem of the relation of the domain of common sense to that of science has notoriously taken the form of opposition of the qualitative to the non-qualitative; largely, but not exclusively, the quantitative.

That this distinction breaks down is clear from Herbert Dingle's (1953) observation that the outstanding scientific achievement of the nineteenth century was the theory of evolution. This theory, he notes (p. 6), "has nothing whatever to do with measurement. It is concerned with qualitative changes, and treats them qualitatively." Even if one disagrees with Dingle's characterization of the theory of evolution, the point is not removed: an eminent historian of science is willing to include in science a theory that he considers to be completely qualitative. Furthermore, there are obvious instances of common-sense inquiry which are quantitatively oriented. For example, a motorist who, with the aid of road maps, seeks the shortest route between two cities is engaged in a quantitative common-sense inquiry.

It seems clear that there is a considerable overlap in the questions and problems investigated scientifically and nonscientifically. It is also clear, however, that at the present time there are a considerable number of questions and problems (e.g., ones involving ethics) which cannot be fruitfully investigated by science. This has led some to assert that at least some questions and problems are, by their very nature, incapable of being answered or solved scientifically. Consequently, such expressions as "the limitations of science" are quite common in discussions of science. But as yet the limits of science have not been adequately defined, for there is hardly a type of question or problem to which science successfully addresses itself today that, at some time in the past, someone did not claim was not susceptible to scientific inquiry. We need not concern ourselves with whether or not such a limit exists, since it is clear that, until it is well defined and generally accepted, it cannot be used to distinguish between scientific and nonscientific inquiry.

It is generally recognized that through the use of science (as contrasted with common sense) we are more likely to obtain the correct answers to questions and better solutions to problems. This is to assert *not* that better results are always obtained by science, but that such results are *more likely* to be obtained by its use. This follows from the superiority of the scientific process of inquiry. This superiority of scientific inquiry derives from the fact that it is *controlled*. *A process is controlled to the extent that it is efficiently directed toward the attainment of desired objectives.* Thomas Huxley [in Wiener (1953, p. 130)] made essentially the same observation when he wrote:

> Science is, I believe, nothing but trained and organized common sense, differing from the latter only as a veteran may differ from a raw recruit: and its methods differ from those of common sense only so far as the guardsman's cut and thrust differ from the manner in which a savage wields his club.

Control of research is exercised in various degrees. Perfect control is an ideal which is approximated more and more closely with the advance of science, but it is never attained. Every inquiry has some controlled and some uncontrolled aspects. Consequently, there are many gradations of inquiry rather than the simple dichotomy: scientific and nonscientific.

It should be noted that, even where scientific inquiry can do a "better" job than common-sense inquiry, it is not always to be preferred. If the cost of the inquiry and the value of the outcome are taken into account, there are many situations in which scientific inquiry is not justified. Also there are many situations where an answer or solution is needed very quickly (e.g., in emergencies). Here, less than the best answer, but an adequate one obtained "in time," is to be preferred to one that is better but late. Most of the prosaic decisions that each of us makes daily about such things as the way to get to work, where to eat, and what clothes to wear do not presently justify scientific inquiry. Science not only reaps the benefits of self-consciousness and control, but must also pay the associated cost. It should be realized, however, that much of the common knowledge and common sense that provide the basis on which today's prosaic decisions are based is itself based on the products of yesterday's science.

Control, though necessary, is not sufficient to distinguish between scientific and nonscientific inquiry. Science is also characterized by the goals of self-perpetuation and self-improvement. It is an on-going institution which pursues an ideal: to increase without limit our knowledge and our ability to answer questions and solve problems. This imposes the requirement on scientific research that it be conducted in such a way as to increase the efficiency of future research. That is, research must be designed to inform and instruct us on how to improve the conduct of research itself. It is for this reason that many reports on scientific research include discussion of how the research ought to have been done in light of the experience gained in having done it the first time. In science, then, every research effort not only has the purpose of answering a question or solving a problem, but also has the aim of testing, evaluating, and improving the research procedures employed.

EXPERIMENTATION AND RESEARCH

Experimentation is sometimes taken to be identical with scientific research. Not all scientific research, however, involves experimentation. Experimentation, as conceived in the nineteenth century, involved the physical manipulation of objects, events, and their properties. Physical manipulation was taken to be identical with control. This is reflected in the writings of F. H. Giddings (1924, p. 55):

> In scientific experimentation we control everything that happens. We determine when it shall occur and where. We arrange circumstances and surroundings, atmospheres and temperatures; possible ways of getting in and possible ways of getting out. We take out somthing that has been in, or put in something that has been out, and see what happens.

But our enthusiasm for experimentation may blind us to the fact that controlled inquiry can be conducted without physical manipulation. For example, consider astronomy. Although the situation may change in the future, up to now the astronomer has not been able to manipulate physically the objects of his study. Control can also be obtained by the conceptual manipulation of symbolic representations (models) of the phenomena under study.

Though control is not synonymous with physical manipulation, some scientists consider it useful to distinguish between inquiries in which control is obtained in this way (as in a laboratory) and those in which it is not (as in a field survey). They tend to restrict the use of the term *experimentation* to research involving physical manipulation and to employ the term *research* to cover experimentation and any other type of controlled inquiry.

With the development in recent years of the techniques of *designed experimentation* (to be discussed in Chapter 10) it has become clear that physical manipulation is not as necessary for experimentation as it was once thought to be; it can be replaced effectively by techniques of classification and randomization. Nevertheless, some physical manipulation does seem to be involved in most experimentation. It is less likely to be so involved in the future.

SCIENTIFIC TOOLS, TECHNIQUES, AND METHODS

Scientific progress has been two dimensional. First, the range of questions and problems to which science has been applied has been continuously extended. Second, science has continuously increased the efficiency with which inquiry can be conducted. The products of scientific inquiry then are (1) a body of information and knowledge which enables us better to control the environment in which we live, and (2) a body of procedures which enables us better to add to this body of information and knowledge.

Science both informs and instructs. The body of information generated by science and the knowledge of how to use it are two products of science. As already indicated, we will not be concerned here with the body of information and knowledge which it has generated; that is, not with the specific theories, laws, and facts that have been developed in the various physical, life, and behavioral sciences. Instead we will be concerned with the procedures by which science generates this body of knowledge, the process of inquiry.

The procedures which characterize science are generally referred to as *tools, techniques,* and *methods.* The common inclination to use these three terms interchangeably conceals some distinctions which are important to understand in discussing scientific procedures.

By a scientific *tool* we mean a physical or conceptual *instrument* that is used in scientific inquiry. Examples of such tools are mathematical symbols, electronic computers, microscopes, tables of logarithms and random numbers, thermometers, and cyclotrons.

By a scientific *technique* we refer to a way of accomplishing a scientific objective, a scientific *course of action.* Techniques, therefore, are ways of using scientific tools. For example, the various sampling procedures . . . are scientific techniques which employ a table of random numbers, a scientific tool. The use of the calculus and graphic analysis are different techniques for finding the minimum or maximum value of a function.

By a scientific *method* we refer to the way techniques are selected in science; that is, to the evaluation of alternative courses of scientific action. Thus, whereas the techniques used by a scientist are results of his *decisions,* the way these decisions are made is the result of his *decision rules.* Methods are rules of choice; techniques are the choices themselves. For example, a procedure for selecting the best of a set of possible sampling designs is a scientific method; and the selection of the most suitable of a set of alternative ways of measuring a property, such as length, hardness, intelligence, or cooperation, involves the use of a method.

The study of scientific methods is frequently referred to as *methodology.* The objective of methodology is the improvement of the procedures and criteria employed in the conduct of scientific research. For this reason, methodology is often referred to as the logic of *science.*

The discussion of methodology is designed to establish the highest possible standards of control in scientific research. It is as important to have methodological standards in science as it is to have standards of measurement. These not only set goals to be sought in scientific performance, but they also provide a basis for adjusting results obtained under less than the best possible conditions. In the measurement of length, for example, no scientist can ever meet all the environmental, instrumental, and operational specifications of the standard of measurement which has been established. But if a scientist knows how the actual environment, instruments, and operations differ from the ideal ones, then—if equipped with adequate theory—he can adjust his results for these deviations. For example, if he cannot measure the length of a metal bar at the specified standard temperature, he can adjust for the effect of temperature by use of the linear coefficient of expansion of that metal. The existence of a standard informs the scientist as to what kind of knowledge is necessary in order to make such adjustments (e.g., the coefficient of expansion). The ability to adjust data to standard conditions makes possible the comparison of results of research conducted under different conditions and the efficient accumulation of the results of scientific research.

As indicated, the role of a methodological standard in science is much like that of a standard of measurement. It performs the following functions:

(1) It provides a basis for determining the extent to which any research is controlled and, hence, scientific. In this way it provides a procedural goal for scientists. The standard at any moment of time represents the best we know at *that* time, not for all time. Standards are themselves subject to continuous modification by what we learn in trying to use them. By making explicit our conception of the best research procedure we facilitate future improvements in both the standard and our efforts to approximate it.

(2) Together with the appropriate theory it provides a basis for adjusting results obtained by use of less than the best known techniques so as better to approximate results that would have been obtained by use of the best known techniques.

(3) It makes explicit the kind of knowledge required to effectively adjust to the standard.

PURE AND APPLIED SCIENCE

The distinction between pure and applied science plays a central role in most contemporary discussions of science. It is generally acknowledged that the distinction is difficult—if not impossible—to make precise. Such a state of affairs is generally a sign that we are trying to treat qualitatively a distinction that is fundamentally quantitative. In other words, it is likely that purse science and applied science represent ranges on a scale and that a point of separation is difficult to specify. What is the nature of this underlying scale?

Pure research is frequently characterized as that which is conducted "for its own sake." For example, according to Norman Campbell (1952, p. 1):

> First, science is a body of useful and practical knowledge and a method of obtaining it. It is science of this form which played so large a part in the destruction of war, and, it is claimed, should play an equally large part in the beneficient restoration of peace. . . . In its second form or aspect, science has nothing to do with practical life, and cannot affect it, except in the most indirect manner, for good or for ill. Science of this form is a pure intellectual study . . . its aim is to satisfy the needs of the mind and not those of the body; it appeals to nothing but the disinterested curiosity of mankind.

It should be observed that the results of pure research are published in one form or another, and hence such research is conducted at least for the sake of those to whom the results are disseminated. "For its own sake," then, means "for science's sake." That is, the research is not expected to yield results which are immediately useful outside the domain of science, but they are intended to be useful within this domain. Hence, an operationally meaningful distinction between pure and applied research depends on the nature of the intended consumers of the research results. Therefore, pure research is research which does not consider uses of its results outside the domain of science. It is relatively rare, however, that the results of "pure" research do not eventually become useful outside the domain of science. Whether or not they are applied depends on others.

If one bases the distinction between pure and applied research on the researcher's intention, we are left with the possibility of two research projects which are alike in all respects except for the intentions of the researchers involved, one pure and one applied. That is, the distinction is based not on a difference in the kind of research conducted, but on a property of the researcher. Furthermore, since the researcher's interest in application of his results outside the domain of science may vary in intensity and degree, this distinction seems ultimately to be quantitative rather than qualitative. This would explain in part the fuzziness of the distinction.

Much of what is thought to be pure research at one time eventually is applied to practical problems outside the domain of science. On the other hand, it is clear that many of the questions to which pure science has addressed itself have been generated out of difficulties encountered in applied research. For example, in trying to estimate the future demand for a specified commodity it becomes apparent that the cost of an error of any given magnitude depends on the sign (positive or negative) of the error. Commonly used estimating procedures assume that such cost of error is independent of whether the error is the result of overestimation or underestimation. Therefore, an inquiry may be started to develop an estimating procedure which can be used effectively where the cost of error depends on both the magnitude and the sign (i.e., direction) of the error. Although the original inquiry may have been "applied," the search for better estimating procedures would normally be thought of as "pure" research.

A related way of distinguishing between pure and applied research lies in the distinction between trying "to answer a question" and "to solve a problem." This distinction will receive further attention in Chapter 2. For the present it is enough to observe that an individual has a problem if he wants something he does not have, has unequally effective alternative ways of trying to get it, and is in doubt as to which alternative is "best." Therefore, in attempting to solve a problem we may engage in research to attain information and instruction in order to decide how best to pursue the objective(s) that define the problem. Put another way, in solving problems we may try to answer questions for the sake of better pursuing a specified set of objectives. If, on the other hand, our concern with a question does not involve use of its answer in pursuit of any specific objective, then we do not have a problem.

When questions, in the sense in which we have just discussed them, are answered by scientific methods, this activity would, then, normally be thought of as pure research. When problems are solved by scientific research, if any of the objectives involved are nonscientific in character, the research is thought of as applied. This does not mean that all problems fall into the domain of applied research. Methodological problems, for example, belong in the domain of pure science, since the objectives involved are scientific in character.

Having tried to make the distinction between pure and applied research meaningful, it should again be observed that to maintain it is very difficult. This is not as serious as it was once thought to be. To a large extent the distinction was made in order to provide status to scientists who considered themselves "pure" at a time when it was thought that pure scientific problems required a greater knowledge and ability for their solution than did applied problems. This type of scientific snobbery has diminished with the growth of the realization that difficulty in science is not related to applicability of results.

QUALITY AND QUANTITY

It is important to observe that qualitative predication may involve quantification. For example, in order to determine the color of an object it may be necessary to measure the wave length of light reflected from it under certain specified conditions.

Any property which can be quantified can also be treated qualitatively. A quality can be thought of as a range along a scale in terms of which the property can be measured. For example, a person can be said to be "tall" if he is over 5 feet 10 inches, "medium" if he is between 5 feet 6 inches and 5 feet 10 inches, and "short" if he is under 5 feet 6 inches.

It is also true that any qualified property is potentially capable of being expressed quantitatively in terms of such a range along a scale. We may never be able to translate all qualities to such measures, but, as science progresses, it converts more and more qualities into equivalent quantitative expressions. But this is not a one-sided development. As science develops more measures, it also requires new kinds of qualitative judgments. For example, height can be measured as a vertical distance; but to do so requires our ability to determine verticality. We can convert verticality into a measure of the angle between a straight line and a radius projected from the earth's center of gravity. This requires our ability to determine straightness, and so on. Quantification at any stage depends on qualification. What is qualified at one stage may be quantified at another, but at any stage some qualitative judgments are required. Consequently, progress in science not only is a function of an increased capacity to quantify efficiently (i.e., to measure) but also depends on an increased capacity to qualify efficiently.

The Particular and the General

One statement can be said to be more general than another if it *implies* and *is not implied by* the other; that is, if the truth of the second necessarily follows from the truth of the first and not conversely. Scientific statements are about things under certain conditions. The larger the class of things to which reference is made, and the more inclusive the set of conditions, the more general is the statement. For example, the statement

All X's have the property Y under conditions (C_1, C_2, . . . , C_n)

is more general than the statement

This X has the property Y under conditions (C_1, C_2, . . . , C_n).

Each statement can also be further generalized by enlarging the range of environments in which it holds.

The less general a statement, the more *fact-like* it is; the more general a statement, the more *law-like* it is. Hence, facts and laws represent ranges along the scale of generality. There is no well-defined point of separation between these ranges.

General statements are of two types. The first type refers to a class of events or conditions each instance of which has been observed. The second type refers to classes of things and/or conditions some of which have not been observed and all of which can never have been observed. If, for example, we observe that each of four pots of water boils at 100° C and make a statement to this effect, then this statement is of the first type. If we infer from these observations that the boiling point of water at standard atmospheric pressure is 100° C, we have made a statement of the second type. The term *law* is normally restricted to general inferential statements of the second type which in addition assert a causal (deterministic or probabilistic) relationship.

A *theory* is a still further generalization. Wolf (1928, pp. 126–127) pointed this out as follows:

> Newton's theory of gravitation (especially in its original causal sense) is an explanation of Kepler's three laws and of Galilei's Law of Falling Bodies; the Kinetic Theory of Gases is an explanation of Boyle's, Avogadro's, and Gay-Lussac's Laws (and of the separate laws which they summarize); and the Undulatory Theory of Light explains Snell's Law of Refraction (and the laws of which this is a summary) by reducing the bending of a ray of light, as it passes from one medium to another of different density, to differences in the velocities of light in the two media.
>
> There is a tendency to distinguish such a more comprehensive law from the less comprehensive laws, which it explains, by calling it a *Theory.*

Perhaps the relationship between theory, law, and fact is best grasped in the context of a deductive system. In a deductive system there are (1) a set of undefined and defined concepts, (2) a set of assumptions (axioms and postulates, or formation and transformation rules), (3) a set of deduced theorems, and (4) instances of the theorems. The assumptions constitute the theory, the theorems constitute laws, and the instances of the theorems are the facts. In the construction of scientific theories the objective is to construct just such a deductive system.

A theory, however, is more than a generalization from which laws can be deduced because, as Campbell (1952, pp. 82–83) observed,

> there are an indefinite number of "theories" from which the laws could be deduced; it is a mere logical exercise to find one set of propositions from which another set will follow. . . . For instance, that the two propositions (1) that the pressure of gas increases as the temperature increases (2) that it increases as the volume decreases, can be deduced from a single proposition that the pressure increases with increase of temperature, and decrease of volume. But of course the single proposition does not explain the two others; it merely states them in other words.

A theory must, according to Campbell (1952, p. 89), satisfy two additional conditions:

> it must explain those laws in the sense of introducing ideas which are more familiar or, in some other way, more acceptable than those of the laws; [and] it must predict new laws and these laws must turn out to be true.

In the assertion of three levels of generality in facts, laws, and theories it is frequently implied that because of differences in generality facts are simplest to confirm, laws more difficult, and theories most difficult. Now this is true in one sense: in the sense that at present the methodology of confirming facts is much more highly developed than is the corresponding methodology for dealing with laws and theories. For example, Churchman (1961, pp. 76–77) observes that

> There are an infinite number of hypotheses contained in . . . [a] theory. Which ones should be tested?
>
>   One might appeal to common sense and assert that the tests should be "spread out" equitably over the interval.

But what do "equitably" and "the interval" mean? Churchman (1961, p. 77) points out that this is not easy to answer.

> In practice, we need a theory of theory-testing . . . most scientists recognize that the mere accumulation of measurements that "confirm" a theory do not add to one's confidence in the theory, for they may merely over-test one or more hypotheses, and under-test the rest. Thus, on a vague level, one feels that a theory ought to be tested under "widely different" circumstances, but this prescription is difficult to define.

There is another sense in which theories are held to be more difficult to confirm than facts. It is maintained by some that the confirmation of facts does not require use of theory but that confirmation of theories does entail confirmation of fact. This is not true. For example, Churchman (1961, p. 81) notes:

> . . . the practice of science shows that such a proposition [statement] as "An observed object X weighs k pounds" or "An observed object X is blue" are, methodologically interpreted, elliptical for "If X is observed under any of the conditions C_i belonging to the class of conditions C, by any observer O_j

belonging to the class of observers O, the recorded observations will all belong to a class of propositions P." The confirmation of this proposition belongs to the last type—the theories. By a similar argument, all other propositions of science are—methodologically interpreted—theories.

The concept of confirmation of even "simple" facts by direct and immediate observation is a methodological myth inherited from the past.

It is maintained by some that, although laws and theories are more difficult to confirm than facts, they are less difficult—or at least no more difficult—to disconfirm than facts. In principle, a law or theory can be disconfirmed by just one contradictory fact. But in practice the fact which appears to contradict the law or theory is itself always subject to doubt. Consequently, there have been many historical instances where facts which appear to contradict laws or theories have been rejected in order to maintain a law or theory in which the scientist had more confidence than he did in the fact. Furthermore, as Churchman (1961) and many before him have shown, the confirmation of a fact itself presupposes a theory and hence the validity of a fact always depends on the validation of the assumed theory. For example, it was once assumed (and still is by some) that, if facts and theory do not agree, then the theory must be false. As the history of science shows, however, the scientist is just as likely (if not more so) to question the validity of the facts as he is to question the validity of the theory.

TYPES OF PROBLEMS

Research that is directed toward the solution of problems can also be divided into two major classes: *evaluative* and *developmental*. An evaluative problem is one in which the alternative courses of action are completely specified in advance and the solution consists of selecting the "best" of these. A developmental problem involves the search for (and perhaps construction or synthesis of) instruments which yield a course of action that is better than any available at the time. For example, the selection of the best of two or more existings drugs for curing a specified ailment is an evaluative problem. Developing a better drug than any available is a developmental problem. In discussing the phases of research we shall consider each of the types of research that have been identified and explore their methodological differences and similarities. But the basis of these comparisons will be laid throughout by a detailed consideration of evaluative problem solving because here, as we shall try to show, we are presently capable of attaining our highest degree of methodological self-consciousness and sophistication.

Applied research has the advantage of being able to formulate criteria of its own efficiency in terms of the objectives for which the problem is being investigated. Because of its lack of specific objectives, pure research cannot formulate such criteria as explicitly. Consequently, pure research makes many implicit assumptions about the conditions under which its results will be applied. In applied research these assumptions are frequently found to be unrealistic. To elaborate a previous example, in pure research the seriousness of various errors can seldom be measured. Hence estimates are made in a way that is "best" only if the seriousness of an error is independent of its sign; that is, if the seriousness of an error of $+x$ is equivalent to the seriousness of an error of $-x$. In applied problems, however, there are few cases in which this condition holds. Hence different estimation procedures are required in applied science, and serious questions about the estimating procedure of pure science are raised.

In general we have the opportunity of making research-design (methodological) decisions more self consciously in applied science than in pure science. This fact is not generally appreciated; to the contrary, it is commonly believed that pure research tends to be methodologically superior to applied research.

THE PHASES OF RESEARCH

The phases of research have traditionally been identified as

1. observation,
2. generalization,
3. experimentation,

or as some variation of these. For example, D'Abro (1951, p. 3) lists the stages of the scientific method as

a. the observational stage,

b. the experimental stage,

c. the theoretical and mathematical stage (in physics).

He then comments (p. 3) on their sequence as follows:

> The order in which these stages have been listed is the order in which they arise in the study of any group of physical phenomena. It is also the chronological order in which they were discovered.

One could take issue with the assertion concerning chronology, for example, on the grounds that atomic theory was apparently formulated in qualitative form by Democritus without his engaging in either of the first two stages. This issue, however, is not as important as the one arising from the implication that the order of the steps is fixed. The position we shall take here is that all stages may and usually do go on simultaneously. Some previous or new theory may suggest and direct new observations. The empirical tradition asserts the primacy of observation in science, but more sophisticated philosophical analysis has shown that observation always presupposes a criterion of relevance, and this criterion, in turn, always involves some theory. This is not to assert the primacy of theory. To the contrary, some modern philosophies of science, such as pragmatism and experimentalism, assert the "cyclic" and interdependent characteristic of these stages of scientific method.*

The various three-stage breakdowns of the research process have been made primarily by scientists preoccupied with pure research. From the point of view of applied research a finer breakdown is necessary. There are almost as many listings of applied-research phases as there are persons who have tried to provide such a classification. Since most such listings are essentially equivalent, it does not make much difference which one is used as long as its meaning is made clear. Here we shall discuss research in six phases:

1. Formulating the problem.
2. Constructing the model.
3. Testing the model.
4. Deriving a solution from the model.
5. Testing and controlling the solution.
6. Implementing the solution.

---

* For detailed discussion of the primacy of observation or theory see Churchman (1961), Churchman and Ackoff (1950), Dewey (1929 and 1938), and Singer (1959).

These phases are not discrete stages each of which is completed before the next is begun. In general all phases go on simultaneously and are completed together. They frequently are begun, however, in the order in which they are listed.

The research process is usually cyclic. For example, if, when testing a model, it is found to be deficient, the formulation of the problem and the model may be re-examined and modified. This leads to new testing and, in some cases, to further revision in the formulation of the problem and the model. . . . Formulating the (applied-research) problem has much in common with the "observational" phase of pure research; "generalization" with "model construction" and "derivation of the solution," and "experimentation" with "testing the model and solution." The control phase of applied research corresponds with efforts to further generalize the results of pure research, and implementation corresponds with efforts to use the results of one piece of pure research in another.

THE PHILOSOPHY OF SCIENCE

Before about a century ago most of what we today call science was called *natural philosophy*. Philosophic inquiry and scientific inquiry were not differentiated from each other, at least popularly, until about the middle of the nineteenth century. In the days when all scientists were philosophers and most philosophers were scientists a great deal of attention was given to the way in which knowledge was acquired. Inquiry into this procedure—which was more philosophically than scientifically oriented—was alternately called *epistemology* and the *theory of knowledge*.

With the separation of science from philosophy there came an increased awareness of the superiority of the methods and techniques of science for acquiring knowledge. Consequently, those who were concerned with the theory of knowledge turned more and more to the analysis of scientific method. Since this inquiry was itself largely speculative in character, it remained philosophic and came to be known as the *philosophy of science*.*

---

* Although the study of scientific method has been a major part of the philosophy of science, it has by no means been the only part. This branch of philsophy has had at least three other types of interest in science:

(1) Conceptual analysis: the attempt to define concepts or problem areas in such a way as to make them susceptible to scientific study.

(2) Examination of assumptions concerning the nature of reality which "underlie" science.

(3) Synthesis: the attempt to fuse the findings of the various branches of sciences into one consistent view of reality, a *Weltanschauung*.

Scientists as well as philosophers engage in the philosophy of science, which is one of the few remaining grounds on which they meet. But even this ground has been shrinking as the study of scientific method itself has become less and less speculative and more and more scientific. Today the breach between the philosophy of science and the science of methodology is wide enough to make it difficult for all but a few to straddle.

This breach is unfortunate. Although most contemporary professional philosophers have little knowledge of present-day science, they do know the history of epistemology and the theory of knowledge and are interested in methodological problems. Scientists, on the other hand, generally know little of this history and are inclined to take for granted their own methods of acquiring knowledge. As a consequence, methodology has developed slowly, and the practices of scientists often fail to incorporate the results that earlier methodological inquiries have produced.*

CONCLUSION

Methodology can be considered to be a special type of problem solving, one in which the problems to be solved are research problems. We will see later that any problem situation, and hence research-problem situations, can be represented by the following equation:

$$V = f(X_i, Y_j),$$

where V = the measure of performance or accomplishment that we seek to maximize or minimize.

X_i = the aspects of the situation we can control; the "decision" or "choice" or "control" variables.

Y_j = the aspects of the situation (environment of the problem) over which we have no control.

Then solving a problem consists of finding those values of the *decision* variables, X_i [expressed as a function, $g(Y_j)$], which maximize (or minimize) V. Theoretically it is possible to formulate *problems in research design* in this way and to find "optimizing" solutions. The attainment of such optima is the objective of methodology. At the present time we can formulate only a few research problems in this way, but this achievement is the product of just a few years of such study of research procedures. Even where

---

* There have been many studies of the development of epistemology and philosophy of science. See, for example, Churchman and Ackoff (1950).

we cannot find such optima, however, we can learn a great deal about the relative effectiveness of different research procedures by attempting to formulate them in this way. Such an effort is the most efficient way we have of precisely defining problems in methodology and of directing scientific research to their solution. . . . In methodology, as in the rest of science, the solution of one problem raises several new ones. But, in general, progress in methodology and science is as much a matter of moving from question to question as it is of moving from answer to answer.

BIBLIOGRAPHY

Campbell, N. R., *What Is Science?* New York: Dover Publications, 1952.

_____ , *Foundations of Science.* New York: Dover Publications, 1957.

Churchman, C. W., *Theory of Experimental Inference.* New York: The Macmillan Co., 1948.

_____ , *Prediction and Optimal Decision.* Englewood Cliffs, N.J.: Prentice-Hall, 1961.

_____ , and R. L. Ackoff, *Methods of Inquiry.* St. Louis: Educational Publishers, 1950.

Columbia Associates, *An Introduction to Reflective Thinking.* Boston: Houghton Mifflin Co., 1923.

D'Abro, A., *The Rise of the New Physics.* New York: Dover Publications, 1951.

Dewey, John, *The Quest for Certainty.* New York: Minton, Balch and Co., 1929.

_____ , *Logic: The Theory of Inquiry.* New York: Henry Holt and Co., 1938.

Dingle, Herbert, *The Scientific Adventure.* New York: Philosophical Library, 1953.

Freeman, Paul, *The Principles of Scientific Research.* London: MacDonald and Co., 1949.

Giddings, F. H., *The Scientific Study of Human Society.* Chapel Hill: University of North Carolina Press, 1924.

Huxley, Thomas H., "Educational Value of Natural History Sciences," in Wiener (1953).

Ritchie, A. D., *Scientific Method.* New York: Harcourt, Brace, and Co., 1923.

Russell, Bertrand, *The Scientific Outlook.* Glencoe, IL: Free Press, 1951.

Singer, E. A., Jr., *Experience and Reflection.* Philadelphia: University of Pennsylvania Press, 1959.

Westaway, F. W., *Scientific Method.* New York: Hillman-Curl, 1937.

Wiener, P. P. (ed.), *Readings in Philosophy of Science.* New York: Chas. Scribner's Sons, 1953.

Wilson, E. B., Jr., *An Introduction to Scientific Research.* New York: McGraw-Hill Book Co., 1952.

Wolf, A., *Essentials of Scientific Method.* London: George Allen and Unwin, 1928.

CHAPTER 23

OBJECTIVITY

*O*bjectivity is a scientific ideal particularly sought by management scientists. Although its meaning is not clear, objectivity is generally believed to be what Winnie the Pooh called a "GOOD THING." It is also believed to require the exclusion of ethical and moral judgments from inquiry and decision making. *Objectivity so conceived is not possible.*

Most, if not all, scientific inquiry involves testing hypotheses or estimating the values of variables. These procedures necessarily entail balancing two types of error. In testing hypotheses these errors are rejecting hypotheses when they are true and accepting them when they are false. Naturally we would like to minimize the probabilities of making them but unfortunately minimizing one maximizes the other. Therefore, setting these probabilities requires a judgment of the relative seriousness, hence value, of the two types of error. Researchers seldom make this judgment consciously; they usually set the probabilities at levels dictated by scientific convention. This attests not to their objectivity but to their ignorance.

The choice of a way of estimating the value of a variable requires the evaluation of the relative importance, hence values, of underestimates and overestimates of the variable. Each estimating procedure contains a (usually implicit) judgment of the seriousness of the two possible types of error. Therefore, estimates cannot be made without a value judgment, however concealed it may be.

The most commonly used estimating procedures are said to be "unbiased." The estimates they yield, however, are best only when errors of equal magnitude but of opposite sign are equally serious. This is a condition that I have virtually never found in the real world.

From *Management in Small Doses* (Wiley, 1986).

In testing hypotheses and estimating the values of variables, science unconsciously equates objectivity with unconsciousness of the value judgments.

The prevailing concept of objectivity is based on a distinction between ethical-moral man—who is believed to be emotional, involved, and biased—and scientific man—who is believed to be unemotional, uninvolved, and unbiased. Objective decision makers are expected to take their heads—not their hearts—into the workplace. To assume that the heart and head can be separated is like assuming that the head and tail of a coin can be separated because they can be discussed or looked at separately.

Objectivity does *not* consist of making only value-free judgments in conducting inquiries and making decisions. It consists of making only value-*full* judgments; the more extensive the values, the more objective the results. A determination is objective only if it holds for *any* values that those who can use it may have. For this reason objectivity is an ideal that can never be attained but can be continuously approached.

Objectivity cannot be approximated by an individual investigator or decision maker; it can be approached only by groups of individuals with diverse values. It is a property that cannot be approximated by individual scientists but can be by science taken as a system.

All this has an important implication for management. The values of all those affected by a decision, its *stakeholders,* should be taken into account in making that decision but this cannot be done without involving them in the decision-making process. To deprive them of opportunities to participate in making decisions that affect them is to devalue them, and this, it seems to me, is immoral. Managers have a moral obligation to *all* who can be affected by their decisions, not merely to those who pay for their services.

CHAPTER 24

RATIONALITY

We often say of people whose behavior we do not expect and cannot explain that they are *irrational*. In this way we absolve ourselves of any responsibility for their behavior.

I have never seen a problem believed to be caused by the behavior of others that could be solved by assuming that *they* were irrational. On the other hand, by assuming that *we* are irrational, solutions to these problems can often be found; for example, during a working visit to India in 1957 I met a number of family planners from the United States who had made no progress in their extended efforts to reduce India's birthrate. Most of them attributed their failure to the irrationality of the Indians.

After hearing this a number of times I suggested to one of the family planners that it could be they who were irrational. I pointed out that a Brazilian woman had recently given birth to her forty-second child. Assume, I said, that the average woman can produce only about half this number, say 20. The difference between 20 and 4.6, the average number of children per Indian family, is much greater than the difference between 4.6 and 0. This, I suggested, was an indication that the size of Indian families was not due to lack of birth control.

The family planner I had addressed thought this argument was ridiculous. He left, terminating our conversation. Fortunately, a distinguished Indian demographer, T. K. Balakrishnan, approached me with apologies for having overheard our conversation. He suggested that we collaborate in research on the possible rationality of Indian reproductive behavior.

We began at the Indian Statistical Institute, but I had to return to the States before our research was finished. Luckily, Glen Camp, one of my colleagues, replaced me in India and helped Balakrishnan finish the work. Briefly, this is what they found.

The average Indian male could expect a number of years of unemployment when he got older. India had no social security program and the

From *Management in Small Doses* (Wiley, 1986).

typical worker did not earn enough to save for these unemployed years. His only hope, then, was to be provided for by his children. It took an average of 1.1 wage earners to support one unemployed adult at the minimal subsistence level, but, because it takes two to produce a child, each family needed at least 2.2 wage-earning children. Because half the children born were female, and females were essentially unemployable in India at that time, 4.4 children were required. To cover infant and child mortality, this number had to be adjusted upward to 4.6 children.

This result could have been obtained by pure chance, but its validity was easy to determine. If family size could be explained even in part by the desire for insurance against old-age unemployment, then families whose first three offspring were male should have few if any additional children. Those families whose first three offspring were female should just be getting started. These inferences were found to be correct.

Those family planners who had attributed irrationality to the Indians had unknowingly expected them to commit delayed suicide by limiting the size of their families.

Consider another example. At one time producers of gasoline advertised heavily in an effort to convince consumers of the superiority of their respective products. There were no significant performance differences between the different brands, but their producers assumed that they could persuade consumers to the contrary and thereby induce them to behave irrationally.

Subsequent research showed that the hundreds of millions of dollars spent on gasoline advertising were wasted; it had virtually no effect on consumers. Behaving rationally, they had no brand preferences. They bought gasoline at those service stations at which they believed the time required to get service was minimized. The oil company that sponsored this research was able to use these findings to increase its market share by locating, designing, and operating its stations to minimize service time. It also made reduced service time the theme of its advertising.

Corporate managers who think that consumers, employees, suppliers, competitors, or government officials are behaving irrationally should think twice and they should think differently the second time.

CHAPTER 25

THE FUTURE OF OPERATIONAL RESEARCH IS PAST

A few years ago I was asked to speak at the Joint Annual Meeting of the Operations Research Society of America and the Institute of Management Sciences. I characterized that occasion as a wake for the profession, whichever name it chose to use. In my opinion, American Operations Research is dead even though it has yet to be buried. I also think there is little chance for its resurrection because there is so little understanding of the reasons for its demise.

This lack of understanding is well reflected in a recent article by John R. Hall Jr. and Sydney W. Hess entitled "OR/MS Dead or Dying? RX for Survival." The authors prescribed five treatments:

1. Practitioners could be more effective if more of the academics' new discoveries in OR/MS theory were made truly accessible to them. The use of short (2 page) readable summaries—refereed to protect the academics' interests—could help to move theory into practice.
2. It would also help if some academics would show less disdain for problems they have "solved before" and recognize the importance to practice of steps outside the problem-solving process (such as preparation of examples and demonstrations of techniques of real problems).
3. Assistant professors could be brought in to help write up the case studies that older practitioners are too busy (or too lazy) to write up.
4. Academics can be given part-time or on-site-jobs with companies in their areas.
5. Internship programs can also foster closer relationships between academics and nonacademic professionals.

From "Reflections on Systems and Their Models," with Jamshid Gharajedaghi, *Systems Research,* March 1996, pp. 13–23.

These recommendations make it clear that the only thing that Hall and Hess find wrong with OR/MS is the relationship between academics and non-academic practitioners. This position is in sharp contrast with that taken by K. D. Tocher. He questions deeply the adequacy of what Thomas Kuhn would call "the paradigm of OR," and doing so Tocher sows the seeds of revolution, not of merely superficial changes. Less generally, but no less tellingly, Jonathan Rosenhead recently called into question the suitability of the OR paradigm in the area of health-services planning. For a number of years now Neil Jessop, John Stringer, John Friend and their colleagues at IOR have done likewise in areas involving the interactions of autonomous organizations. K. D. Radford recently offered a sketch of a new paradigm for OR.

Because there is more questioning of the paradigm here than in the United States, I have the impression that Operational Research, unlike Operations Research, may not yet be dead. Perhaps in the land of its birth OR may have a renaissance, but, in my opinion, not without a radical transformation. In this, the first of my presentations, I deal with the death of OR. In the second, I consider how it might be resurrected.

THE DENOUEMENT

The life of OR has been a short one. It was born here late in the 1930s. By the mid-60s it had gained widespread acceptance in academic, scientific, and managerial circles. In my opinion this gain was accompanied by a loss of its pioneering spirit, its sense of mission and its innovativeness. Survival, stability and respectability took precedence over development, and its decline began.

I hold academic OR and the relevant professional societies primarily responsible for this decline—and since I had a hand in initiating both, I share this responsibility. By the mid 1960s most OR courses in American universities were given by academics who had never practiced it. They and their students were text-book products engaging in impure research couched in the language, but not the reality, of the real world. The meetings and journals of the relevant professional societies, like classrooms, were filled with abstractions from an imagined reality. As a result OR came to be identified with the use of mathematical models and algorithms rather than the ability to formulate management problems, solve them, and implement and maintain their solutions in turbulent environments. This obsession with techniques, combined with unawareness of or indifference to the changing demands being made of managers, had three major effects on the practice of OR.

First, practitioners decreasingly took problematic situations as they came, but increasingly sought, selected, and distorted them so that favored techniques could be applied to them. This reduced the usefulness of OR, a reduction that was well recognized by executives who pushed if further and further down in their organizations, to where such relatively simple problems arose as permitted the application of OR's mathematically sophisticated but contextually naive techniques.

According to Hall and Hess

> . . . this decline in visibility has not stemmed from a wave of firings or other reductions in OR/MS ranks. Instead OR/MS talent is increasingly being dispersed to the various corporate functions. The original reason for centralization was that OR/MS was felt to need protection to establish itself. Today, the only companies still maintaining central OR groups are those that are large enough to be able to use "internal consultants" who are available to back up the analysts down the line.

The dispersion that Hall and Hess note is a fact, but their reasons for it are a fiction. I submit that OR was once a corporate staff function, because corporate executives believed it could be useful to them. It was pushed down because they no longer believed this to be the case, and they correctly perceived that if it had any use, it was in the bowels of the organization, not the head. My observation of a large number of American corporations reveals that when it could no longer be pushed down, it was pushed out.

A second effect of the technical perversion of OR derived from the fact that its mathematical techniques can easily be taught by those who do not know where, when and how to use them. This, together with the fact that in the late 1960s use of quantitative methods became an "idea in good currency," resulted in these techniques being taught widely in schools of business, engineering and public administration, among others. This has deprived OR of its unique incompetence; an increasing portion of it is done by those who do not identify with the profession.

These nonprofessionals are not as obsessed with the techniques nor as immune to reality as the professionals. When required to make a choice, they are more likely to embrace reality than techniques; therefore, they tend to move up in their organizations, not down.

According to Hall and Hess, the decline of visibility of professional OR in organizations "is more a sign of institutional acceptance than a sign of real decline." If one were to take this criterion seriously, one would be forced to conclude that such professions as economics and engineering, which have not declined in visibility, enjoy less institutional acceptance than OR. No. What this dispersion signifies is that OR has been equated by managers to mathematical masturbation and to the absence of any substantive knowledge or understanding of organizations, institutions or their management.

The third effect of OR's immersion in techniques is that those who either practice or preach it have come to be more and more like each other. The original interdisciplinarity of OR has completely disappeared. In his recent presidential address to this Society, Professor Michael Simpson correctly referred to OR *as a discipline*. OR's isolation from other disciplines was (and is) encouraged by professional societies. In several countries, including this one, serious consideration has been given to registering only qualified practitioners and to accrediting academic programs. Nothing could be more effective in removing whatever vestiges of interdisciplinarity there are in the practice of OR.

In the first two decades of OR, its nature was dictated by the nature of the problematic situations it faced. Now the nature of the situations it faces is dictated by the techniques it has at its command. The nature of the problems facing managers has changed significantly over the last three decades, but OR has not. It has not been responsive to the changing needs of management brought about, to a large extent, by radical changes taking place in the environment in which it is practiced. While managers were turning outward, OR was turning inward—inbreeding and introverting. It now appears to have attained the limit of introversion: a catatonic state.

Many practitioners do not accept my characterization of the state of OR or the environment in which it is practiced. Supporting evidence and argument are required. I tried to provide them in my book "Redesigning the Future," but here I summarize very briefly some of the essential points made there.

THE CHANGING ENVIRONMENT OF OR

Systems thinking, expansionism and objective teleology provide the intellectual foundation for what may at least tentatively be called the *Systems*

Age. The world-view they yield does not discard that of the Machine Age but incorporates it as a special case. Machines are understood as instruments of purposeful systems: purposeful systems are no longer conceptualized as machines. The Post Industrial Revolution is as logical a consequence of systems thinking as the Industrial Revolution was of mechanistic thinking. In this second revolution man seeks to develop and use instruments that do *mental* rather than physical work: artifacts that *observe* (generate symbols), communicate (transmit symbols) and *think* (process symbols logically). Together these technologies make possible the mechanization of *control, automation.*

Systems thinking brings special attention to organizations: purposeful systems that contain purposeful parts with different roles or functions, and that are themselves parts of larger purposeful systems. This focus reveals three fundamental interrelated organizational problems: how to design and manage systems so that they can effectively serve their own purposes, the purposes of their parts, and those of the larger systems of which they are part. These are the *self-control,* the *humanization* and the *environmentalization* problems, respectively.

Now OR has been and is almost exclusively concerned with organizational self-control. It has virtually ignored the other two types of problem and the relationship between them and self-control. Furthermore, it employs a Machine-Age approach to the self-control problem. Its method is analytic and its models are predominantly of closed mechanical systems, not of open purposeful systems. This is clearly revealed when one considers OR's use of two concepts: *optimization* and *objectivity.*

OPTIMIZATION IN OR

I begin this discussion of optimization by retelling one of what my students call "Ackoff's Fables." Two years ago, an OR group that was highly placed in an important public agency asked me to review one of its major projects. Most of the members of the group had received degrees in OR from three of the major centers of OR education in the United States.

The project involved a very large intrasystem distribution problem. Those who worked on it were very proud of the number of variables and constraints included in the LP transportation model they had developed. As usual, the researchers complained of the fact that they had not been able to obtain either the quantity or quality of data that they would have liked. As a result it had been necessary for them to engage in a bit of data enrichment.

After the team members had presented the problem, the model and their way of solving it, they showed me what they referred to as their "evaluation of the results." Over a reasonably long period of time they had recorded the decisions actually made and implemented by the responsible managers and had fed these decisions into their model and calculated the total related operating costs. They had then compared these costs with those associated with the optimal solution derived from the same model.

Lo and behold! The optimal solutions were consistently better than those of the managers. Using these differences they had estimated an annual saving which they had used successfully in convincing management to adopt their model and optimizing procedure.

Of minor significance was the fact they had not taken into account the not insignificant costs of their research and its implementation. Also of minor significance was the fact that they also had not taken into account of the unreliability and inaccuracy of the data about which they had complained. Of *major* significance, however, was the fact that even if these costs had been taken into account, their evaluation would have been a *farce*.

The optimal solution of a model is *not* an optimal solution of a problem unless the model is a perfect representation of the problem, which it never is. Therefore, in testing a model and evaluating solutions derived from it, the model itself should never be used to determine the relevant comparative performance measures. The only thing demonstrated by so doing is that the minimum or maximum of a function is lower or higher than a non-minimum or non-maximum.

All models are simplifications of reality. If this were not the case, their usefulness would be significantly reduced. Therefore, it is critical to determine how well models represent reality. In this project the team had not done so.

I put the following question to its members: Suppose you could not conduct an adequate test of your model, what would you do? After considerable squirming the group's leader said he would ask managers to accept it *on faith*. Voilà and Q.E.D.!

This was not the end of the matter. The researchers went on to tell me how the managers had invariably modified the optimal solution to take into account factors that were not taken into account in the model.

Furthermore, the team confessed that it had not carried out any analysis of the nature of the adjustments made by managers or their effects. When I pressed for an explanation of this oversight, I was told that the nature of the factors considered by the managers precluded their inclusion in a mathematical model. *Voilà* again!

Then came the climactic revelation. After about six months the managers had discontinued use of the model because of a significant change in the environment of the system. This change was political in character. When I asked why they had not tried to incorporate the relevant politics into their model, I was told that such changes are neither quantifiable not predictable.

It should be apparent by now that if the researchers had, in fact, solved a problem, it was not the problem that the managers had.

The Need for Learning and Adaptation

The structure and the parameters of problematic situations continuously change, particularly in turbulent environments. Because optimal solutions are very seldom made adaptive to such changes, their optimality is generally of short duration. They frequently become less effective than were the often more robust solutions that they replace. Let us call this cross-over point the moment of death of the solution. Donald A. Schon has convincingly argued that the life of solutions to many critical social and organizational problems is shorter than the time required to find them. Therefore, more and more so-called optimal solutions are still-born. With the accelerating rate of technological and social change dramatized by Alvin Toffler and others, the expected life of optimal solutions and the problems to which they apply can be expected to become increasingly negative.

For these reasons there is a greater need for decision-making systems that can learn and adapt quickly and effectively in rapidly changing situations than there is for systems that produce optimal solutions that deteriorate with change. Most Operational Researchers have failed to respond to this need. As a consequence, the application of OR is increasingly restricted to those problems that are relatively insensitive to their environments. These usually involve the behavior of mechanical rather than purposeful systems and arise at the lower levels of the organization; hence the movement of OR down to them.

The Omission of Aesthetics

There is a second very subtle deficiency in OR's concept of optimality that derives from the concept of *rationality* on which it is based. The conventional concept of an optimal solution to a problem is one that maximizes expected value. Expected value is expressed as a function of three types of variable: first, the *probabilities of choice* associated with each of the available courses of action; second, the *efficiencies* of each of these courses of action for each possible outcome; and third, the *values* of each of these outcomes. The probabilities of choice that maximize the expected value are said to be both a rational and optimal choice. Rationality and optimality so conceived are seriously deficient because they do not take into account two other types of variable. Let me explain.

A positively valued outcome is called an *end* or *objective*. Any course of action that has some probability of producing an end is called a *means*. In OR's concept of optimality the value of a means is taken to lie exclusively in its efficiency for ends; that is, the value of a means is taken to be purely *instrumental, extrinsic*. On the other hand, the value of an end is taken to lie in the satisfaction its attainment brings, to be purely *non-instrumental, intrinsic*. OR does not acknowledge, let alone take into account, the intrinsic value of means and the extrinsic value of ends.

Means and ends are relative, not absolute, concepts. Every means is also an end and every end is also a means. For example, going to school is a means of obtaining an education, an end. But obtaining an education is also a means of increasing one's income, an end. Increasing income, in turn, is a means of supporting a family, and so on.

Every means has intrinsic value because it is also an end, a potential source of satisfaction. And every end has extrinsic value because it is also a means; it has consequences.

That means have intrinsic value is commonplace knowledge. For example, we have preferences among shoes that are identical in all respects except color. We like certain colors more than others. Such preferences among means have nothing to do with their efficiencies but with the satisfaction their use brings. We often prefer a less efficient means because of the satisfaction its use brings. Persistent efficiency-independent preferences among means are called *traits*. Traits, in turn, are elements of that general characteristic of personality called *style*. Style has to do with the satisfaction we derive from what we do rather than what we do it for. It is apparent to all but (apparently) an optimizer that the pursuit of an objective is often more satisfying than its attainment. Herein, of course, lies the attractiveness of games.

To the extent that OR's concept of optimality fails to take the intrinsic value of means, traits and style into account, it is seriously deficient. How they can be taken into account is much too big a subject to deal with here. But let me say a little about it.

In 1936 the eminent psychologists G. W. Allport and H. S. Odbert identified 17,953 traits. It is apparent, therefore, that it is not feasible to measure, let alone include in a model, every relevant aspect of the styles of the decision makers and all others who hold a stake in a decision. This presents a problem that is taken up in Part II.

Now consider ends. Every end that is less than an ideal has consequences with respect to which it can be considered a means. Every consequence of an outcome is itself a means to further consequences, and so on to an ultimate consequence. A maximally desired ultimate consequence, of course, is an ideal which is the only kind of an end that can have purely intrinsic value. Therefore, the instrumental value of any end that is less than an ideal lies in the amount of progress towards one or more ideals that its attainment represents. For example, if an ideal of science is omniscience, then at least part of the extrinsic value of the outcome of any scientific research lies in how much it advances us toward this ideal.

Again, to the extent that OR's concept of optimality fails to take extrinsic value of ends, progress towards ideals, into account, it is seriously deficient.

In a recent article I tried to show that noninstrumental values of means and instrumental values of ends are *aesthetic* in character, and that aesthetic, as well as ethical, values should be incorporated into our theories of decision making. My reasons for doing so were not philosophical; they were pragmatic.

I believe the current worldwide concern with deteriorating *quality of life,* and of such aspects of life as work and education, derives from decreasing stylistic satisfaction and loss of a sense of progress. More and more people are coming to realize that optimization of all the quantities of life does not optimize the quality of life and that growth is a limiting objective.

In addition, there is a widespread belief that much of the accelerating rate of change is getting us nowhere. There is a diminishing sense of progress towards such ideals as peace of mind, peace on earth, equality of opportunity, individual freedom and privacy and the elimination of poverty. A sense of progress towards ideals gives meaning to life, makes choice significant. But today more and more people believe either with Jacques Ellul that they are no longer in control of their futures, or, as the Nobel laureate George Wald wrote, with part of the younger generation, that there may be no future. For them choice is meaningless. Quality of life is degraded by resignation to a future that is believed to preclude progress towards ideals.

Those of us who are engaged in helping others make decisions have the opportunity and the obligation to bring consideration of quality of life—style and progress—into their deliberations. OR has virtually ignored both the opportunity and the obligation.

Beyond Problem Solving

My third point about problem solving is as obvious as my second point about style and progress was obscure. Managers are not confronted with problems that are independent of each other, but with dynamic situations that consist of complex systems of changing problems that interact with each other. I call such situations *messes*. Problems are abstractions extracted from messes by analysis; they are to messes as atoms are to tables and chairs. We experience messes, tables, and chairs; not problems and atoms.

Because messes are systems of problems, the sum of the optimal solutions to each component problem taken separately is *not* an optimal solution to the mess. The behavior of a mess depends more on how the solutions to its parts interact than on how they act independently of each other. But the unit in OR is a problem, not a mess. Managers do not solve problems; they manage messes.

Effective management of messes requires a particular type of *planning*, not problem solving. The inappropriateness of OR modelling to the type of planning required has been presented effectively by K. D. Tocher and Jonathan Rosenhead in the articles already referred to. Furthermore, the *design* (or redesign) of organized systems so as to reduce or eliminate messes is not a preoccupation of OR. Planning and design are predominately synthesizing, rather than analytic activities; they involve putting things together rather than taking them apart. Moreover, there is no such thing as an optimal plan for, or design of a purposeful system in a dynamic environment. The objective of such efforts should be to produce systems that can pursue ideals effectively and do so in a way that provides continuing satisfaction to the participants.

The Paradigmatic Dilemma of OR

Now for my fourth point: the type of model employed in OR implies a particular paradigm of problem solving. It consists of two parts: *predicting the future* and *preparing for it*. Clearly, the effectiveness of this approach depends critically on the accuracy with which the future can be predicted. It helps us little, and may harm us much, to prepare perfectly for an imperfectly-predicted future.

Therefore, the paradigm of OR should be one that involves "designing a desirable future and inventing ways of bringing it about." The future depends at least as much on what we and others do between now and then as it does on what has already happened. Therefore, we can affect it, and by collaboration with others—expanding the system to be controlled—we can increase our chances of "making it happen." The wider the collaboration, the more closely we can approximate the future we have jointly designed. It is this perception by Fred Emery and Eric Trist that gave rise to their work in social ecology.

Prediction and preparation were the principal modalities of the Machine Age: design and invention are emerging as the principal modalities of the Systems Age. Prediction and preparation involve passive adaptation to an environment that is believed to be out of our control. Design and invention involve active control of a system's environment as well as the system itself.

The models currently employed by OR are evaluative in nature; they enable us to compare alternative decisions or decision rules that are "given." In design and invention, however, the alternatives are "taken," created. Creative solutions to problems are not ones obtained by selecting the best from among a well- or widely-recognized set of alternatives, but rather by finding or producing a new alternative. Such an alternative is frequently so superior to any of those previously perceived that formal evaluation is not required. If it is, however, then the evaluative models of OR may have a use. The challenge, therefore, is not so much to improve our methods of evaluation, but to improve our methods of design and invention.

The point of the views I have expressed up to this point is not that OR's concept of problem solving is useless, but that it should have been taken as a starting-point of OR's development, not as its end-point. To have taken it as the end-point was to have aborted OR's development and to have initiated its retreat from reality.

The Disciplinarity of OR

My fifth point relates to an allegation I made earlier: that although OR began as an interdisciplinary activity, it has become uncompromisingly unidisciplinary. This, I believe, has contributed significantly to its decline.

Colin Cherry observed that up until the time of Leibniz one person could know the entire body of scientific knowledge. As science expanded it became necessary to subdivide both its pursuit of knowledge and the knowledge it produced. Disciplines began to emerge, slowly at first, but with increasing speed. A few years ago the U.S. National Research Council had identified about one hundred and fifty of them.

Subjects, disciplines, and professions are categories that are useful in filing scientific knowledge and in dividing the labor involved in its pursuit, but they are nothing more than this. Nature and the world are not organized as science and universities are. There are no physical, chemical, biological, psychological, sociological or even Operational Research problems. These are names of different points-of-view, different aspects of the same reality, not different kinds of reality. Any problematic situation can be looked at from the point-of-view of any discipline, but not necessarily with equal fruitfulness. The higher in the evolutionary scale is the object of study, the larger is the number of disciplines that are likely to make a constructive contribution to that study. For example, a doctor may see the incapacity of an elderly woman as a result of her weak heart; an architect, as deriving from the fact that she must walk up three flights of steep stairs to the meager room she rents; an economist, as due to her lack of income; a social worker, as a consequence of her children's failure to "take her in"; and so on. Planning such an old lady's future ought to involve all these points-of-view and many others. Progress in handling messes, as well as problems, derives at least as much from creative reorganization of the way we pursue knowledge and the knowledge we already have as it does from new discoveries. Science's filing system can be reorganized without changing its content, but doing so can increase our access to and understanding of that content.

The fact that the world is in such a mess as it is is largely due to our decomposing messes into unidisciplinary problems that are treated independently of each other. Effective treatment of messes requires the application of not only Science with a capital "S," but also all the arts and humanities we can command. OR provides no such treatment. Its interdisciplinarity is a pretention, not a reality.

OBJECTIVITY IN OR

OR does not incorporate the arts and humanities largely because of its distorted belief that doing so would reduce its *objectivity*, a misconception it shares with much of science. Immanuel Kant showed that thought and observation could not be separated. C. G. Jung argued that neither thought nor observation could be separated from feeling, the source of value judgments. C. West Churchman, I believe, showed the validity of this argument. To think of objectivity in terms of thoughtless and feelingless observations, as some classical empiricists did, is to think of the scientist as a camera or tape recorder. To think of objectivity as observationless and feelingless thought, as some classical rationalists did, is to think of the scientist as an unprogramed computer. The scientist can no more act like a machine than a machine can act like a scientist.

Objectivity is *not* the absence of value judgments in purposeful behavior. It is the social product of an open interaction of a wide variety of subjective value judgments. *Objectivity is a systemic property of science taken as a whole, not a property of individual researchers or research.* It is obtained only when all possible values have been taken into account; hence, like certainty, it is an ideal that science can continually approach but never attain. That which is true works, and it works whatever the values of those who put it to work. It is *value-full*, not value-free.

This concept of objectivity has an important implication for OR. The clients of OR are usually organizations. These organizations have purposes of their own, and so do their parts and the larger systems of which they are part. Therefore, organizations clearly have responsibilities to themselves, their parts and their containing systems. These purposes are often in conflict. Such conflicts are frequently conceptualized by managers and the researchers who serve them as games to be won. In my opinion, such a formulation is irresponsible, unprofessional, and unethical.

It seems to me that it is the responsibility of managers and their researchers to try to dissolve or resolve such conflicts and serve all of an organization's stakeholders in a way that reflects the relative importance of the organization to them, not their relative importance to the organization. This cannot be done without involving them or their representatives in the organization's decision making. To fail to take all stakeholders into account, as OR usually does, is to devalue those who are not considered or involved in the decision process but who are affected by it. Their exclusion is a value judgment, one that appears to me to be immoral. Science has a moral responsibility to all those who can be affected by its output, not merely to those who sponsor it.

SUMMARY

Now let me attempt a constructive summary. I have tried to make the following points.

First, there is a greater need for decision-making systems that can learn and adapt effectively than there is for optimizing systems that cannot.

Second, in decision making, account should be taken of aesthetic values—stylistic preferences and progress towards ideals—because they are relevant to quality of life.

Third, problems are abstracted from systems of problems, messes. Messes require holistic treatment. They cannot be treated effectively by decomposing them analytically into separate problems to which optimal solutions are sought.

Fourth, OR's analytic problem-solving paradigm, "predict and prepare," involves internal contradictions and should be replaced by a synthesizing planning paradigm such as "design a desirable future and invent ways of bring it about."

Fifth, effective treatment of messes requires interaction of a wide variety of disciplines, a requirement that OR no longer meets.

Sixth and last, all those who can be affected by the output of decision making should either be involved in it so they can bring their interests to bear on it, or their interests should be well represented by researchers who serve as their advocates.

POSTSCRIPT

Let me close with a very personal postscript. I doubt the persuasiveness of the arguments I have presented here. In the early 1970s I persistently argued similarly with the faculty in OR that I had assembled at the University of Pennsylvania. Despite three years' effort I was unable to convince them of the need for radical change. A minority of the faculty and I felt this need for change so deeply that we separated from the OR faculty and initiated a new graduate program in what we called "Social Systems Sciences." This name was selected for three reasons. First, it was the only one we proposed that no other department of the University objected to, for obvious reasons. Second, we could not conceive of a profession, a discipline or a society using such an awkward name, and we wanted to preclude such use. Finally, it suggests, however vaguely, what we are about. Nevertheless, we would not have changed the name if we could have changed OR.

If I could not persuade a faculty that I had assembled to change its concept of OR, you can understand why I am not very hopeful here. But I would point out one thing. The OR Program at the University of Pennsylvania is only a fraction of the size it was when the separation occurred and it no longer has a research center associated with it. The new program in Social Systems Sciences is now much larger than the program in OR is or ever was. Of course this does not prove I was right; but it does suggest that if I was wrong, it was not a costly error.

BIBLIOGRAPHY

R. L. Ackoff, "The Social Responsibility of Operational Research," *Operational Research Quarterly, 25* (1974), pp. 361–371.

_____ , *Redesigning the Future,* New York: John Wiley & Sons, 1974.

_____ , "Does Quality of Life Have to Be Quantified?" *General Systems, IX* (1975), pp. 213–219.

_____ , "Optimization + Objectivity = Opt out," *European Journal of Operational Research, 1* (1977), pp. 1–7.

_____ , "Resurrecting the Future of Operational Research," *Journal of the Operational Research Society, 30* (1979), pp. 189–199.

_____ , and F. E. Emery, *On Purposeful Systems,* Chicago: Aldine-Atherton, 1972.

Allport, G. W., and H. S. Odbert, "Trait-Names: a Psycholexical Study," *Psychological Monographs, 211,* (1936).

Cherry, C., *On Human Communication,* New York: John Wiley & Sons, 1957.

Churchman, C. W., *Prediction and Optimal Decision,* Englewood Cliffs, NJ: Prentice-Hall, 1961.

Ellul, J., *The Technological Society,* New York: Vintage Books, 1967.

Emery, F. E., and E. L. Trist, *Towards a Social Ecology,* London: Plenum Press, 1973.

Friend, J. K., and W. N. Jessop, *Local Government and Strategic Choice,* London: Tavistock, 1969.

Friend, J. K., J. M. Power, and C. J. L. Yewlett, *The Inter-Corporate Dimension,* London: Tavistock, 1974.

Hall, J. R., Jr., and S. W. Hess, "OR/MS Dead or Dying? RX for Survival," *Interfaces, 8* (1978), pp. 42–44.

Jung, C. G., *Psychological Types,* New York: Harcourt and Brace, 1926.

Kant, I., *Critique of Pure Reason,* London: Macmillan, 1929.

Radford, K. J., "Decision-Making in a Turbulent Environment," *Journal of the Operational Research Society, 29* (1978), pp. 677–682.

Rosenhead, J., "Operational Research in Health Services Planning," *European Journal of Operational Research, 2* (1978), pp. 75–85.

Schon, D. A., *Beyond the Stable State,* New York: Random House, 1971.

Simpson, M. G., "Those Who Can't?" *Journal of the Operational Research Society, 29* (1978), pp. 517–522.

Stringer, J., "Operational Research for Multiorganizations," *Operational Research Quarterly, 18* (1967), pp. 105–120.

Tocher, K. D., "Systems Planning," *Philosophical Transactions of the Royal Society,* London, A287 (1977), pp. 425–441.

Toffler, A., *Future Shock,* New York: Bantam Books, 1971.

Wald, G., "A generation in search of a future," Boston: *The Boston Globe,* (March 8, 1969).

EPILOGUE

THE ROLE OF BUSINESS IN A DEMOCRATIC SOCIETY

THE SOCIETAL VIEW OF BUSINESS AS A SOCIAL SYSTEM

Let us consider the systemic view of an enterprise from the perspective of its containing system, society. For reasons that will become apparent, this view has come to be called the *stakeholder view of the firm.* Imagine a visitor from another planet who, although he does not know any of Earth's languages, has been sent to find out what a corporation is. He cannot talk or read about corporations; all he can do is observe what they do. In all likelihood his description would reflect the stakeholder view of the firm as shown schematically in Figure E.1.

In this view, the firm is seen as a set of transactions, for example, an exchange of money for work with *employees,* an exchange of money for goods and services with *suppliers,* an exchange of goods or services for money with *customers,* an exchange for money received at an earlier time for money paid at a later time with *investors* and *lenders,* an exchange for money paid at an earlier time for money received at a later time with *debtors* (e.g., banks, and other companies in which the corporation has invested), and an exchange of money for the use of services and facilities from a source which exercises some control over the corporation, *government.*

The particular stakeholders identified are not the essential part of the stakeholder view of the firm; different observers will recognize different stakeholders for even the same firm. What is essential is the view of the firm as engaged in a set of transactions with various stakeholders, however they are identified.

This chapter is drawn from the essay of the same name in *The Portable MBA,* in Eliza G. G. Collins and Mary Ann Devanna (Eds.), pp. 335–360 (Wiley, 1990).

Figure E.1
A Stakeholder View of the Firm

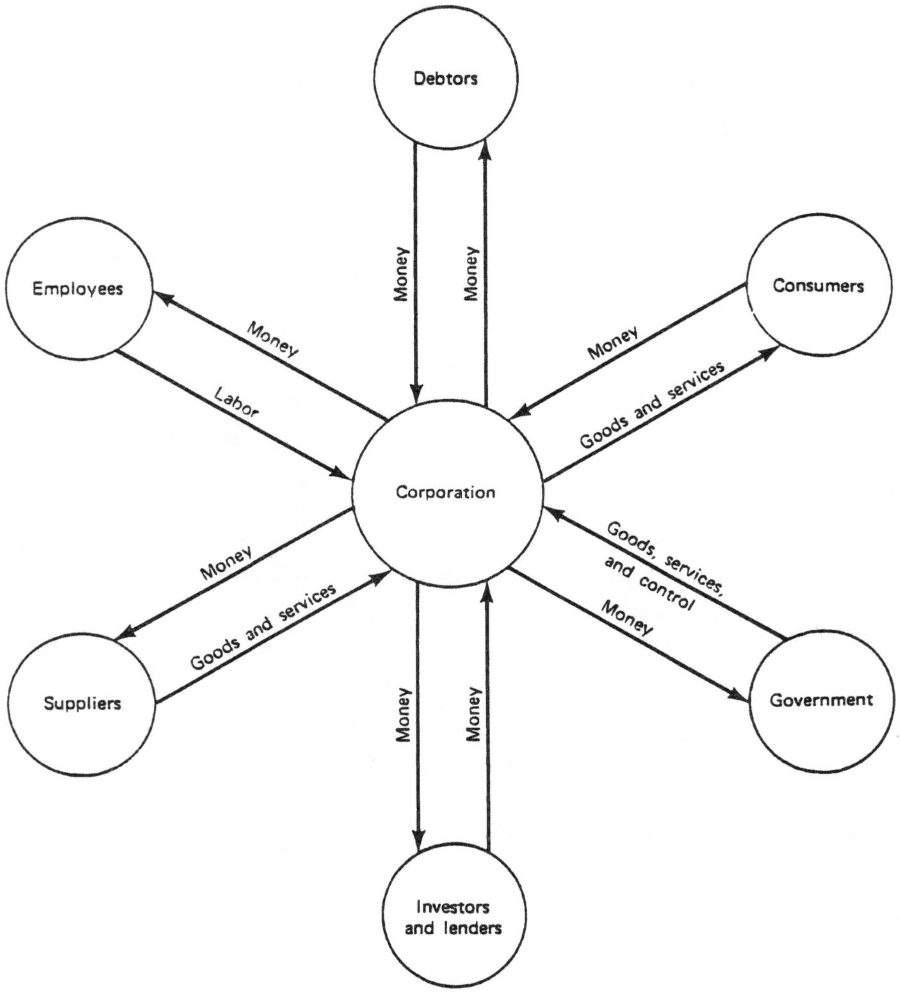

One stakeholder group, larger than all the others combined, is almost always ignored: *future generations.* They may be the ones most seriously affected by what is done today. How can their interests be taken into account when we do not know what their interests will be?

We do know one thing about future generations: They will be interested in *making their own decisions,* not in having had us make their decisions for them. Future generations should be allowed to make their own decisions. This requires *keeping their options open.* Managers should not make decisions that reduce the range of choices available in the future, but they do so continually. In many of their decisions, they do not take into account even their own future interests.

In addition to its transactions with stakeholders, the corporation either adds value to the goods and services supplied to customers or makes them more accessible to customers without changing them (as is the case with a retail establishment). The flows in and out of a corporation are flows of resources. The flows constitute either *consumption* of resources by the corporation or *distribution* of the means to acquire products or services for consumption, or the products and services themselves.

The difference between the amount of resources consumed by a corporation and the amount of consumption it makes possible, is the amount of wealth *it creates.* Then, in society's systemic view of a corporation, its principal social functions are the *production and distribution of wealth.* Identification of the production of wealth as a corporate function is nothing new, but the focus on its distribution function is relatively new.

The principal means by which most businesses distribute wealth is compensation for work: employment. Furthermore, employment is the only way of distributing wealth which can also create it; all other means of distributing wealth consume it, rather than produce it. When private enterprises, taken collectively, fail to provide enough employment in a society to distribute wealth equitably and, therefore, to enable it to maintain political stability, governments frequently intervene and take over some enterprises, nationalizing them. Its purpose in doing so is to maintain or create employment rather than wealth. It is not surprising, then, that government-owned enterprises are seldom as productive as those that are privately owned and operated.

In an increasingly international and competitive environment, businesses must continually increase their productivity if they are to remain competitive. Increased productivity means less employment unless it is accompanied by increased demand. Therefore, the only way of assuring stable, much less increasing, employment in a competitive environment is through growth. Thus, growth becomes a means, not an end as it was in the organismic view of the firm. To what is it a means? *Development.*

From Efficiency to Effectiveness: Adding Value

To understand the difference between *growth* and *development,* it is useful to understand the distinction between *efficiency* and *effectiveness.* Science, technology, and economics focus on *efficiency,* not *effectiveness.* Both efficiency and effectiveness are determined relative to one or more ends (goals, objectives, or ideals). The *value* of these objectives is not relevant to the determination of efficiency, but is essential for the determination of effectiveness. The effectiveness of behavior is a function of both its efficiency for one or more outcomes and the values of those outcomes. The difference between efficiency and effectiveness is reflected in the difference between *growth* and *development*. Growth does not necessarily imply an increase in value; development does. A company can grow without increasing in value, but it cannot develop without increasing its value.

Hierarchical organizations where decisions are made without consulting those affected by the decisions provide limited developmental opportunities for employees. In the absence of developmental opportunities, the satisfaction one can derive from work is also limited.

In today's environment, we see more and more organizations that are driven by competitive pressures for increased productivity strive to create self-directed workforces within the confines of a traditional hierarchical organization. This pursuit rarely works. Managers must begin to rethink organizational design issues with an eye to creating democratic systems to support development and not just growth. The circular organization that is discussed next is designed to accomplish this purpose.

DEMOCRACY IN BUSINESS: THE CIRCULAR ORGANIZATION

From the preceding discussions, we can conclude that there is a need for participation of employees in making decisions that affect them directly. Providing opportunities for such participation may well be the most profound type of cultural change currently taking place in business. Perhaps more than any other, this change reflects the shift from thinking of businesses as organisms to thinking of them as social systems.

Participation implies democracy. Although most economically advanced countries are committed to democracy in the public sector, most of their organizations—corporations in particular, but even government agencies—are organized autocratically, not democratically. Explanations for this inconsistency usually center on the theory that hierarchy is required in organizations in which labor must be divided and managed efficiently, and hierarchy is believed to require centralized control, hence, autocracy. Decentralization does not reduce the authority concentrated at the top of an organization; however, it does increase the amount of authority located at lower levels. Keep in mind that this lower level authority can be overridden by the higher level authority.

The essence of democracy is the absence of an ultimate authority—what we call circularity of power. Democracy requires that anyone who has authority over others be subject to their collective authority. This requirement is met by a structure called a *circular organization*.

The Design of a Circular Organization

The design of a circular organization, as discussed here, should be treated as a theme around which each organization should write its own variation, one adapted to its unique characteristics and conditions.

The central idea in a circular organization is that every person in a position of authority—each manager and supervisor—is provided with a *management board*. We will first consider the composition of these boards, then their responsibilities, and finally, how they operate (see Figure E.2).

Composition of Management Boards. The suggested *minimal* requirements for the composition of these boards at every level of the organization except at the top are:

1. The manager whose board it is
2. His/her immediate superior
3. His/her immediate subordinates

Therefore, in the board of any manager who has more than two subordinates, the subordinates constitute a majority.

Any board has the right to add members drawn either from the organization or outside. For example, it has been quite common for boards of functionally defined units—like marketing or finance—to invite other functional managers to participate on their boards as either voting or nonvoting members. Boards of units that have internal consumers of their products or services have frequently invited some of their customers to participate. In some cases, even external customers have been invited to be part of boards. In widely dispersed organizations—for example, in multinational corporations where different units are in different countries—representatives of various external stakeholder groups have been

**Figure E.2
A Circular Organization**

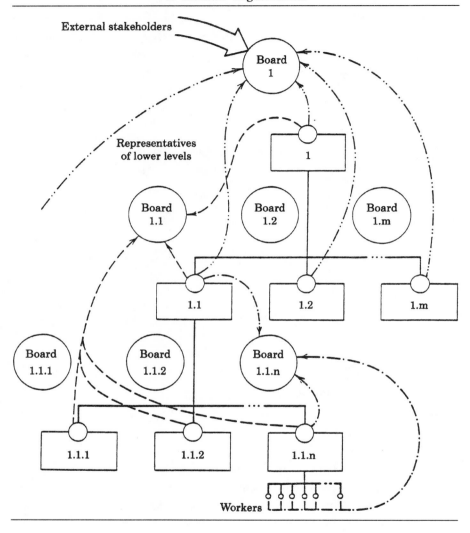

invited to participate. These have included representatives of relevant communities and consumer or environmental groups.

Chief executive officers (CEOs) of corporations already have boards on which only the shareholders and management are generally represented. The circular organization suggests adding to most of them all executives who report directly to the CEO, and representatives of other major stakeholder groups, for example, customers, suppliers, creditors, and the public at large.

Where an executive is supported by a staff, a separate staff board is usually established. If an executive has a chief of staff, then it will be that chief's board with the executive participating. If the executive acts as chief of staff, his or her immediate superior is generally not a member of the staff board.

In a unionized organization, union officials at each level of the organization are usually invited to participate on boards at the same level—shop stewards at lower levels, department representatives at higher levels, and union executives at the highest levels. (The role of unions in a circular organization is discussed next.)

Participation in boards is generally compulsory for managers/supervisors, but voluntary for others. Something is wrong with boards that fail to attract a majority of their manager's nonmanagerial subordinates. In such cases, the performance of the managers whose boards have this characteristic should be evaluated by their superiors.

Managers other than those at the top and bottom of an organization will interact directly with five levels of management through their participation on boards: two higher levels and their own level in their superiors' boards, and two lower levels in their subordinates' boards. Such interaction makes it possible to achieve a degree of coordination and integration of management that conventional organizations seldom attain.

Responsibilities of Management Boards.   Boards normally have the following responsibilities:

1. *Planning* for the unit whose board it is
2. *Making policy* for the unit whose board it is
3. *Coordinating* the plans and policies of the next lower level
4. *Integrating* its own plans and policies and those of its immediately lower level with those made at higher levels
5. *Making decisions* that affect the quality of working life of those on the board

In addition, most, but not all, boards are given the power of:

6. *Evaluating the performance* of the manager whose board it is, and *removing* him from that position.

Now consider each of these functions in turn. Each board has responsibility for planning and making policy for the unit whose board it is. *A policy is a decision rule,* not a decision. For example, "Hire only college graduates for managerial positions" is a policy; hiring such a person is a decision. Boards do not make decisions other than those directly affecting the quality of working life of its members; except for these, managers make the decisions, not boards. In general, boards are analogous to the legislative branch of government, and managers to the executive branch. Note that Congress can make decisions regarding its own quality of worklife, but only policies with regard to the quality of life of others.

Managers may, of course, consult their boards on decisions to be made, but responsibility for decisions other than those directly involving the quality of the working life of the board's members belong with the manager alone, not his or her board. The use of boards in a consulting role is common, as is their use to facilitate communication up, down, and across. Because they are used as communication channels, the need for separate staff and other types of meetings is frequently reduced. The number of meetings a manger must attend is usually reduced in a circular organization.

Each board is responsible for coordinating and integrating the plans and policies made at the level below it. Since the managers at this level participate in the board and generally constitute a majority, coordination is self-coordination with participation of two higher levels of management. Integration involves preservation of hierarchy: No board can make a plan or policy incompatible with a higher level board's output. However, it can appeal for revision of such output since it contains members who participate in two higher level boards. Moreover, because its members have an extended vertical view of the organization, boards are not likely to make plans or policies that are either harmful to lower levels of the organization or incompatible with those made at higher levels.

No board is permitted to implement a plan or a policy that directly affects another unit of the organization at the same or a higher level without either agreement of that unit or, where such agreement cannot be obtained, approval of the lowest level board at which the affected units converge going up the hierarchy.

Quality-of-worklife decisions are those that directly affect the satisfaction employees derive from their work, and their perception of its meaningfulness. Responsibility for the amount of work done and its quality remains with the manager. However, when employees are given power over their quality of worklife, significant improvements in the quantity and quality of their work are usually attained, often with more dramatic improvements than have been obtained by programs explicitly directed at increasing productivity and quality.

The most controversial responsibility that boards can assume is for evaluating and improving the performance of the manager whose board it is. Where boards have this responsibility, managers cannot retain their positions without their board's approval, hence approval by a majority of their subordinates. Because this function is so controversial, only about half the corporations that have implemented the circular organization have initially given this responsibility to the boards. Some have added it after running without it for a year or more, and some have never adopted it. Without this provision, complete democracy in the workplace cannot be attained.

In few cases have boards removed their managers. Removal has not been necessary because the boards enable subordinates to obtain most of what they want from their manager through constructive criticism. Once each year, the subordinates on a board meet without their superiors to discuss what their manager could do to enable them to do their jobs more effectively. The subordinates are precluded from telling their boss what he or she should *not* do; they must confine their opinions to what might be done that would enhance their own, not their manager's, performance. When they have organized their suggestions, they meet with and present their proposals to their manager. In some cases, these evaluative groups use a facilitator who makes the presentation for them.

"Receiving managers" are expected to respond to the suggestions in one of three ways—accept, reject, or agree to consider further. In most cases, managers accept about 75 percent of the suggestions. These ideas usually involve aspects the manager had not thought of, the virtue of which he or she sees immediately. For example, one such group suggested that their manager use his full vacation allowance so they would not feel guilty if they used theirs. The manager was surprised to learn that his failure to use his vacation allowance was preventing his subordinates from using theirs. He accepted the suggestion and implemented it. Another suggestion involved more flexible budgets, particularly with respect to the purchase of minor equipment and external services. Again, the manager agreed, and appropriate changes in budget control were made.

Second, the manager can reject a suggestion but is required to explain fully. In most cases, refusal involves constraints imposed on the manager from above, of which subordinates are unaware. The subordinates do not have to agree with, but should understand, the reasons for rejection of their suggestion. However, in few cases did such explanations not produce the understanding required for gracious acceptance of the rejection.

Finally, the manager can ask for more time to consider a suggestion and commit to providing a response by a specific time.

These constructively oriented evaluations have generally brought manager and subordinates closer and have bound them into a more collaborative relationship. Such sessions emphasize the fundamental change in the concept of management that is implicit in the circular organization: *The principal responsibility of managers is to create an environment and conditions under which their subordinates can do their jobs as effectively as their capabilities allow.* It is not to supervise them. That is, the principal responsibility of a manager is to manage over and up, not down, to manage the *interactions* of their units with the rest of the organization and its environment, not to manage the actions of their subordinates. If subordinates require supervision beyond an initial break-in period, they should be replaced by persons who do not require it.

Managers who do not have the support of their subordinates have difficulty implementing their decisions. Such managers do not perform as well as they could. On the other hand, subordinates who approve of their manager try to make him or her look as good as they can.

Note that in a circular organization, a group of subordinates cannot fire their manager; they can only remove him or her from that position. A manager can fire a subordinate. This potential means that managers cannot hold their positions without the approval of both their managers and their subordinates.

Modes of Operation of Management Boards

Each board should prepare its own operating procedures, but most boards operate in similar ways. Most boards, for example, operate by *consensus* rather than majority rule. The advantage of consensus over split decisions is apparent. What is not apparent is how consensus can be obtained where there is a significant initial divergence of opinions. Before considering how to obtain consensus in such situations, consider the nature of consensus, in particular, how it differs from complete agreement.

In situations where a change from current practice is contemplated, different proposals are not unusual, nor is the lack of agreement as to which is best. In such cases, boards have been offered the following choice: They can either retain their current plan, policy, practice, or design—whichever irrelevant—or permit one of the proposed changes to be selected at random. In most cases, they unanimously support a random choice. In other words, there is complete agreement that any of the alternatives is better than what is currently being done. In such cases, there is no agreement as to what is *best,* but complete agreement as to what is *better.* This procedure is consensus. Consensus, in this sense, can be reached relatively easily in at least 75 percent of the situations requiring a decision.

In the first "fall back" procedure, *a test of the alternatives* being considered is designed, one that *all* board members accept as adequate and fair. For example, in one company, agreement could not be reached as to whether plant maintenance in a multi-plant operation should be placed under the plant manager or a corporate manager of engineering. A multi-plant test was designed that all board members considered to be good and fair. The test was conducted and the findings were implemented across the system.

In most cases, such differences of opinion are based on different beliefs concerning a question of fact. The fact involved in the maintenance case involved the relative efficiency and responsiveness of maintenance personnel under two different organizational arrangements.

In some (but few) cases, either time is lacking that is required to design and conduct a test because a choice must be made quickly, or agreement on a test cannot be reached. Each board must decide how it wants to handle such cases. Most boards adopt a procedure much like the one described next.

When it is apparent that consensus cannot be reached through discussion, and a test is not practical, the chairperson goes around the room asking each person to state his or her position succinctly. Then, the chairperson states what decision he or she will make if consensus is not reached. Next, he or she goes around the room again for a restatement of positions. If consensus is reached among all but the chairperson, even if it is on a choice that differs from that the chairperson, that choice holds. If consensus is not reached, the chairperson's decision holds. Note that with this procedure, the lack of consensus on a decision other than the chairperson's constitutes consensus on the chairperson's decision.

Most boards are chaired by the manager whose board it is. In a few cases, boards use a rotating chairmanship. In no case that I know has a board selected as chairperson the superior of the manager whose board it is.

Each board either designates one of its members as recording secretary or engages an assistant or secretary to the manager whose board it is for this purpose. Minutes of each meeting are usually prepared and distributed shortly after that meeting. In most cases, every meeting begins with a review of tasks previously assigned. The "secretary" of the board is responsible for maintaining this list and distributing it to all board members.

Agendas for coming meetings are prepared by the secretary using input from any of the board members.

After the initial "break-in" period, most boards schedule monthly meetings which usually last about three hours. Additional meetings are called when required either by the manager whose board it is or by any of its other members.

Common Questions about Management Boards

Since managers may have as many as 10 or more boards to attend, when can they work? When one executive who had installed boards throughout his company was asked this question, his reply was essentially as follows: "The 10 boards in which I take part meet once per month for three to four hours each. Say four hours. That makes 40 hours per month. If I worked only 40 hours per week—like most managers, I work closer to sixty—this would be only 25 percent of my time. According to a number of studies of how managers spend their time, most managers spend no more than 20 percent of their time managing. Therefore, the question that should be asked is: What do I spend the other 55 percent of my time doing?"

He continued: "There is a better answer. In my boards, I plan, make policy, coordinate the plans and policies at the level reporting to me, integrate these with those made at my level, and evaluate and guide the performance of my subordinates two levels down. What should I be doing that is more important than this? Moreover," he concluded, "boards eliminate a number of other meetings, including staff meetings. I spend less time in meetings now that I did before boards were introduced."

Does it take any special skills to run board meetings? It does. For this reason, most organizations that initiate boards provide managers at all levels with training in group skills. Such training usually takes only two or three days. In many cases, these sessions are made available to union and nonmanagerial personnel as well.

Does it help to have a skilled facilitator at board meetings? It often does, at least in the first few meetings. A facilitator can help establish the rules of procedure and keep the meetings flowing smoothly. Once the manager for the board gains confidence in her ability to run the meetings, she can take over. It often helps for the facilitator to remain as an observer for the first few meetings run by the manager. This transition time enables the facilitator to make constructive suggestions to the manager in charge.

At Metropolitan Life, a special training program was developed and conducted to provide the large number of facilitators that the company required. Most of those trained had previous experience facilitating various types of quality-improvement groups.

Have any of the organizations that started boards discontinued them? To the best of my knowledge, only two have, and both for the same reason. Shortly after their initiation, and before they were operating throughout the organization, the chief executive officers were replaced, and their replacements discontinued the boards along with many other innovations initiated by their predecessors.

What is the principal obstruction to the successful implementation of boards? Lack of commitment by middle managers. These managers seldom "buy in" unless they have been exposed to a presentation about boards and have had an opportunity to discuss them with someone experienced in their use. For this reason, appropriate education of managers, particularly those in middle ranks, is very important. Since there may be a large number of managers, and they may be geographically dispersed, videotapes of relevant presentations and discussions have often been used to inform and motivate managers. Availability of an experienced person to answer questions also helps.

What is usually done with managers who do not fully cooperate despite indoctrination? As previously noted, participation in boards is usually required of managers. Evaluation of their participation in boards is a significant part of their performance evaluation. Where boards have been introduced with unambiguous commitment of the senior executive, rarely do managers, once indoctrinated, fail to participate fully. In a few cases, uncooperative managers have been moved to nonmanagerial positions.

How do circular organizations affect the readiness, willingness, and ability of enterprises to change? Organizational resistance to change is a familiar phenomenon. Implementation of decisions involving significant organizational changes are often diluted or subverted during their establishment, because those who actually effect implementation do not "buy into" the decision. No matter how much authority decision makers in large organizations have, they seldom have the ability to oversee each step in the implementation of their decisions. Therefore, the larger the organization, the more difficult to obtain implementation as intended. *Power-over* and *power-to* differ significantly. For example, the last Shah of Iran, one of the most powerful rulers on Earth, in the sense of *power over,* often complained of his inability to have his decisions implemented as he intended. The more democratic a culture and the more educated its members, the more negatively correlated are *power-over* and *power-to.* The circular organization does not reduce *power-over,* but it does increase *power-under* and, therefore, *power-to.*

What is done with boards where such groups as quality circles already exist? In some cases they run in parallel, but in most, the quality circles are incorporated into boards, thereby reducing the number of meetings required.

Where in an organization is the best place to introduce boards? Wherever you are. Boards have been initiated at every level of an organization and have subsequently spread throughout. In some organizations, Anheuser-Busch, for example, boards were initially established at the top. After the executives involved had experience with it, each started a board of his own. Then, they moved down layer by layer. This diffusion took more than a year to reach the lower levels.

At Kodak, the first boards were established in a unit where the manager was at the fifth level of the organization. Boards then spread up, down, and across. At Alcoa's Tennessee Operations, boards were simultaneously established at the top and bottom with the participation of the union at both levels. Boards subsequently moved up and down the organization until they met at the middle. In some smaller organizations, all managers have been indoctrinated at the same time, hence boards were initiated all over the organization at the same time.

In some cases, managers below the top of an organization initiated boards without the participation of their immediate superiors, who usually begged off, claiming to be too busy to be involved. However, as the boards manifested their value, most of these superiors began to participate.

Participating senior executives are not always able to attend all the board meetings of their immediate subordinates because of other demands on their time. In such cases, they keep informed through minutes of meetings, and they are notified when their attendance at an upcoming meeting is critical.

Is it easier or more difficult to introduce boards in a unionized company? Both. Where unions have collaborated, they make it easier to involve the workforce. Where they are opposed, it is difficult but possible to introduce boards. In a few such cases, unions have eventually come to support the idea and participate fully.

Are there certain types of organizational structures on which a circular organization cannot be superimposed, for example, a matrix organization? No. The concept has been used by organizations with just about every type of structure. This should not be surprising; democracy is associated with a wide variety of government structures.

Does the introduction of a circular organization involve a significant change in a corporation's culture? It does. In a circular organization, managers are no longer either commanders or supervisors, but are required to be leaders, facilitators, and educators. These are roles to which many managers are not accustomed. It takes time to make the conversions, but the rewards can be immense. For example, at the time boards were introduced in Alcoa's Tennessee Operations, in the early 1980s, these operations were scheduled to be shut down because of their low productivity and poor quality of product. In less than two years, their productivity and product quality improved so much that corporate headquarters reversed its decision and initiated a modernization program for the operations. At the end of 1987, the most advanced aluminum sheet rolling mill in the world opened at these operations.

Examples of Circular Organizations

During the 1980s, A&P closed all its supermarkets in the Delaware Valley, the metropolitan area of Philadelphia. The reason was lack of profitability. Subsequently, in a joint effort with Locals 27, 56, 1357, 1358, and 1360 of the United Food and Commercial Workers to which the A&P employees had belonged prior to losing their jobs, a new chain of supermarkets was designed. They used boards at all levels. The new chain, called *Super Fresh,* was initiated mostly in the old facilities. It is now the fastest growing chain in the area and is profitable. This chain is being extended, replacing traditional A&P stores.

Armco's Latin American Division (ALAD) was also reorganized around the use of boards and has experienced significant improvements in performance as well as morale. The same has been true of a number of other organizations including Metropolitan Life, Central Life Assurance, Clark Equipment, several new units of Alcoa, a variety of departments and divisions of Kodak, and Anheuser-Busch. Democracy and efficiency are not inimicable.

SUMMARY

In this chapter, we have conceptualized the business enterprise as a social system. This means a corporation has responsibilities both to the society of which it is a part, and to its parts, its members. Its principal social function is the production and distribution of wealth. Its principal means of distributing wealth is through compensation for work—employment. The principal objective of a corporation conceptualized as a social system is its own development: To develop is to increase one's desire and ability to satisfy one's own needs and legitimate desires, and those of others. Business enterprises are also seen as having an obligation to encourage and facilitate the development of their members. Continuous development involves continuous progress in science and technology (the pursuit of truth), economics (the pursuit of plenty), ethics/morality (the pursuit of the good), and aesthetics (the pursuit of beauty). Science, technology, and economics focus on the *efficiency* with which ends are pursued. Ethics/morality and aesthetics focus on the *effectiveness* of such pursuits. Effectiveness takes into account the value of the needs pursued as well as the efficiency of their pursuit.

We have seen how the pursuit of corporate ethical/moral and aesthetic objectives requires providing employees at all levels with opportunities to participate in making decisions that affect them directly, and in exercising collective control over those who control them separately. Such opportunities for participation and exercise of control are best provided by a circular organization. In this type of organization, every employee has an opportunity to participate in his or her boss's board. These boards plan, make policy, coordinate horizontally and integrate vertically plans and policies, improve quality of worklife, evaluate the performance of the manager whose board it is, and, with their manager's immediate superior, control occupancy of the position held by that manager. This type of organization makes it possible to convert corporate autocracies into industrial democracies without sacrificing any of the values of hierarchy.

Moreover, the boards of a circular organization facilitate the management of interactions. They make it possible to convert management from directing the actions of subordinates to the creation of conditions under which subordinates can perform as effectively as possible. This feat is accomplished by managers coordinating the interactions of their subordinates, and the interactions of the units they manage, with other organizational units at the same and higher levels of the organization. Systemic management is the management of interactions. It is based on knowing that the performance of a system is not the sum of the performances of its parts but is the product of their interactions with each other and their environments.

Systemic management replaces supervision, direction, and command with leadership. Systemically managed corporations contribute to the development of all their stakeholders and to the society of which they are part. Therefore, they are increasingly in a position to lead society in its quest for an improved quality of life for all.

BIBLIOGRAPHY

Ackoff, R. L., *Creating the Corporate Future,* New York: John Wiley & Sons, 1981.

_____ and W. B. Deane, "The Revitalization of ALCOA's Tennessee Operations," *National Productivity Review* (Summer 1984), pp. 239–245.

Allport, G. W., and H. S. Odbert, "Trait Names: A Psycholexical Study," *Psychological Monographs,* No. 211,1936.

Beer, S., *The Heart of Enterprise,* New York: John Wiley & Sons, 1981.

Burnham, J., *The Managerial Revolution,* London: John Day, 1941.

Singer, E. A., Jr., *On the Contented Life,* New York: Henry Holt, 1923.

_____ , *In Search of a Way of Life,* Columbia University Press, New York, 1948.

Work in America: Report of a Special Task Force to the Secretary of Health, Education, and Welfare, Cambridge, MA: The MIT Press, 1973.

INDEX